PUBLIC SERVICE IN A GLOBALIZED WORLD

T0049422

To the Trainers of CSTDI and LBSNAA

Public Service in a Globalized World

Central Training Institutes in India and Hong Kong

AHMED SHAFIQUL HUQUE
McMaster University, Canada and City University of Hong Kong, China

LINA VYAS
City University of Hong Kong, China

Routledge
Taylor & Francis Group

LONDON AND NEW YORK

First published 2004 by Ashgate Publishing

Reissued 2018 by Routledge
2 Park Square, Milton Park, Abingdon, Oxon OX14 4RN
711 Third Avenue, New York, NY 10017, USA

Routledge is an imprint of the Taylor & Francis Group, an informa business

First issued in paperback 2018

A Library of Congress record exists under LC control number: 2004017610

Notice:
Product or corporate names may be trademarks or registered trademarks, and are used only for identification and explanation without intent to infringe.

Publisher's Note
The publisher has gone to great lengths to ensure the quality of this reprint but points out that some imperfections in the original copies may be apparent.

Disclaimer
The publisher has made every effort to trace copyright holders and welcomes correspondence from those they have been unable to contact.

ISBN 13: 978-0-815-39128-9 (hbk)
ISBN 13: 978-1-138-62027-8 (pbk)
ISBN 13: 978-1-351-15092-7 (ebk)

Contents

List of Figures

List of Tables

Preface

Good governance has become an essential precondition for the survival, operation and progress of modern states, and one of the key ingredients for an efficient and effective public service. Generally, officials are recruited on the basis of open competitive examinations that test their merit and public service receives the benefit of the best and the brightest talent available in the country. This advantage can only be sustained by a continuous process of updating and upgrading the knowledge and skills of public service employees. Most governments rely on central training institutes to perform these tasks. Thus, training for public services occupies a critical place in the operation of modern governments, and central training institutes have the responsibility of sustaining the quality of public services.

The task has become more challenging with the advent of globalization, which has exerted a converging pressure on countries to adopt similar structural adjustments and administrative reforms to operate according to standard rules and procedures applicable across countries. A natural consequence has been a tendency for training programs to concentrate on those areas ranked high on the list of priorities of internationally powerful actors, at the expense of knowledge and skills essential for serving the public in the country and solving local problems. This book examines the operation and performance of central training institutes in India and Hong and finds that the centralized approach may become less and less relevant, as specialization and problem based decisions become critical.

Central training institutions provide the lead and set the agenda for ensuring a constant supply of competent public officials in most countries. While central training institutes have the potential of catering to the needs of diverse groups in the public service, weaknesses in the structures and evaluation systems have affected their performance. This argument is substantiated through the presentation of detailed information on the central training institutes in India and Hong Kong, analysis of the changes experienced by them, and examination of the strategies employed for coping with the changing circumstances. The study is based on extensive field research conducted in India and Hong Kong. An examination of their publications and interviews with trainers and trainees indicate that although the two institutes operate in radically different circumstances, their objectives and priorities are similar in nature. Both institutes are striving to attain competitive advantage in a world of open markets, free movement of people, skills and capital and harmonization of practices of public administration.

The study deserves attention for several reasons. Public administration in changing societies has often been affected by the dearth of capable administrators and it is worthwhile to examine the process of enhancing capability through training. The role of central training institutes in performing this task has not been examined on a wide scale. And the findings are expected to generate debates as well as provide suggestions for further research in this important area.

We are grateful to several institutions and individuals for encouragement, assistance and support received in the course of this study. The Department of Public and Social Administration at the City University of Hong Kong has been a constant source of support throughout the duration of the study, while the Institute on Globalization and the Human Condition at McMaster University provided invaluable assistance at the writing stage. We would also like to acknowledge extremely helpful cooperation received from the Lal Bahadur Shastri National Academy for Administration, India and the Civil Service Training and Development Institute, Hong Kong. Staff, trainers and trainees at these two training institutes deserve much of the credit for facilitating our understanding of the challenges in public service training.

Among individuals, there are many who have extended help through advice, encouragement, comments and criticism of earlier drafts. B. S. Baswan, Director of the Lal Bahadur Shastri National Academy for Administration provided invaluable support and logistical help in the collection of data in India. Patricia Tam, Senior Training Officer of the Civil Service Training and Development Institute in Hong Kong was a key contact and generously gave her time and advice. Our friends and colleagues in the academic world have contributed in various ways. We must express our gratitude to Muhammad Yeahia Akhter, Brian Brewer, Will Coleman, Arie Halachmi, Ian Holliday, Randhir Jain, Jermain Lam, Joshua Mok, Martin Painter, and Habib Zafarullah. We would like to register our gratitude to the referees who evaluated the manuscript for Ashgate Publishing Group. Special thanks are also due to Kirstin Howgate, Senior Commissioning Editor, Ashgate, for bringing this project to fruition. We are grateful to Carolyn Veldstra for editorial help.

Finally, we would like to thank our spouses Yasmin and Anand, and register our appreciation for our children Shineen, Ariqa and Arjun. Their support and understanding went a long way in keeping our spirits high. With all the help, cooperation and advice, we remain responsible for any shortcomings in the book.

Ahmed Shafiqul Huque   July 2004
Lina Vyas

Chapter 1

Introduction

Globalization has ushered in societal, political, and cultural changes of great magnitude and its impact is becoming increasingly obvious. In this context, good governance has become an essential precondition for the survival, operation and progress of modern states. In order for modern states to operate effectively, training for public service personnel is critical. Public sector employees must be knowledgeable, skilful, compassionate, and be able to make sound decisions and implement them.

Traditionally, the scope of training for public service was somewhat limited. The nature of daily activities did not change often, and academic preparation, combined with standardized training through government facilities, were considered adequate for most officials. Furthermore, it has typically been assumed that the objectives, approach, content and direction of training, and the operation of training institutes would be determined based on the features, requirements and agenda of a particular country. Two completely different cases such as India and Hong Kong—the two main examples in this book—would be expected to have strikingly different arrangements for training personnel in the public service. One of the only things these places ostensibly share is a history of British colonial rule. However, as the effects of globalization become more extensive, the activities of public servants are becoming more diverse and complex, and there have been radical changes in the nature, approach, methods and implications of public service training. In response to these changes, many countries are moving toward more centralized training, and the emphasis in training has shifted to common areas.

This book argues that one of the most striking impacts of globalization on public service has been this standardization of administrative procedures and practices across countries, and that the role and operation of central training institutes for public service are converging. However, there is a lack of standardization of practices within central training institutes. Detailed information about central training institutes in India and Hong Kong, and analysis of the changes that have occurred, will substantiate this theory. Both places are striving to attain competitive advantage in a world of open markets, free movement of people, skills and capital, and harmonization of practices in public administration. On examination, the fact that they are trying to set similar goals and achieve them is clearly reflected in publications from central training institutes in India and Hong Kong, and in interviews with trainers and trainees—although success in these attempts may differ.

Public service training in central institutes serves as a useful basis for analysis because these organizations set the public service agenda for a country. By examining the role of central public service training institutes in such strikingly diverse settings as India and Hong Kong, this study will help assess the real value of such institutes across a range of countries, and is expected to shed light on a number of important areas including training plans, needs analysis, procedures and methods. With areas of concern identified, recommendations will be made to help governments plan effective responses to the challenges of both globalization and internal forces, and enhance public service capabilities in developing countries.

Public Service Training

The development of people into competent employees of an organization depends on a range of factors, including the organizational context or environment in which those human resources employ their talents. There are various methods and mechanisms that organizations can use to develop their employees' skills for achieving organisational goals. One of the most effective means is an effective system of training and development of public employees.

For the past several decades, as part of the globalizing process, the world has seen rapid technological change, poor economic growth, economic reforms, increased market competition, civil service and administrative reforms, high unemployment rates, and shortage of skilled labour. There are different ways of responding to these challenges, which depend primarily on the nature and capability of respective governments and their available facilities. An examination of governmental efforts to develop their human resources and training programs provides a valuable perspective on how governments are specifically responding to these challenges, what priorities are being established, and what patterns are being reinforced from within.

The recruitment and retention of competent public employees is critical in order to meet the needs of the country and facilitate the achievement of the objectives of the government. It is an extremely important and difficult task to find employees with appropriate skills and abilities. The task does not end with careful recruitment and suitable placement of public employees. Training priorities also have to be adjusted and altered in response to changes that are occurring both internally and externally to a country. Employee skills can deteriorate or be rendered obsolete with the passage of time, advancement of technology, or change in circumstances, and the organisation may undertake new activities that would necessitate a change in the types of jobs and the skills necessary to perform them. Other factors that can precipitate change in training include changing organizational structure, dealing with problems of growth, implementing decentralization, changing demands of technology, contingency planning, increased inter-unit knowledge requirements, or a need to integrate policy and philosophy.

Ideally, training is planned with future requirements in mind, to the extent that is practical. Because these challenges are common in most countries of the world, the point worth investigation is whether central training institutes are adopting identical or diverse approaches for addressing these changes. Either way, the reality that a large number public service employees will assume increased responsibilities in the forthcoming years of their employment, it is clear that a sustained commitment from governments to continually train and upgrade employee skills is absolutely necessary if public organisations are to remain effective.

To explore this issue, this book concentrates on the leading centres for training of civil servants in India and Hong Kong. An examination of the training programs conducted by the Lal Bhadur Shastri National Academy of Administration (LBSNAA) in India and the Civil Service Training and Development Institute (CSTDI) in Hong Kong form the cornerstone of this study. The main objectives of this study are to identify changing priorities in training needs, strategies adopted to anticipate future training needs, methods used to prepare civil servants to cope with changing times, and finally, more broadly, to provide insight into training trends and future training requirements.

Training and Human Resource Development

Every year a large segment of government budgets are spent on training public officials. To meet the labour requirement for each position, four basic tasks must be performed. Employees must be recruited to fill vacancies, retained with a satisfactory career package, developed to fill more senior posts, and deployed to positions where they are most suitable and useful. Training is a course of action that results in developing skills, behavior, awareness, understanding and ability in human resources, which helps in increasing the effectiveness of employees to work in their present government positions as well as prepares them for the prospective government. Training is part of a process of development that advances and maintains individuals within an organization. Training of public servants prepares them to fulfil their administrative duties and helps them understand their responsibilities—but beyond merely developing their skills, training can affect employee attitudes and values such that it can guide their actions in a desired direction.

Training comes in different forms, and can be delivered at different levels. 'Training is a tool; it is instruction in a myriad of forms and settings, in which both technical and conceptual knowledge and skills are imparted to employees, both non-managers and managers' (Shafritz, 2001, p. 306). Pre-entry training prepares a prospective candidate for entrance into the public service. Orientation training introduces an appointee to the basic concepts of the job, new work environment, organisation, and its goals. In-service training has the twin aims of stimulating the employee to make his best effort, and helping him to improve his performance (Avasthi and Maheshwari, 1996, pp. 352-353). Post-entry training is expected to further upgrade and refine the skills of employees and prepare them for undertaking more responsibilities and challenges. In some cases, post-entry training may not be directly related to the work of the employee, but is aimed at improving general managerial skills or exposing employees to new and innovative ideas.

Human Resources Development (HRD) deals with the human side of management and reflects the integrated use of (a) training and development, (b) organisation development, and (c) career development to improve individual, group and organisational effectiveness. Among the elements of HRD, training and development aims to identify and develop, through planned learning, the key competencies that enable individuals to perform current or future jobs. The primary emphasis is on individuals in their work roles, and it is intended to help achieve planned individual learning. Organisation development focuses on promoting positive work relationships and helping groups initiate and manage change, while career development is intended to help align individual career planning and organisational career management processes to achieve an optimal balance of individual and organisational needs.

Even when organisational objectives are well-defined, it is not always easy to decide on the specific nature and content of training programmes. 'What kind of training program will be offered and what emphasis will be placed on employee development are usually based on several key criteria: (1) that training be job- or career-related; (2) that it be relevant to enhancing advancement potential; (3) that it be useful in improving organizational effectiveness; and (4) that it be of sufficient relevance and interest to employees. In the public sector, decisions about training programs are more often focused on the first criterion mentioned- job-or career-relatedness' (Shafritz, 2001, pp. 306-307).

Because public organizations are continually challenged by change, strategic, cohesive and comprehensive human-resources policies and programs enable them to anticipate and respond effectively in a systematic and integrated way. Training can prepare public officials for this task. However, it is not always clear exactly why governmental objectives in this regard are successful or not. It is difficult to tangibly identify and demonstrate the results produced by training, and few skills can be easily or accurately quantified and measured. The general outcome of training is clearly positive, but the degree of success in achieving objectives through training is variable.

Studying Central Training Institutes

There are a number of objectives for this study of national training institutes for public service in India and Hong Kong. First, the study is intended to develop an insight of the current trends in training and how future training needs are being identified in different contexts.

Second, it will add to the debate on how globalization is affecting governments and public service. The LBSNAA and the CSTDI have undergone several significant changes in recent years to keep up with the demands of the times, and are striving to ensure continuous improvement in their respective programs, as well as guarantee the quality of the civil service, through providing appropriate training. Government training has always needed to make constant adjustments, but it can be argued that globalization has added to the complexity of, and accelerated the adjustment process because an increasing number of areas need attention. This situation is typical for government training programs around the world.

Third, while India and Hong Kong are different in many respects, it is worth investigating if the common British colonial tradition has left a strong influence on the training systems of the two former colonies. As expected, on examination of the two diverse systems, a few common elements were unravelled.

Fourth, this study can be used to illustrate the point that, irrespective of the differences in the level of development and political system, there are a number of universal principles and processes for developing efficient and effective public officials. Training must be properly planned and delivered in order to be effective in different kinds of settings.

Finally, the conceptual ideas developed in this research, based on the two cases, could be tested and applied to other places, subject to certain modifications. Various principles and procedures of training developed in one part of the world may also prove worthy of consideration for adoption in other countries. 'The influence of Western patterns of administration in the newly independent countries is well known and easily understandable. Less obvious is the growing interest in the larger countries concerning administrative machinery originated in smaller nations' (Heady, 1991). This book seeks to initiate a process of assessing administrative institutions after a period of maturation in the post-colonial period, based on their roles and contributions.

The Cases

India and Hong Kong are different in many respects. While India is a sizeable country that has celebrated fifty years of independence, Hong Kong is a self-contained, small autonomous unit of the People's Republic of China. There are marked differences in terms of their respective economic development, political systems, and demographic composition of society.

However, as previously stated, on examination of these two diverse systems, several common elements emerged. Their training institutes share some common goals, values and objectives, but they differ in how and to what extent they are to be achieved. Globalized economic influences and technological changes, affecting both places, have resulted in similarities in policy, approach, and identification of future training needs. Operating within a global context has placed common demands on policy managers, and as a result, the nature and role of public administration, when viewed country by country, appear similar.

The Foundation of Analysis

This study is built upon a foundation of theoretical discussion underpinned by empirical findings. Theoretical discussions focus on the concept of civil service training and its related concepts on defining the area of the study. Empirical findings were based upon original data collected from primary sources in India and Hong Kong.

A list of the training programs conducted during 1995-2000 was the basis for studying the trends within and content of public service training programs in the two cases. Published information on the different training packages offered during that period was obtained through the Internet and personal visits to the training institutes. Questionnaires related to feedback on the training programs and future developments were sent out to the trainers and trainees of the two institutes. This was followed up with personal interviews with the trainers, ex-trainers, and trainees who were identified to be potential information providers for this study. Snowball sampling and convenience sampling, for questionnaires and interviews respectively, were adopted while identifying the potential information providers for the study.

Information related to the institutes and the staff helped to assess the standard and qualifications of the trainers. The trainers and trainees were interviewed to receive feedback on the training programs and also to find out how they benefited by the training provided. The interviews focused on how training changes the attitude, personality and output of personnel.

Primary data was obtained for the core of the study, which consisted of collecting and analysing information in order to examine the background and operation of the two training institutes, and to arrive at conclusions regarding the nature of services provided by those institutes. Extensive investigations were conducted into the two target institutes of training, the LBSNAA in India and CSTDI in Hong Kong. Information was obtained on the training policies over the past five years and primary respondents were asked to identify what they regarded as training priorities for themselves and the other government departments over the next five years.

Although the Department of Personnel and Training in the Ministry of Personnel has the overall responsibility for public service training in India, it operates as a clearinghouse and performs functions mainly related to administrative co-ordination. Rigorous training programs are conducted at a number of regional institutes such as the Lal Bahadur Shastri National Academy of Administration (LBSNAA, located in Mussoorie), IAS Staff College (located in Simla) and the IAS Training School (located in Delhi). The LBSNAA, described as 'India's premier research and training institute on administration and public policy' had been selected for this study. While the CSTDI imparts much of the training for higher civil servants in Hong Kong, the task is performed by a number of agencies and institutes in India.

Research Methods

The research was based primarily on the qualitative method. Qualitative methods are branded by using a small number of cases to uncover facts about the social world. Researchers using these methods seldom employ mathematical means to analyse data. Instead, they seek to interact with the respondents in their own language and on their own terms. 'Qualitative research is a particular tradition in social science that fundamentally depends on watching people in their own territory and interacting with them in their own language, on their own terms' (Kirk, 1986, p. 9). In contrast to the quantitative methods, qualitative methods lay considerable emphasis on the situation and often the structural contexts (Strauss, 1987, p. 2) where the data is being collected.

Qualitative research tends to be associated with researcher participation while quantitative research tends to be associated with research aloofness. Quantitative surveys are based on highly structured interviews using a predetermined questionnaire and closed questions with considerable effort devoted to the formulation of unbiased questions. Interaction between the interviewer and the respondents is minimal to prevent the interviewer from possibly affecting the respondents' answers. There is less emphasis on the role of the researcher. In contrast, qualitative interviewers often use open-ended questions to gather information from respondents. The researcher plays an active role and is deeply involved in the interviews. Qualitative methods also ensure participation of officials from different ranks in the public services to get a more broadly representative sample.

Because this is a qualitative study, themes and concepts are used to analyse data instead of numbers. The questionnaires did not require elaborate statistical calculations. Furthermore, the interviews contributed towards verbal data and it was not possible to quantify all observations. Nevertheless, percentages were calculated and numbers presented wherever possible and necessary.

Sources of Data

Interviews, questionnaires and documents constitute the main modes for collection of data. Interviewing is a powerful research tool for gathering information and opening windows on experiences of the interviewees. Rubin and Rubin (1995, p. 4) pointed out that 'researchers put together the information they find from qualitative interviews to form explanations and theories that are grounded in the details, evidence and examples of the interviews'. Interviews are usually defined as conversation with a purpose (Berg, 1998, p. 57). Interviews involve a set of assumptions and understandings about the situation, which are not usually associated with casual conversation (Denscombe, 1998, p. 109).

This study is based on semi-structured and one-on-one interviews. Semi-structured interviews allow the interviewer to focus on a number of specific issues, while still leaving room for flexibility. Open-ended questions are helpful because they allow the interviewees to develop their ideas and speak more freely.

Officials from different ranks in the public service were invited to participate in the interviews. Potential respondents were chosen by a convenience sampling method, and it helped choose respondents that were readily available. Each of the interviewed participants was asked for further recommendations. Follow-up interviews were conducted in some cases when more information was required for further analysis. The field research helped gain useful insights into the normal patterns from some deviant cases.

Using a questionnaire for conducting relevant research is often regarded as an appropriate strategy when there is need to collect standardized data for a considerable amount of targeted respondents in many different locations (Babbie, 1995; Denscombe, 1998, p. 88). Open-ended self-administered questionnaires allowed respondents to register their views. Each questionnaire was accompanied by a letter explaining the goals of the research, encouraging respondents to answer all questions to the best of their ability, and ensuring complete confidentiality. A large quantity of data from a considerable number of people was collected in this way.

The use of in-depth interviews serves a different purpose than the structured questionnaire. Structured questionnaires set out beforehand all the relevant questions about the issues that are being studied, and must predict to some extent how the subjects will respond. Respondents have defined options from which to choose. Interviews, on the other hand, can be based on a wide variety of formats. The major difference lies in the degree of structure that is imposed on the respondents. Interviews range along a continuum from highly structured interview schedules, which permit no deviation, to the largely unstructured, undirected exploratory interviews. The purpose of questionnaire was to measure characteristics or opinions of the respondents on the defined research questions.

Documents, referring to any written sources of data, were also used for research. Documents provide background knowledge to the researcher and at the same time can be treated as source of data and an alternative to questionnaires, interviews or observation. Documents can be divided into six categories: books and journals; government reports and official statistics; personal documents such as letters, memos, diaries and autobiographies; historical sources like records and archives; mass media including newspapers and magazines; and internet resources (Dencombe, 1998, pp. 159-165).

A document search was carried out as part of the preliminary research, and continued throughout the study. Published information on past and present training programmes was obtained through Internet sources and personal visits to the training institutes. The literature reviewed included secondary data from books, journals, newspaper clippings and research reports. Data was collected from various sources on the existing training arrangements in India and Hong Kong. Analysis of the reports and views of the past training programs provided valuable information about the success or failure of the institutes in achieving their proposed objectives.

These aforementioned sources were supplemented through reviewing material published by governments, non-governmental organizations, and professional associations, which are relevant to the training of public service employees. The Internet was regularly searched in order to keep the database of the study up-to-date. In this way, the literature review helped to construct a framework for developing the study.

Using more than one single data collection method to focus on the same research topic is called triangulation. The basic rationale of using triangulation is that there is no single data collection method that could be regarded as 'the best' and 'universally accepted' for application to all situations. Using more than one method at the stage of data collection can enhance the validity of data collected, and improve the overall quality of research because it helps the researcher access and consider diverse perspectives on the subjects and issues being examined. As Sarantakos (1993, p. 155) stated, triangulation allows a researcher to 'obtain a variety of information on the same issue; to use the strength of each method to overcome the deficiencies of the other; to achieve a higher degree of validity and reliability; and to overcome the deficiencies of single-method studies'.

Because this study obtained information through a variety of methods, using separate qualitative and quantitative methods, it created a condition conducive to independent external validity—data obtained in different ways could be compared and analyzed based on their consistency or reliability.

The study achieved a response rate of about 60 per cent. According to Babbie (1998), for a survey questionnaire, 'a response rate of 50 per cent is adequate for analysis and reporting. A response rate of 60 per cent is good and a response rate of 70 per cent is very good' (p. 262). A snowball sampling method was used when the questionnaires were distributed, and a convenience sampling method was subsequently used to select interviewees. Snowball sampling begins by identifying respondents who meet the criteria for inclusion in the study, who are then asked to recommend others who may meet the criteria, thereby depending on referrals from existing subjects. Snowball sampling is especially useful in trying to reach populations that are inaccessible or hard to find. A convenience sample involves choosing cases to study that are readily available to the researcher, and is practical for setting up interviews.

Analysis of Data

Organization of qualitative data involves dealing with a huge amount of words. The basic principle of qualitative analysis is to reduce the amount of raw data while simultaneously preserving the meaning of its content. Thus, the data must be arranged in systematic ways that allow for quick location and retrieval of specific points and arguments.

The first batch of data collected for this study after an extensive literature review was obtained from government documents and publications regarding training in the public services. Such data formed the foundation for our understanding of the historical background of civil service training in India and Hong Kong.

From the interviews held with public service trainers and trainees, data was organized around of the need to evaluate and assess training needs. Where possible, frequency and percentile analysis was conducted to identify trends. For example, this has been done where interview questions and responses were directly related to benefits attained from training.

Questionnaires were sent to line managers and employees in the public sector, and the resulting data was classified and later analysed. The questionnaires focussed on evaluating training, and involved a comparison of the syllabi, number of trainees and how consistent training was with the officially defined requirements of the country.

The information and data was analyzed to assess the role of central training institutes. The impact of public service training was considered in terms of efficiency and effect of training on workplace performance. A review of the data identified different areas such as effectiveness of training programmes; past, present and future trends; training priorities; process of identification of training needs; training techniques and mechanisms and future direction of public service training as important areas.

Framework for Study

The analytical framework for the study is presented in Figure 1.1. Most countries have centralized training institutes. The LBSNAA and CSTDI, as central training institutes, train personnel from different departments in governmental organizations. These institutes are responsible for designing and conducting relevant training programmes and they must update them in accordance with changes in governmental policy, public demand, and society. They analyze training needs and also anticipate future training needs. They are approached by the different departments of the government to help upgrade the skills of personnel in accordance to the changing environment.

Generally, senior public servants head central training institutes and supervise the operation of the various units. The head is assisted by a group of officials who help with training and management. These institutes are normally divided into several sections and each section specializes in its own area of training. Training is conducted at either the institute or at the trainees' workplace.

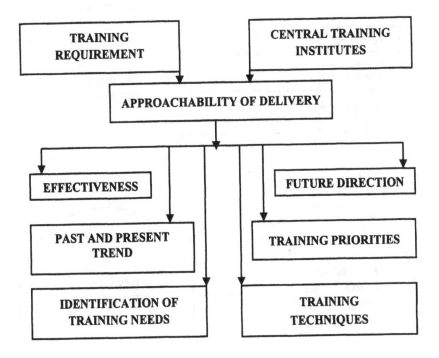

Figure 1.1 Analytical Techniques

The aims and objectives of training institutes can be achieved with the help of appropriate policies, programs, projects and action plans. Potential areas of training and development must be identified and corresponding programs and plans must be developed. Effective training plans anticipate what skills and knowledge a specific group of civil servants will need. Figure 1.2 shows a schema of an effective training process and its desired outcomes.

The schema in Figure 1.2 was developed based on an overview of the CSTDI and LBSNAA. By reviewing the aims and objectives, one can discover if an institute has identified skills and habits that must be imparted to employees to keep up with changing times. To examine the aims and objectives required a careful examination of the people, processes and structure of each institute. Finally, all of this enabled an in-depth examination of the policies, programs, projects and action plans of each institute.

A systematic approach to training needs analysis for central training institutes, looking specifically at anticipation and response, will be discussed in the following chapters. The ability of CSTDI and LBSNAA to anticipate training needs is as important as their ability to develop forward-looking training programs in response.

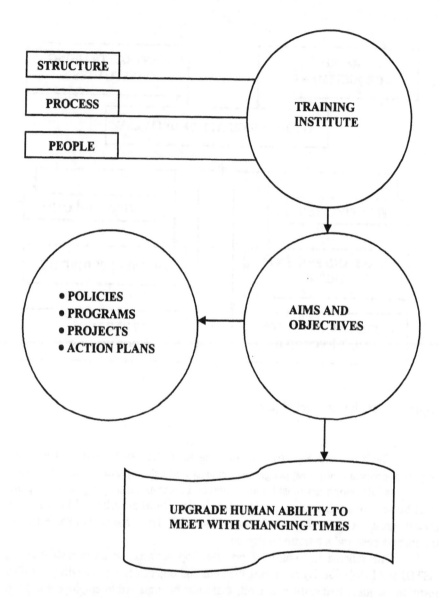

Figure 1.2 Training Process and Outcomes

Training institutes need to conduct intensive studies to help anticipate future training needs. Once the training needs and trainees are identified, programmes can be implemented, within budgetary restrictions. The problems intended to be resolved through training programmes, the methods for offering the programmes, and the potential outcomes have to be considered carefully beforehand. An evaluation of the training after it has been conducted helps to identify possible future plans, and reflecting on the outcome gives an idea of the merits and drawbacks of what was implemented.

Figure 1.3 suggests that formulating and implementing training packages is a continuous process followed by most training institutes. The foremost requirement for any training plan is the identification of training needs, which helps the providers of training to consider the actual requirement of the workforce. Training programmes become more focused following the identification of training needs. An estimate of the cost to be incurred is made and the effects and benefits from the training package are considered. Finally, training is conducted, followed by evaluation of the outcome to assess the achievements and drawbacks of the training programmes. The evaluation results are taken into consideration in formulating new training plans. Identification of future training needs and implementation of new training packages is a continuous process and the entire procedure and steps mentioned above are repeated while responding to each new need.

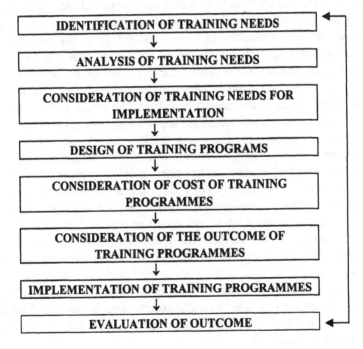

Figure 1.3 Anticipation and Response to Training Needs

Rationale, Plan and Analysis

This study concentrates on the training trends and the ability of the government central training institutes to anticipate training needs with special reference to India and Hong Kong. The aim of the study is to understand the actual role played by each of the institutes in imparting training to employees in the public service. It also tries to understand the degree to which new and projected training requirements are addressed and approached.

The study seeks to examine past and present training programmes and identify the future training needs of the civil servants. This analysis could help provide a basis for preparing the labour force needed to cope with challenges faced by public service in the new century, and was done by evaluating the degree of effectiveness the training given in India and Hong Kong. Training is often neglected but at the same time is essential for efficient and effective public service. Training programmes are not always effective, and officials may not be able to acquire the required skills. This points to the need for emphasising training for commitment of public services and political accountability. This is an area, which has remained neglected in conventional training programmes.

In brief, this book examines the training needs assessment procedures and evaluation techniques used to judge the effectiveness of training programs. It reviews the training methods and training procedures in India and Hong Kong. The book goes on to compare and contrast training trends in India and Hong Kong by reviewing the implementation of related policies. It is also pertinent to consider whether and in what way the training of civil servants is affected by the recent changes and demands for new skills. Finally, an attempt will be made to determine if it is possible for the central training institutes to identify the training priorities for public services in the near future by considering the present and past trends.

The book is based on the assumption that there are a number of universal principles and processes for developing efficient and effective public officials. This assumption is tested against the background of two extremely diverse places. The pattern and trend of training at the central training institutes of Hong Kong and India will also reveal the impact of globalization on public service training. A number of questions are addressed: Is public service training in India and Hong Kong conducted within a framework based on similar principles? Do the public service training institutes in India and Hong Kong employ similar strategies and procedures for the identification of training needs and conduct of training programmes? Are similar training techniques and mechanisms used in public service training in the two cases? Has public service training in India and Hong Kong developed in response to similar government objectives and priorities? Are there shared perceptions about the future directions of public service training in India and Hong Kong?

These issues are examined within the framework of the following key questions: How effective are the training programmes provided by the central training institutes in India and Hong Kong? What has been the trend of training in the past and what is it likely to be in the future? Is there a common framework, based on similar principles, that underpins public service training? With reference to India and Hong Kong, the following areas are emphasized: Are there similar processes for the identification of training needs and the conduct of training programmes for public service? Are similar training techniques and mechanisms used in the two cases under study? Are there shared perceptions about the future directions of public service training?

Training of public servants is believed to facilitate the entire efficient operation of public services. Identifying training needs and trends and anticipating and responding to future training needs enhances the efficiency of government operations. These factors and other associated ideas lead to interesting conclusions by studying a developing nation, India, with one that has achieved a high level of development in certain areas, Hong Kong. A parallel examination of such diverse countries contributes to a good understanding of the trends in most parts of the world. It is quite common for many countries to underemphasize the actual process of administration while overemphasizing the overall objectives, and thus fail to strike a balance between the two. It will be interesting to note the state of affairs in India and Hong Kong in this respect.

The research questions have been addressed with reference to two different frameworks. First, a schema of 'Training Needs Anticipation and Response' explains how training programs are considered and implemented. This framework also helps assess the trends and directions of training. Does an analysis of the past and present training programs assist in identifying trends for the future? Secondly, the effectiveness of training programmes may be evaluated by using a framework of 'Training Process and Outcomes'. This schema is useful for studying the structure, processes and people involved with the central training institutes, their aims and objectives, and their efforts to upgrade human skills to cope with changes in both the workplace as well as imposed by the internal and external environment. The two frameworks are described in detail in the following chapter.

A number of problems were encountered in conducting research for this study. Access to information was one of the major problems. Collection of secondary data collection was not much of a problem, but arranging and conducting interviews with trainers and trainees in India and Hong Kong required elaborate plans and negotiations. For various reasons, trainers and trainees were reluctant to share their views and remained non-committal. It was difficult to schedule appointments with senior public officials, and some of the information provided appeared to be similar to those found on official publications. Consequently, there were several instances of information gap and important and urgently required data was not available instantly. This added to the time required to complete the research.

Another word of caution should be stated on the generalization of the findings from this study. The main findings are based on the circumstances and experiences of public service training facilities in India and Hong Kong. This factor may make generalisations that are actually mores specific to these contexts. Moreover, the research for this study was confined to the training provided by the two major central training institutes. There are other institutes providing training for officials employed in the public services, both in India and Hong Kong.

Finally, this study research is narrowly focused and is limited in scope. Public service employees are exposed to various types and levels of training offered by a range of training providers—local, national and international. There are different formats for imparting general and specialized skills. This study restricts itself to the central training institutes of the two cases under study.

The book is divided into seven chapters. This introductory chapter sets out the purpose and significance of undertaking such a study. The methods used to collect, analyze and interpret information are stated, and the layout of the study presented.

The second chapter explores the concept of training, with reference to current debates and its implications in a globalizing world. Various interpretations of training as impacted by the forces of globalization are discussed to establish a framework for analysis. The content includes a review of the literature related to public sector training and outlines the theoretical framework and the relevant areas related to training. The main purpose of this chapter is to explore the intellectual and academic interpretations of public sector training, which provides a framework for the study and provides a context for the discussion in the subsequent chapters.

The third chapter presents a detailed discussion on the need for, significance of, and organization of centralized training programs. The issues are examined with reference to the nature and role of central training institutes and their potential for contributing to the development of effective and efficient public service training systems.

The fourth chapter presents an in-depth view of the LBSNAA. A substantial amount of data obtained through field research are used to describe and explain the organization and operation of the institute, and to highlight the framework of training, content, method, and features of public service training in India. The purpose of the fifth chapter is the same as the fourth, but it focuses on the CSTDI in Hong Kong. Chapters four and five thus give a detailed account of this study's major findings. The data is presented, in accordance with the framework stated earlier, with reference to the effectiveness of training programs; past, present and future trends of training; training priorities; process of identification of training needs; training techniques and mechanisms and future direction of civil service training are discussed. The views and comments of the respondents are also presented in these chapters.

The sixth chapter brings together the findings from the field research in these two different settings. It discusses the similarities and differences in the environment, mindset, facilities and the behaviour of trainers and trainees and their interaction with the public to assess the impact of globalization on the role and efficacy of central training institutes. The chapter examines the role of central training institutes in India and Hong Kong by evaluating their training trends, techniques, and ability to anticipate future training.

The last chapter brings together the various ideas and insight obtained from the research. An attempt is made to highlight prominent trends and recommend strategies for coping with the demands and pressure exerted by the forces of globalization, while continuing to serve indigenous needs to make public services effective. Central training institutes operate in the face of such tension, and are often found to devote attention toward the global trends while neglecting local needs and demands in public service training.

Chapter 2

Training for Public Services

Organizations and their human resources are constantly changing and both must develop new skills to maintain effective operations. During times of financial difficulty and rapidly changing technology, it is even more important for organizations to create a flexible and adaptable labour force, competent at using new technology and methods. The fundamental purpose of training is to provide organizations with manpower sufficiently skilled to meet the demands of a shifting work environment. The aim of training, in general, is to avoid persistent and economically damaging shortages of skills, including those that could inhibit technological developments.

Training has long been recognized as an important instrument in human resource development. Employee training and development is not only an activity that is desirable but also one that an organization must commit resources to if it is to maintain a viable and knowledgeable workforce. Training is a process of involving a sequence of programmed behaviour and facilitating the application of knowledge. It gives employees an awareness of the rules and procedures that should guide their behaviour, and attempts to improve their performance on an existing job or prepare them for an intended job. Training is directed towards maintaining and improving skills for current jobs and role performance requirements.

In other words, training is the process of changing employees' behaviour at work through the application of learning principles. This behavioural change usually focuses on knowledge or information, skills or activities, and attitudes or belief and value systems.

The Evolution of Training

Training is not solely a product of recent administrative and industrial development and advancement. As early as 1872, the first factory school was established at Hoe and Company, a manufacturer of printing presses in New York City. Miller notes that Hoe and Company needed to increase production, as there was no time to train machinists by the apprenticeship method, it was necessary to establish a factory school (1987, p. 8). In 1888, 1901, and 1907, Westinghouse, General Electric and International Harvester, established their own factory schools. However, one cannot assume that a full understanding and utilization of systematic training was in place at that time. In his book *The Principle of Scientific Management*, Frederick Taylor was one of the first to link training, among other factors, with high productivity. He argued that when tasks are set according to a rubric, managers can select the appropriate employee, 'train them', monitor their activities, and thereby increase productivity (Taylor, 1911).

However, it was not until the mid-1940s that training was conceived as a viable tool to increase employee and organizational effectiveness. When industrialized countries needed to increase their level of production during the war, fewer able men were available. Females and older people who did not have the required skills were the only alternative. Through the implementation of training, it became obvious that most of these workers could learn and become productive members of the organization (Nadler, 1984, p. 1).

Training in the public sector has been a common practice for many years. In 1941, a committee representing American and Canadian civil servants reported that, only exceptional agencies have given systematic attention to teaching their employees how to perform their duties most effectively. In 1944, the Assheton Committee in the United Kingdom found that 'neither inside nor outside the civil service has there been much systematic post-entry staff training' (United Kingdom, 1944, p. 6). Thereafter, the United Kingdom Government established training programmes on a scale far exceeding anything known in the history of Britain (United Nations, 1966, p. 4). In the first decade after the end of World War II, some countries created institutions and began more or less comprehensive programmes for public service training. Instead of being scarce, disorderly, and chaotic, 'training had become an aspect of personnel administration which attracted much attention and which was the subject of much experimentation' (United Nations, 1966, p. 4).

However, evidence of systematic public sector training is found in the *Employee Training Act, 1958* in the United States of America. The Act is considered as one of the pioneer steps in emphasizing on the importance of training. This was followed by the establishment of training agencies in New York, California and other locations in the country. Prior to that, the *Twelfth Biennial Report of the State of California Personnel Board*, published in 1937, recommended training as a critical activity. The Report stated that the Board 'will provide for the training of the employees in the specific duties of their jobs for the purpose of keeping them abreast of the best techniques and latest developments in their jobs and also to prepare them for promotion. Such training should not only include training in specific skills and abilities, but also should teach a broad understanding of the functions of the governmental activity and the fundamental principles, which govern public administration' (cited in Qureshi, 1967, p. 97).

Some less or non-industrialized countries also realized the importance of training. In a World Bank report published in 1983, Samuel Paul states that from the early 1960s to the 1980s, the number of administrative training institutions increased from 70 to 280 in developing countries (p. 1). The recognition of the importance of training and an increase in the number of training institutions does not necessarily imply that these bodies are effectively utilized in developing countries for several reasons.

First, training does not operate in a vacuum. It operates within and in conjunction with the administrative system it serves. Therefore, it must be supported by other administrative reforms, such as an informed selection and appraisal system, career-planning system, the level of salary and other incentives, and improved manpower planning systems (Commonwealth Secretariat, 1979). Some other factors that affect the success of training in most developing countries are:

(a) the absence of a national training policy.
(b) an inadequate educational systems, in that the supply of educated and trained personnel is seldom related to the demands of the economic and social development (United Nations, 1978).
(c) an administrative culture of governments that lack appropriate incentives for self development of first line and middle level managers, where improvements in personal capacity are recognized with increased responsibility and rewards (Sherwood and Fisher, 1984).
(d) public personnel systems that are inadequate as they do not provide substantive personnel policies that can guide career development and performance appraisal processes (United Nations, 1978).

These factors, among others, affect the success of and may pose obstacles to the implementation of effective training programmes.

The design and implementation of training programmes is based on various theories of learning. There are three principal groups of learning theories, which stem from three different models of man. The first group is labeled the mechanistic (or behaviourist) theories. According to this set of theories, the purpose of education is to produce prescribed behaviour, i.e. the behaviour that determines the performance of the learner. These are commonly known as 'stimulus-response' theories (Knowles, 1984, p. 47). This group of theories has grown far beyond earlier models of classical conditioning theories. There has been a sustained influence of mechanistic theories on training; it has greatly inspired the development of 'competency-based training', 'behavioural objectives', and 'trainer accountability'. It also has served to highlight the belief that learning through reinforcement is an efficient and effective means for internalizing new behaviours and skills (Kerrigan and Luke, 1985, p. 67).

Another line of thinking is social learning theory, which provides the theoretical basis for the behavioural modeling method used in custom-tailored formal training. The theory advocates that individuals respond to particular external reinforcers, and that this choice is based on one's expectations of outcomes and the intrinsic values one places on the outcomes (Kerrigan and Luke, 1985, p. 67).

The second set of learning theories is known as cognitive theories. These theories view humans as intelligent beings who are capable of thinking critically and solving problems. The purpose of training, thus, is to enhance the capacity of the brain to engage in critical thinking and problem solving (Knowles, 1984, p. 50). In other words, cognitive theories assume that adult learning occurs through problem solving. Research supports the notion that most adults engage in learning activities in the hope of solving a problem, rather than with the intention of learning a particular subject (Kerrigan and Luke, 1985, p. 70).

The third set of learning theories is known as the organismic (or humanistic) theories. These theories hold that human beings have their own genetically determined, unique and individual potential. The purpose of learning, therefore, is to encourage each individual to develop his or her full and unique potential (Knowles, 1984, p. 52). Learning, according to organismic theories theory, relies on the learner's capacity to experience and reflect. It assumes that learning can occur anywhere, that 'learning' and 'doing' are interdependent, and that as a person's capacity to learn from experience increases, s/he becomes less dependent on external conditioning or crisis-oriented problems (Kerrigan and Luke, 1985, p. 72).

The Concept of Training

Training may be viewed as a planned process whose organizational purpose is to provide learning experiences that will enhance the employee's contribution to the goals of the organization (Heneman,1986). There are three important elements in of this definition. First, the term process indicates that training should be a series of predetermined, interrelated steps rather than a haphazard activity undertaken for uncertain purposes. These steps include (1) determining training needs, (2) specifying training objectives, (3) designing training contents and techniques, (4) evaluating the effectiveness of training and (5) modifying the training process, if necessary, for future applications. The likelihood that training will be effective is directly related to the degree of planned processes within the organization. The second important element in the definition given above is related to learning. Successful training programmes must be able to answer questions such as 'What is training?' and 'How can we help learning to persist on the job?'. Finally, the definition implies that training needs requires periodic evaluation and the ultimate criterion of effectiveness, though difficult to measure, would help employees contribute to organization goals..

Training involves preparation for a particular job. Training is not an end in itself; its only purpose is to serve as a means of improving present job performance. Therefore, it follows that, in analyzing training needs, attention should be paid first, to the job and what it requires and second, to the jobholder and how s/he is performing those requirements.

In general, training is a process that aims to improve specific knowledge or skills that can be achieved, and will show benefits in the short term. Training, in both formal and ad hoc forms, is an activity that takes place continually within an organization and involves anyone in a supervisory position. It may range from someone showing a new employee how to operate a machine through formal training courses, to lectures, instructions and demonstrations.

Training is defined as the systematic acquisition of skills, rules, concepts, or attitudes that result in improved performance in another environment (Goldstein, 1986, p. 101). Baron (1981, p. 88) views training as 'the systematic development of the attitude/knowledge/skill behavior pattern required by an individual in order to perform adequately a given task or job'. Training is a process by which organizations can improve the levels of knowledge and skills of their employees to the point where they are able to achieve high productivity, quality of output and lower cost. This helps them to achieve competitive advantage and to provide excellent service (Cowling and James, 1994, p. 9). Training may also be defined as the acquisition of job-related skills. It is significant because it offers employees opportunities for advancement within the organization and can serve to improve morale and individual performance. For the organization, it is an important means of enhancing capabilities and efficiency. Training is one of several social control mechanisms in an organization. Thus, one of primary functions of training is to socialize individuals into the organization and to help them develop appropriate expectations for role performance in their specific positions (Jahns, 1981, p. 103).

According to Taylor, 'Training is basically concerned with improving the competence of an organization's employees. An organization with a well-trained workforce is better placed to defend, maintain or increase its market share nationally or internationally. It is concerned with the development of skills that may be any combination of physical, social or cognitive in nature. As such training should be an integral part of the investment plan of an organization, whatever in its size, since the company's employees are among its most important and expensive assets. The skills of a company's workforce are essential for its success' (cited in Revans, 1982, p. 78).

The *Handbook of Training in the Public Service*, issued by the United Nations, places emphasis on the importance of both teaching and learning. 'Training certainly is teaching with clearly defined objectives, but it is also learning. Unless something has been learned as well as taught, there is no training' (United Nations, 1966, p. 15). With particular reference to the civil service, the handbook states, 'Training is the reciprocal process of teaching and learning a body of knowledge and the related methods of work. It is an activity in which a relatively small group of persons acting as instructors impart to the larger mass of civil servants knowledge which is believed to be useful in the work of the latter, and at the same time the instructors assist the large body of civil servants to perfect skills which are useful in their work. In brief, training imparts knowledge and develops skills' (United Nations, 1966, p. 15).

The Ends of Training

There are different views on the purpose of training. Smith thinks that its purpose is to effect change in the behaviour of the employee (1974, p. 145). Leonard Nadler used it specifically to include only the learning process by which an individual will improve his or her present job performance (1984, p. 1). However, according to Irwin Jahns training can serve many functions, such as helping employees grow and develop their potential, and assisting organizations change successfully (1981, p. 109).

There are several ways to approach a consideration of the purposes of training. In reference to the individual who is being trained, the purpose is to prepare the employee to work in a satisfactory manner. A person may enter public services knowing practically nothing about the duties involved. In that case the purpose of training is to teach each person how to do the task and to teach the entire group to work together as a team in the implementation of the programme of the agency (United Nations, 1966, p. 57). The success or otherwise of the training is reflected in the efficiency of the workforce, and the quality of service provided by the employees for the people.

The purposes of training may also be considered with reference to particular programmes. Thus, on-the-job training has specific objectives, which may be expressed in terms of teaching employees how to use prescribed forms, file documents, or meet the public. Formal training courses may be designed to serve many ends, ranging all the way from the explanation of new sets of rules to national development (United Nations, 1966, p. 57). It is useful also to consider the objectives of the training in broad terms. The people responsible for conducting the training have certain goals in mind and hope to accomplish particular results. The goal or the expected results are not the same for every training activity, but there are some which are fairly constant and which recur in the formulation of the purposes of training. The United Nations (1966, pp. 57-59) summarized the general purposes of training in public service in the following categories (cited in Vadhanasindhu, 1994, pp. 18-21):

Efficiency and Competence

One of the rationales for training people is to increase efficiency. In the tradition of scientific management, efficiency is understood to be synonymous with economy in operations, or with improved performance without increased costs, which means that the purpose is to accomplish the objectives of government with minimum use of personnel, resources and materials. Training is an activity through which public services are led to understand ways, in which they may speed up their work, eliminate waste motions, employ manpower and material resources to greater advantage, and reduce costs.

Scaling-down of Learning Period

Training aims to speed up the learning process when personnel are allocated new duties. Learning by trial and error methods may be risky, costly and time consuming. A government operating under normal conditions with abundant resources of educated manpower can afford it, but such conditions do not prevail in developing countries. Training offers a solution by bringing public service officials to satisfactory standards of performance in a relatively short period of time.

Abolition of Defect and Weaknesses of Public Servants

Training is one of several ways to attack and eliminate the traditional faults attributed to public service officials. The purpose of training in this sense is to identify the specific habits or attitudes, which are considered to be inefficient and ineffective, and then design training programmes to help eliminate each of them. Generally, public service officials are criticized for over-concern with precedent, remoteness from the rest of the community, inaccessibility and faulty handling of the general public, lack of initiative and imagination, and procrastination and an unwillingness to take responsibility or to make decisions. Moreover, fear of the media and publicity, an excess of caution and a tendency to perfectionism, are deficiencies common in developing countries. The practice of taking bribes and deference to family and personal relationships poses additional problems in such countries. Many of the problems traditionally found in the public service are associated with poor handling of the clients/customers that they come into contact with in the course of their work, and this suggests the need for the improvement of communications, human and public relations through training programmes.

Morale-Building

Training is one of the best means to improve the morale of the employees of an organization, although this aspect of training does not receive much exposure in discussions on the issue. To the employee, selection to participate in a training course means that the supervisor is interested in her/him as a useful contributor to the organization. It also means an opportunity for self-improvement and to raise one's standard of performance on the job. In the past, selection for participation in training may have had the opposite effect, since the employee could have interpreted it as an indication that the supervisor considered her/him to be incapable of performing the duties. Nowadays, the widespread confidence in training has the effect of bringing satisfaction to those who participate. Training presents a possibility of improving group morale or *esprit de corps* by assembling the employees of a particular office or employees holding similar positions in different offices. A training course brings the participants into contact with others in the profession that does not usually occur in the normal course of their work. They have the opportunity to become acquainted with each other in their capacity as learners. This tends to deepen their sense of attachment to the organization and develop team spirit, while providing better appreciation for the goals of their organization.

Career Growth

Training can assist in developing employees in ways that enable them to take more responsible positions and to advance, by way of reassignment and promotion, through a satisfying and rewarding career. This aim of training poses some of the most difficult operational problems faced by trainers. Since the primary purpose of training is understood to be the improvement of an employee's performance in his/her current job, there is some contradiction in looking upon training as a means of career development. To use training as a method of preparing employees for advancement does not necessarily mean that they shall be trained for the higher position. It may only mean that better accomplishment in a present position will serve as the strongest recommendation for promotion and that the other objectives of training, such as an improvement in morale, will also contribute to the same end. The purpose of training under this consideration has been expressed as an effort to broaden the horizons of the officers, prepare them for higher responsibilities and to enable them to reach the full limit of their potential.

Advancement of Public Administration

Training can also be a means to improve or reform the standard of public administration in a country. It can be an aid to achieve quick results with relatively small expenditure, resulting in savings in time and effort. For instance, the clerical staff from different departments might be subjected to training and taught modern methods in handling the business in public offices. They can immediately get the opportunity to put the training into practice. If the employees could successfully act in this way, one training course might result in sweeping improvements in conducting public business. The introduction of administrative reforms is not so easy and immediate. The trainees might face problems and may be prevented from putting the reforms into operation by their supervisor, if they have not undergone similar training themselves.

Phases of Training Development

Training programmes involve at least four phases: analysis of training needs, curriculum design, implementation/delivery and evaluation of training programs. Support for this form of arrangement has developed over the years, escalating their loyalty to what has come to be known as the basic system requirement, accepting that training interventions will be a regular phenomenon throughout an organization's life.

Needs Assessment
- Conduct job/task analysis
- Conduct personal analysis
- Conduct organizational analysis
- Conduct demographic analysis

↓

Curriculum Design
- Establish learning objectives based on required needs
- Select format and content appropriate to type of training
- Sequence instruction to best achieve learning objectives

↓

Delivery
- Establish positive training environment
- Use instructional techniques appropriate to learning
- objectives
- Instruct consistent with principles of adult learning
- Transfer skills

↓

Evaluation
- ➤ reaction
- ➤ learning
- ➤ behavior
- ➤ results
- Modify previous steps based on results

↓

Anticipating Future Needs
- Conduct organizational analysis
- Conduct analysis of social and economic change
- Reconsider function of government
- Consider technological change

Figure 2.1 A Systematic Approach to Training

Needs Assessment

Steadham and Clay (1985) define needs assessment as a process in which the needs of a particular group or organization are identified, analyzed, and evaluated for the purpose of planning a constructive intervention in the form of training or other activities. Needs assessment is a diagnostic process by which one discovers what problems or deficiencies need to be addressed. In relation to training, needs assessment is a process focused on training related needs used to discover employee and organizational needs that can be addressed through training. However, there is no straightforward approach to the detection of specific training needs. For instance, there is much controversy around whether more emphasis should be given to employee or organizational needs.

In order for training to be effective in achieving the organization's mission and objectives, an employee development plan, which recognizes both the organization's and employee's perspectives, must be developed. In order for the plan to incorporate both perspectives, a negotiation process must take place (Austin, 1984, p. 53). The negotiation process should include:

(a) knowing the organization's mission, and the current of training;
(b) knowing the employees' interpretation of their own operational goals and their training needs; and
(c) assessing how other factors contribute to the agreement or disagreement between the two perspectives (p. 55).

If training is to be effective, a careful diagnosis of what kind of training is essential. Needs assessment ensures that training is relevant to both short-term performance deficiencies as well as the long-term career development needs of employees. It must consider the level of training demanded by different types and levels of employees and the most effective methods and techniques for conducting the training. The largest difficulty, but also the most important issue, faced by most trainers is to ascertain employees' training needs. There are various ways by which to assess needs. According to Shafritz and associates (2001, p. 323), the following techniques are commonly used:

(a) Survey of employees
(b) Interviews of employees, supervisors, or work experts
(c) Review of performance evaluation and assessment of career data
(d) Model career planning
(e) Job Analysis
(f) Human resources information systems approach.

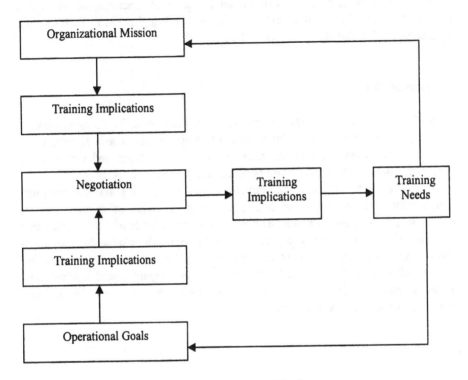

Figure 2.2 Negotiating Training Programme Needs

Source: Adapted from Austin, Brannon and Pecora, Managing Staff Development Programs in Human Service Agencies, 1984, p. 54.

An employee survey involves written individual opinion questionnaires, in which they are asked to estimate their skill levels, corresponding training needs and interests. The second technique involves extensive interviews of a sample of individuals, supervisors or work experts in special occupational or job categories. The interview may be directly concerned with the training needs or may ask indirectly how one would handle a certain kind of task in a given situation. The interviewer is required to identify training or skills need level that is related to job performance. The third technique involves a review of performance records in which supervisors consider performance records and determine the most relevant training programme. Using the fourth technique, a career model is formed with each functional and occupational work category plotted out against time and career grade objectives and with approximate work assignments and training programme objectives. The model is planned and formulated by experts and has a list of courses required, from which the supervisor selects the appropriate programme. The fifth technique, human resource information system approach, relates training to position redesign, employment, and placement options. Finally, functional job analysis examines managerial positions on the basis of functions, activities and tasks performed. This involves extensive survey work and position analysis on a continuing basis (Shafritz, 2001, pp. 323-324).

Curriculum Design

In whatever way the needs assessment process is completed, its outcome must be the basis for the design phase. The product of comprehensive needs assessment or analysis is the foundation for all subsequent training actions and provides the operational definitions of successful performance (Foley, 1985, p. 143).

The key to success in any training package is a well-planned curriculum, which may take the shape of a single course, a series of related courses. Curriculum development begins when need assessment leads into the formulation and identification of learning objectives and an approach suitable for training is chosen. Learning material must be developed to be consistent with identified training objectives, the intended audience, and the organizational environment. Training may take place on the job or in classrooms, and must be logically sequenced to achieve training objectives.

Delivery

Appropriate needs assessment and design phases are critical for success at the delivery stage. A successful delivery, while it builds on the findings of needs assessment and stems from the developed curriculum, must be effective in its own right. This phase is concerned with carrying out what has been agreed upon in the earlier two phases, especially the design phase. The format for delivering training is determined during the curriculum design. A proper format may include on-the-job training, classroom instruction, programmed learning or computer assisted instruction. A positive training environment is to be created and a proper transfer of skills is essential (Tompkins, 1995).

Evaluation

The final component of a systematic training process is evaluation of training efforts to determine whether training programmes and courses are accomplishing their stated objectives. Evaluation allows actions and corrections based on feedback about performance deficiencies, and introduce change in attitudes and/or alteration of behaviour. It makes it possible for training and development staff to identify areas where particular courses or training programmes may be strengthened. Evaluation is also a useful source of data for assessing the cost-effectiveness of training programmes. Different questions are asked at various levels and these are outlined in the following table:

Table 2.1 Steps in Evaluation

Level	Question
Reaction	Were the learners pleased with the programme?
Learning	What was learned from the programme?
Behaviour	Did the learners change their behaviour based on what they learned?
Results	Did the change in behavior positively affect the organization?

Source: Adapted from Kirkpatrick, 'Evaluation in Training', 1967, pp. 87-122.

These questions can assist in the modification of programmes to enhance the quality of training.

Anticipating Future Training Needs

Looking ahead is extremely important for training programmes, although it must be recognized that it is difficult to predict the future needs of potential trainees. Hall explains the notion of future-oriented job analysis in relation to succession planning. The organization's work objectives and strategies are examined in order to anticipate the job demands and necessary skills required for the future. 'Thinking through this link between the organization's basic objectives and need for future employees skills is the core of strategic planning and must be the basis for identifying the future training and development need of individuals. However, for new and drastic changes, where the required inputs are not available, the trainers should look upon the working of similar structures to learn from their experience. Comparative studies or learning from the experience of others greatly aid in preparing for ones own future' (Hall, 1986).

In public service training, it is the duty of the government to anticipate future training needs and formulate programmes accordingly. The goal of organizational analysis is to identify micro-level training needs so that resources can be concentrated in a particular area. At the same time, the requirements of economic development and technological change should be considered. Training institutes monitor changes taking place throughout the world and trainers are sent to international conferences to keep them informed of the latest developments.

The Benefits of Training

Civil Service systems and civil servants are usually defined as human capital, that is, the manpower resources of the national system of public administration, which is traditionally perceived as the bureaucratic organization that implements government decisions and policies. Although the nature of the system of public administration and civil services varies according to the political system, the idea of the civil service and civil servants as human capital is accepted globally.

Civil service training is assumed to increase the value of civil servants as human capital and manpower (Alam, 1990, p. 54). Through a process of teaching and learning, the participants in training programmes acquire cognitive knowledge, skills, rules, concepts and attitudes that will improve their performance in their professional administrative roles. An effective career in service is dependent upon many factors, one of them being the education and training provided for public servants.

Training is usually conceived as the responsibility of three partners: the participant's work organization, the participant, and the agency providing training. Public service training has also been categorized in many ways depending on target groups and objectives. There is general training and expert training, training of officials from different levels of public administration (federal, state, regional and local level), from different hierarchical echelons (higher, middle and lower level public servants) and the training of public officials at different stages of their career (pre-service training, induction training, on-the-job training or in-service training). Thus, there are many types of training, using many methods, at many stages of an individual's career. Basic training prepares employees for entry into the public service. Orientation or induction training introduces employees to the job and the organization prior to the assumption of a particular position. Post-entry training is aimed at improving performance in positions already held or to prepare employees for promotion. Special training may be required due to the installation of new systems or processes. Senior officials may also receive training in the form of individual study, conferences and seminars. Training may take place at the work site, in relevant institutions, or in other countries. Training programmes are offered by governments, private sector organizations, schools and universities, or by public administration institutes. Training may be sponsored by government agencies, national scholarship programmes, or technical assistance programmes. Variations in the training process are almost infinite.

Public servants, irrespective of their hierarchical position, must possess the conceptual knowledge, skills and attitudes relevant to the performance of their jobs (Paul, 1985). Training refers to a process of developing or augmenting these areas in a person with a view to enabling him or her to apply them in his work situation. Even if the educational preparation of a civil servant is adequate at the time of his entry into government service, training may still be required to induct and adapt him to his new job, and upgrade his skills at different stages in his career to match his changing task requirements.

Training is a well-articulated effort to provide for increased competence in the public service by imparting professional knowledge, broader vision, habits and aptitudes. Avasthi and Maheshwari identify several benefits of training:

(a) Training helps the entrant by inculcating occupational skill and knowledge, making him familiar with the objectives of the department to which he belongs, and his potential contribution is the furtherance of the department's goal.

(b) There are constant changes in the goals and techniques of the department. The broad goals are defined by legislation and are, therefore, occasionally modified and revised. Training adjusts the employee to the new environment.

(c) Training makes up for the deficiencies of the recruits. The public servants have to meet their personnel requirements from the existing supply. Training forges and shapes the existing material into the desired instrument of a good administration. Thus, the deficiencies of the new appointee may be corrected by imparting to them necessary training.

(d) The government must impart training in activities and occupations, which are peculiar to it and have no parallel in the private enterprise. The Government must train the appointee in their skills.

(e) In an era marked by spectacular advances in the field of knowledge, training helps keep the employee informed of latest development in his special field and, thus, keeps his knowledge up-to-date.

(f) Training helps broaden the vision and outlook of the appointees by constantly holding out to them wider, national objectives and their potential contribution towards the realization of the same.

(g) Training equips those already in the public services for higher positions and greater responsibilities that inevitably develop upon the existing personnel in view of the expanding functions of modern government and the demand for increased competence in the public services.

(h) Training is vital to a career service, which provides for the recruitment of persons of young age and their subsequent promotions. It is indeed, implicit in idea of career services that efforts would be incessantly made to develop the capacities of the recruits.

(i) Training sets the tone and quality of the organizations. It enhances the efficiency of the employees, by developing their capacities; the efficiency and prestige of the department go up. Work is not only done well, but also done quickly and to the satisfaction of the people.

(j) Training helps build integrity and morale in the public employees by inculcating in them the right mental attitudes to questions of personal and public conduct. It is imperative that the Civil Services should build up a higher standard of integrity than that generally prevailing in the community.

(k) Training fosters homogeneity of outlook and esprit de corps in the employees. It is conducive to cohesion with regard to method of work, and approach to problems' (Avasthi and Maheshwari, 1996, pp. 350-351).

A systematic programme of training is essential in public administration, since it makes possible the establishment of a career corps of civil servants skilled in general administration, who can man the senior positions in a wide range of substantive and functional fields. The development of such an administration corps will make available the range of managerial competence required at the top levels of each ministry, and will provide career incentives for the ablest public servants. In its broadest sense, training is a key to national development (Vadhanasindhu, 1994, p. 14).

Training Models

Training can be based on a number of models. On the one hand, a high degree of joint interchange among attendees is experienced during the training process in the andragogical approach. On the other hand, professionals take up the responsibility for the training process in the pedagogical approach. However, there are also other options for designing and conducting training.

Irwin Jahns identified five training models, each of which is differentiated by a division of responsibility between trainers and organizations and by different premises concerning the role of performance expectations throughout the training process (1981, p. 109). Among Irwin Jahn's models, the menu model suggests that packaged training activities and events are offered by the training provider to be purchased by organizations. The training supplier, depending on his experience, assesses the training needs and designs the training programme to be purchased as a package. The organization has the responsibility for deciding what it needs, and for selecting the appropriate training package.

In the special-order model, the training provider offers technical expertise and designs training activities and events that will meet the specific requests of an organization. In such cases, the organizations must be aware of its own needs. The training provider is responsible for delivering a complete package that meets the needs identified by the organization. Thus, the provider is not concerned with the kind of needs as they are simply delivering a prepared package.

While in menu and special order model, training needs are assessed by the organization, in the diagnostic model, it is the training provider who assesses and diagnoses training needs and prescribes an appropriate course of action. The responsibility of the organization is limited to the identification of deficiency or dissatisfaction, the selection of a training provider to assess the problem and prescribe the solution, the satisfaction of the training provider's request for information regarding its diagnostic and prescriptive services, and acceptance or rejection of the implementation of the prescription. The responsibility of the training provider is to conduct an objective diagnosis and develop appropriate prescriptions for the client organization.

The collaborative model is similar to the diagnostic except that both the training provider and the client organization are involved in a greater interchange of efforts. They are jointly engaged in assessing needs, prescribing solutions, implementing a plan and evaluating the results. Besides solving problems or removing dissatisfaction, the intention of this model is to enable the client organization to enhance its own abilities to conduct future efforts independently.

The organizational learning model builds on the collaborative strategy, and its primary intention is to increase the client organization's ability to engage in the training process, independent of external guidance, direction or control. The resolution of any given training need or problem is secondary to the client organization's goal of attaining self-sufficiency in problem solving. The client organization is responsible for demonstrating full commitment to increase its self-help abilities. On the other hand it is the responsibility of the training provider to assist the client organization in this task. Treffman (1978), as well, proposed five different training models. Although some of his models are categorized under 'education' rather than 'training' they all fall under the five broad categories of training (p. 1). The pre-entry education model includes any type of education one obtains prior to assuming the responsibility of a new position in an organization. The orientation-training model emphasises the process by which new members become acquainted with the rules and regulations of the organization. The major concern of the induction-training model is the process by which a newcomer to a specific position learns the responsibilities of that position and others in the organization. The in-service training model is concerned with the changing aspects of organizations and how current organization members learn adaptive responses to the new changes. Finally, the continuing education model is directed mostly by the individual, which may or may not be related to the specific role s/he plays in the organization.

Treffman's five models reflect the pattern of training structure and procedures generally followed by central training institutes in most countries. The need for the training and retraining public service employees at every phase of their career, to help in upgrading and keeping up with the requirements of the services and the departments they serve as well as for upholding the national policies and programmes, reflects a common pattern.

Types of Training

Training may be informal or formal. Informal training is based on working and learning from mistakes as one performs one's tasks, leading to the acquisition of administrative skills through practice. It is self acquired education (Sachdeva and Gupta, 1990, p. 178). This training 'occurs in the day to day relationships of employee and superior; in conferences and staff meetings of employee, newspaper and organization publication; at meetings of professional associations, and in the reading and study that the employee undertakes at his own volition or at his supervisor's suggestion. Because such training is connected with the regular tasks of the employees, he can best integrate with his own experience and thereby profit from it. Since there is no compulsion, connected with it, his motivation is positive. Its influence, whether good or bad, is profound' (Mandell, 1954, p. 568). The ultimate success of informal training, however, depends upon the experience and seniority of the supervising official and interest on the part of the participants. Owing to the phenomenal increase in the number of tasks and activities required of governments, senior public service officials now find themselves too busy to devote time and attention to the young officials sent out for field training. The latter are consequently denied the benefit of learning from their senior colleagues' experienced, and are left to learn through trial and error. The training sequences and their rationales are shown below:

Table 2.2 Sequences and Rationale for Training

Training Sequence	Rationale
Pre-training	• To construct an entry-level test by which to assess whether or not potential trainees meet training entry requirements. • To develop a diagnostic test that will reveal a trainee's pre-training profile made up of knowledge, skills and attitudes. • To aid the formulation of training objectives.
During training	• To aid in the assessment of trainees at each stage of training to ensure they reach (the) requisite levels and standards in the enabling objectives.
Immediate post-training	• To allow a check to be made that all the objectives of the training programme have been realized.
On-job: Short to medium term	• To assist the trainer in ascertaining whether or not, in the short to medium term (one week to one year) the actual or potential performance gap has been closed and that training has transferred credibly to real on-job conditions.
On-job: Medium to long term	• To help the organization in assessing whether or not training is contributing to corporate, economic, strategic, social and political goals.

Source: Adapted from Roger Buckley and Jim Caple, The Theory and Practice of Training, 2000, p. 95.

Formal training purports to inculcate administrative skills through well-defined courses at various stages in the public official's career. Such training is usually provided through administrative schools or academies. It consists of actual instructions in certain skills or procedures. There are different categories of formal training.

Table 2.3 Types of Training

Category	Nature and Scope	Duration
Pre-entry training (PET)	Training given to new entrants either prior to recruitment or during probation before the first job assignment. Focus on induction/subjects relevant to the general functions of administration. Usually a combination of classroom training and field work/attachments.	Generally long term: 6 months to 3 years.
In-service training (IST)	Training provided after entry into the service at different stages in a public servant's career. Covers both general administration/management training and functional/specialized training.	Generally short term: Few days to 6 months.
Project related training (PRT)	Training offered to different categories of personnel in a development project. Includes both technical and managerial training. Usually organized by donors.	Generally short term: Few days/months or a year depending on project needs.
Self Development (SD)	Training on a part-time or full-time basis at the initiative of a public servant, but with the formal support/approval of the government, using facilities outside of government.	Generally long term: Duration depends on the qualification to be acquired.

Source: Adapted from, Jonathan, Topkins, Human Resource Development, 1995; Shafritz J. M., Hyde A.C., Rosenbloom D.H., Riccucci N.M, Personnel Management in Government, 1992; Austin, Brannon and Pecora, Managing Staff Development Programs in Human Service Agencies, 1984.

Pre-entry Training

Pre-entry training prepares a prospective candidate for entrance into public service. Viewed in this light, even education imparted in schools and universities is pre-entry training, as it seeks to fit its recipient for all sorts of jobs in the public sector. However, the term 'pre-entry training' is restricted to vocational or professional instruction. Pre-entry training encourages trainees to apply previous academic and employment experience to new concrete job situations through direct participation, on a systematically planned and scheduled basis, in the work of organizations appropriate to the particular interests of trainees. This type of training also provides, if appropriate, for trainees' participation in supplementary, academic, and professional activities that will contribute further to their development.

Orientation

Orientation, in the form of information about plans and procedures, and introduction to relevant people, is necessary when personnel are introduced to a new or changed working environment. The process involves sponsorship by an experienced worker or supervisor, provision of information, open responses to questions, and a relationship based, overall, on guidance (Torrington, 1983, p. 166). The object of orientation training is to introduce an appointee to the basic concepts of his or her jobs, new work environment, and organization and its goals. The importance of orientation was highlighted by Morstein Marx a half century ago: 'It is clear that significant advances in the functional efficiency of the administrative state cannot be expected without corresponding changes in the working style of the administrative system. In this respect, perhaps, the most important thing is the acceptance within the higher civil service of a reorientation towards its role. The men of the top cadre must shift their attention from watching processes to measuring their impact, from getting things done to giving each citizen his due, from the technology of administration to its effect upon the general public, for utility to ethics. Not what is being said but what is being done, will decide whether the administrative state will stand out eventually as a benefactor or as a destroyer. It is for the civil servant to realize that much of what can be done must be his doing' (Marx, 1954, p. 66). This emphasis is on a very specific kind of reorientation that involves a more cooperative industrial model that is aware of the implications of its actions.

In-service Training

In-service training has the twin aims of stimulating the employees to make their best effort and of improving performance. For practical purposes, this is a common approach to training on the job, with trainees working directly in the production, operation or service environment. Special space and equipment are not required, while controls and reinforcements are operational and real, and the trainees can earn while learning.

Post-entry Training

The distinction between post-entry training and in-service training is somewhat unclear. Post-entry training, for the most part, is not directly related to the work of the employee, but is definitely of help to an organization. For example, training in engineering for a personnel specialist in a public works of highway department. Conversely, training in personnel work or public administration in this instance would be considered in-service training. Yet training in engineering, in our example, might be as valuable to the employee as the more closely related work in personnel management Though not directly concerned with the immediate tasks of the employees, the post-entry training is of value to the organization.

Project Related Training

Project related training focuses on the training requirements of all personnel in a given development project. A distinction between levels here is secondary. It includes both technical and managerial training. Such training programmes are usually organized by donors who sponsor the relevant projects.

Self-Development

Self-development refers to organized efforts to support individual training through the facilities available outside the training system of the government. Thus, public servants may be encouraged to undergo specialized training in certain useful subjects at academic or specialized training institutions. Study leave and other incentives are offered by the government to motivate employees for engaging in self-development.

Strategies and Learning Tactics

Prior to deciding the strategies and tactics, it is important to take into consideration the skill level of those being trained. In accordance with skill level, various methods can be adopted to train personnel such as, lectures, demonstrations, role-playing, learning packages, discussions, and computer based learning. There are advantages and disadvantages of each of these strategies adopted for training.

A lecture is a talk or presentation, usually supported by visual aids, in which information about practices, procedures and policies are described and explained to the audience. The trainer has full control of the contents and sequence of the training imparted. A large number of people can be trained simultaneously, and substantial output can be delivered in limited time. However, this method is not appropriate to teach skills and the interaction between the trainee and the trainer is limited. This type of training may sometimes be considered boring and monotonous by the attendees.

The demonstration is an illustration by live performance of a task, skill or procedure, accompanied by explanation and interpretation by the trainer. Usually, it is a follow up of issues dealt with in the training session in order for public servants to try out new skills before they apply them on the job. This method has the advantage of being comparatively easier, attracting the attention and interest of the trainees. It also speeds up the rate of adaptation by the attendees. However, it can be time consuming to obtain material and set up demonstrations. This method requires the trainers to possess a high level of competence.

Role-playing replicates the essential features of real work situations, in as near a form as is practicable. Trainees are required to use equipment, solve problems, follow procedures and act out roles as if they were actually performing the job. This method introduces an element of realism and involves a high level of activity, which arouses interest and motivates trainees. Real life experiences of both trainers and trainees can be drawn upon. However, the preparation and conduct of such exercises can be time consuming and expensive. Moreover, the trainer must possess extensive knowledge of the requirements of the job to be able to direct, manage and control the exercises.

A learning package is a collection of learning materials, which might include case studies, assignment exercises, directed readings and other material used by individual trainees as a distant learning tool. This package can be used with a widely dispersed target group and the contents of the package can be made attractive to assist motivation. However, the trainee might feel cut off and assessing assignments and exercises can be difficult and time consuming.

Discussions are group activities led by the trainer, in which the participants examine suggestions, attitudes, ideas related to work and performance. This method gives the trainees an opportunity to express their views and listen to those of others. It involves a high level of participation and the knowledge level of trainees is exposed. However, this method requires special competence of the trainers for stimulating the group, directing the discussion, controlling participants and managing time.

Computer-based learning or online training is a method for providing continuous training. This involves a group of learners and a tutor who are linked by computers, and exchange ideas and opinions in discussing the subject matter being studied. This method is highly flexible and cost effective, and can cater to a large number of people being trained at the same time. However, the initial expenditure needed for equipment can be high. The administration of such packages could be difficult due to the isolation of trainees from other learners and tutors (Buckley, 2000, pp. 168-173).

Preconditions of Training

Appropriate and successful training contributes to organizational effectiveness as it enables public service employees develop job competencies in order to meet established goals and standards. It also prepares them to cope with increasing demands arising from a changing internal and external environment.

The performance of an individual on the job is influenced both by ability and motivation. For instance, if an employee scores high on ability but is low on motivation, the level of performance will be lower than expected. Training deals primarily with improving ability. It cannot do a great deal to improve an individual's motivation, which depends on other factors such as compensation, working conditions, and personality. Training plays only a partial role in determining the overall level of an individual's performance. Therefore, it is important to identify the preconditions necessary to ensure the effectiveness of training.

Training Policies and Management of Institutions

A national policy on training and on the design and management of training programmes is a prerequisite for effective training. When training is organized haphazardly and training concepts, content, and methodologies are not properly adapted to the local environment, both training and the training institutions usually fail to make the impact expected of them.

The Education System

The training system can only build on what the education system of a country can offer. In fact, a sound education system can back up the training system. When the educational foundation of the young entrants into the public service is weak or inappropriate to the country's needs, training becomes an extremely difficult task. To some extent, this mismatch may be due to inadequate manpower planning by the government, which may have neglected the development of certain categories of manpower needed for smooth operation of public services.

A Pool of Skilled Manpower

A reasonably good supply of educated manpower is a necessary precondition for effective training. Some less developed countries are plagued by a general shortage of educated manpower. This is not necessarily a problem emanating solely from a weak education system. Demographic factors, as well as the past and current policies of a country, may have led to a situation of continuing manpower shortage which makes it difficult for the public services to attract an adequate supply of manpower with relevant skills. Under these conditions, competition for trained manpower becomes intense and a rapid turnover or depletion of personnel in the public sector renders training less effective.

Personnel Policies and Systems

Training is unlikely to be effective as long as the personnel policies and systems existing in the country do not support this activity. For example, if training is not integrated with the career development plans of public servants and an effective system of performance evaluation, a rational process cannot be developed. The reluctance of ministries to sponsor people for training and the lack of motivation on the part of public servants to take advantage of training opportunities largely contribute to this problem.

Favourable Administrative Culture

Effective training requires an administrative system that is performance-oriented in its patterns of authority and communications, attitude towards work, and values.

'Every government has an administrative culture, which is the combined outcome of informal work socialization and the interaction of complex administrative structures over a long period of time' (Moris, 1977). Several studies of training in industry have documented the decisive influence of 'organizational climate' on training effectiveness. Personnel policies and administrative culture are variables that promote effectiveness by stimulating a genuine demand for training. Training effectiveness is optimized when the preconditions are satisfied.

Pitfalls in Training

Several pitfalls can hinder the achievement of the objectives of training programmes. The first potential problem is the (a) the failure to properly identify training needs and (b) a strong tendency to follow the syllabi and methods followed by the traditional public service organizations. A careful and timely revision of the syllabi is essential. Second, the absence of a strong and coordinated training policy for public enterprises and neglect to integrate training programmes of different types leads to the insufficient use of resources. Third, weak personnel policy and failure to link training to career development of individual public officials gives rise to further complications. Fourth, difficulties can arise from an inadequate training program that either fails to meet expanding needs or uses inappropriate content or training materials. Another common problem is the failure to treat investments in training as a long-term project and the reluctance of governments or top management to allocate adequate funds for training. Finally, evaluative measures are lacking, making it difficult to assess the impact or relevance of training, both at the central and training agency levels. Need identification is an important area, which requires a careful diagnosis of the existing state of affairs and the demands of the future.

Institutional Categories

In most countries, public or government-owned training institutions are influenced by the British or American models. However, in Francophone Africa, the Ecole National D'Administration has a dominant influence on the approach and operation of training institutions. Autonomous institutions including Institutes of Public Administration as well as Administrative Staff Colleges can also be found in some countries.

Table 2.4 A Typology of Training Institutions

Category	Types of Training	Target Groups	Training Duration	Professional Staff
Civil service training Academy (Government owned and managed)	Pre-entry training (PET). In-service training (IST). Non-degree classroom work and field attachments.	New recruits to public service. Middle and senior level personnel.	PET: 3-24 months. IST: 1-12 weeks. Short seminars/ workshop.	Experienced public servants deputed as trainers and academic trainers.
Ecole Nationale D' Administration -Francophone	PET Classroom work and field attachments.	Pre-entry candidates, mostly for the public service.	1-3 years.	Experienced public servants and academic specialists.
University School Department of Public Administration	Mostly PET (degree/diploma programmes). Part-time IST.	Students and middle level administrators.	1-2 years.	Permanent faculty / part-time visiting faculty from public service.
Autonomous Institutions of Public Administration	Mostly IST, some PET. Classroom work, some field projects (may lead to degree).	Middle level government personnel and public enterprise managers.	1-9 months. Short programs/ seminars.	Permanent academic faculty and visiting practitioners.
Administrative Staff College	IST. Classroom work.	Senior and middle level personnel in government. Public / private enterprise managers.	1-12 weeks. Short seminars for top levels.	Permanent faculty with academic and practical experience and some visiting faculty.
Management Training Institute	PET, IST. Project related training. Classroom work and field projects and attachments (leading to degree/diploma in PET).	Young people interested in private / public enterprises. Middle / senior level personnel from government. Programme / project personnel.	PET: 1-2 years. IST: 1-12 weeks. Short seminars for top level.	Permanent faculty with academic and practical experience and visiting faculty.
Sectoral Training Institute/Centre	IST, PRT (PET rarely). Classroom work and field projects.	Middle level and technical personnel. Programme and project personnel.	1-9 months. 1-2 years.	Academic specialists and practicing sectoral administrators.

Civil Service Academy

This type of institution is heavily engaged in induction training, long-term pre-entry training for new recruits in the major administrative cadres of government, and in-service training mostly for middle-level personnel (http://www.apnic.net/). Their programmes cover general and functional administration. The foundation courses for new recruits have a strong general orientation (such as the study of national environment, economics and law). As well these institutions offer functional courses in financial management or project management for middle-level personnel that have a more specialist focus. If the institution is meant to service the work area of a single ministry or department, the technical or specialist orientation in training will be even stronger.

Ecole Nationale D'Administration

Ecole Nationale D'Administration or ENA is based on the French model and provides inter-ministerial career development for potential senior civil servants. The typical programme usually extends over 27 months and is divided into two parts: the internship period, which lasts 12 months, followed by the study period that lasts 15 months (http://www.ena.fr/ena.php). Generally, the ENA offers long-term pre-entry training programmes. Its training has a generalist orientation with emphasis on several subjects such as administrative theories, politics and economics, personnel management, development planning, financial management and international relations. The Civil Service Ministry of the French government supervises the ENA. In some cases, it also offers short-term training programmes of a specialized type.

Higher Educational Institutions

The primary task of higher educational institutions is to prepare young graduates for careers in government through pre-entry training. A degree or a diploma is awarded to the successful graduates. Courses in such institutions cover both general and functional administration areas. Some of these departments are also active in in-service training that is often devised as part time courses for employees in the public service. One of the most prominent institutions of this type, the National College of Public Administration and Governance at University of the Philippines, is engaged in both pre-entry and in-service training (http://www.upd.edu.ph/~ncpag/aboutthecollege.html).

Autonomous Institutes of Public Administration

Autonomous Institutes of Public Administration are generally larger than university departments teaching public administration, but smaller than most civil service academies. In-service training is the primary task of such institutes, though some do offer pre-entry training in the form of a degree or a diploma. The Indian Institute of Public Administration is engaged only in in-service training, whereas the Saudi Arabian Institute of Public Administration and the Brazilian Institute of Public Administration offer pre-entry training as well. Their curricula for pre-entry training are quite similar to those of the universities offering courses in similar subjects. However, for in-service training, autonomous Institutes of Public Administration concentrate more on specialized areas (project planning, appraisal and management, and performance budgeting) and have adopted a new curriculum to suit their needs. As they are engaged in the training of public enterprise personnel, enterprise management concepts and tools have influenced their curricula.

Administrative Staff College

Staff Colleges are designed as hybrid institutions in most countries, patterned along the lines of those in the United Kingdom. These institutions are exclusively engaged in training senior officials in both public and private sectors. The Administrative Staff College of India, the East African Staff College, and the Philippines Executive Academy have all followed this model. The curricula of such colleges focus both on public administration and management and they are known for their extensive use of the syndicate method of teaching. Joint programmes on management and policy problem for both private and public sector senior officials are seen as a useful forum for mutual interaction and learning, apart from the substantive acquisition of knowledge and skills.

Management Training Institute

Management Training Institutes are mainly engaged in pre-entry and in-service training for both public and private enterprises. Courses on the contextual problems of public enterprises have been added to their curricula to make training more relevant to their mission. Recruitment of graduates of such institutes by public organizations has become a common practice. A more recent development in the engagement of some of these institutes is in-service training work for the public services. The Indian Institute of Management (IIM) in Ahmedabad has offered this form of training to middle and senior level officials in the government. The IIM's in-service training covers both general administration and management topics based on field research and consulting experience (Paul, 1983, p. 89).

An overview of the various types of central training institutions allows us to place the two cases in this study in specific slots. The Lal Bahadur Shastri National Academy of Administration (LBSNAA) in India represents the Civil Service Training Academy model. It is involved in induction training, classroom work and field attachments. The induction course is long and lasts for two years. The LBSNAA appoints permanent trainers and draws upon the talent of visiting trainers from various branches of the public service. The Civil Service Training and Development Institute (CSTDI) in Hong Kong resembles the Administrative Staff College. It concentrates mainly on in-service training and targets middle to senior level personnel in the government. The duration of courses is short and training is conducted by a small number of permanent trainers who are supported by external experts.

A Strategic Approach to Training

Certain strategies can be employed in order to overcome these kinds of weaknesses and problems. Target groups should be selected and given training on areas identified as appropriate and beneficial. The approach, methods, content and orientation of public service training programmes must be consistent with the needs of the country and goals of the government. Financial support and commitment to training at the policy making level is also essential. The training policies must be farsighted and address the needs of the future.

The strengths and weaknesses of public service employees and the needs of the organization should be taken into account while planning training and development. The ideal characteristics of a strategic approach towards training and development include a number of elements. There must be an awareness of organizational goals and a commitment to training for the purpose of developing employees to meet these goals. An informed and regularly updated analysis of operational requirements and job competencies is important. This is helped by the establishment and statement of clear objectives and intended outcomes relevant to workplace, and which must be able to be evaluated. Other critical elements include skilled training personnel capable of effective delivery and management of training; regular evaluation of training activities at programme and strategic levels; a continuous learning culture in which employees constantly improve their knowledge, skills and abilities through self-learning, experience sharing, mentoring and formal training; joint responsibility between managers and staff for identifying and meeting training needs within overall constraints; and a variety of training modules and development methods to suit different circumstances and learning styles (adopted from United Nations, 1996, p. 3).

Concluding Observations

Training is offered in a variety of formats through different kinds of institutions and its key purpose is primarily to induce more effective behaviour. Training programmes are carefully developed and delivered on the basis of assessed needs. The need for initial and subsequent training is determined at various stages of an employee's career in the public service.

An overview of the published secondary literature reveals a number of critical elements in public service training. It is necessary to establish a proper sequence of the different phases of training. The processes and procedures of the different areas of training must be clearly presented and developed fully. This chapter has tried to present the combination of factors contributing to the different phases of the training activity and make it more valuable.

The advent of globalization has rendered the task of training for public services more difficult. Central training institutes are now forced to cater to the needs and demands expressed by external agencies and cannot afford to ignore them. The continued pressure by the international community for convergence and conformity has forced several countries to rethink and reformulate their training agenda. As a result, many of the benefits and expected outcomes of the various types of training programmes are coming under pressure. The next chapter takes a closer look at the organization and operation of central training institutes and the challenges they face.

Chapter 3

Centralized Public Service Training

Introduction

There are many training institutions in the world, taking a variety of forms. At the international level, the United Nations Institute for Training and Research (UNITAR), the United Nations Development Program (UNDP), the International Labour Organization (ILO) and several other agencies promote training through research, seminars, conferences, loaning of experts (Subramaniam, 1990, p. 111). At the national level, almost every country has a national training academy, school or institute.

The organization and coordination of training facilities in the government are normally undertaken by a central personnel institute, but in many cases it may not be in a position to undertake the extensive functions expected of the agency. In addition, in some countries, there is no such central personnel agency. From the earliest years of technical assistance programs offered by developed countries and international agencies, the concept of a National Institute of Public Administration has been regarded as the best practical alternative. It may be located within the government structure, affiliated with a university, or set up as an autonomous body (United Nations, 1978, p. 7). Such an institute forms the focal point for the improvement of public administration. It becomes a meeting place for advocates of reform, whether they are ministers, public servants, members of university faculties or public corporations. It can, at the same time, act as a teaching institute, a center for research, and a repository of the documentary base of experience and ideas drawn from other countries.

In the twenty-first century, training is one of the basic challenges faced by most countries as the forces of globalization bring countries in closer contact. It exposes the weaknesses of existing institutional constraints, and compels governments to search for alternatives. Trainers have to be aware of the requirements of recipient departments and must develop curriculum without unnecessary emphasis on dogma. For the purpose of achieving meaningful change, training can be designed so that it revolves around action and reflection at both the national and regional levels. Central training institutes need to continuously review and, if necessary, expand their training and research programs. Priority given to areas where training is most needed is beneficial, and they also have to work towards meeting the specific needs of the country by developing new training programs. The main aim of these institutes is to increase the level of efficiency in the public service, and to prepare the public servants with the skills and knowledge required to handle their jobs, duties and responsibilities. The institutes also aim at increasing the administrative awareness of the public employees and support the development of the national economy. The primary role of training institutes has greatly grown in importance and relevance in recent years, largely in response to globalization and the increasing complexity of developmental issues.

Generally, training institutes have the sole function of teaching civil servants how to do their jobs. Training centres specialize in job-oriented and intensely practical courses. They do not pretend to offer academic instructions similar to the universities, nor do they claim or need autonomy within the administration that they serve. Many training centres work behind the scene without attracting much attention. This study examines the role of central training institutes and analyzes their role in developing human resources in a country.

The primary functions or activities performed by training institutes are teaching, research, and consultation. The secondary functions include documentation, publication and serving as a source of information. Central training institutes also perform a number of other relevant functions, such as the recruitment of public servants and the organization of conferences and seminars. An account of the functions of the training institutes is summarized in the table below.

Table 3.1 Functions of Training Institutes

I.	**Primary or Major Functions**
A.	Teaching
B.	Research
C.	Consultation
II.	**Secondary Functions**
A.	Documentation
B.	Publication
C.	Serving as an information centre
III.	**Special Functions**
A.	Organization and conduct of conferences and seminars

All central training institutes in anglophone countries, or in countries where technical assistance is strongly influenced by the British or American tradition, perform the key functions outlined above. These institutes are engaged in teaching courses of one kind or the other, although, there is variation in the nature and level of instruction provided. An institute's role may be limited to pre-entry training or it may be engaged in a more in-depth job related training.

Research is one of the essential functions of training institutes. Any subject worthy of being taught must be firmly grounded in research. The findings of the research are used in the production of textbooks and other instructional materials. The practical application of research is highly beneficial to trainees. The research function merges into consultation or advisory services. By exercising its academic freedom to engage in research in any subject deemed to be important, the training institute may come out with recommendations for improvement and draw the attention of the government, media or public. The term 'consultation' is applied to this process when the government departments request the institute to undertake the inquiry.

Central training institutes generally act as a repository for books, documents and journals. Government departments, local government bodies, universities, professional associations, citizen's organizations, community groups and other bodies compile, document and disseminate a considerable amount of information in the course of performing their functions. Many of these materials are not published for sale in the market and are issued as unbound pamphlets and leaflets. These are collected and housed in the libraries of central training institutes and made available to trainers and trainees. Thus, valuable collections of documents relating to public affairs are collected and retained for reference at training institutes.

Publishing is another function of central training institutes. They publish various items including catalogues or prospectus, instructional material, monographs, and professional journals.

Central training institutes organize conferences and invite people from outside the agency to participate. Such conferences usually bring together senior public officials and external experts to promote the efficacy of their programs. These meetings offer opportunities for in-depth discussion on administrative problems and the mapping out of programs for identifying problems and devising solutions for bringing about improvements in the administrative system. In response to the dynamics of political and economic development, central training institutes have thus assumed diverse functions of great importance.

The Location Factor

Training is not a secluded function; it must be carried out in close coordination with other government programs, with agencies such as universities and other public and private institutes. Within the government, there are many departments and agencies involved with training and they share the responsibility of assuring that good training is provided for the public service. Training is always an activity that requires coordination among a number of interested parties. Even though a central training agency may be assigned a large share of the responsibility, it cannot function without the cooperation of numerous other partners (Vadhanasindhu, 1994, p. 30).

There are differing opinions about the ideal location of training institutes for public services, particularly regarding their relationships with the government and education system. A group of experts assembled by the Brookings Institute in 1961 identified several different types of organizational settings; but the report on the conference stated that: 'no pattern was singled out as "ideal", since the choice of setting and affiliation depends heavily on situations peculiar to each country' (Robinson, 1961, p. 39). When the first training institute in a particular country is designed and organized, it is essential to locate it carefully within the governmental and educational system. The location of the training institute will impact on its function and its success in accomplishing the tasks allocated to it. The advantages of incorporating the training institute into the government system include strong political and administrative support; greater protection against rival establishments; relatively easy access to clients or potential trainees; acceptance by the rest of the public service; greater opportunities for research and consultancy in government; easier access to information about governments; and the relatively easy provision of practical field work for its trainees (Reilly, 1979, pp. 117-19).

Most government training centers enjoy these advantages, especially the significant factor of political and administrative support. A national or central training institute, located as part of a powerful civil service commission, will likely have uninterrupted access to the highest level. This, in turn, can mean access to all kinds of benefits, including aid from abroad, freedom from interference by the government, updated developments in training, and recognition as the main training institute of the country. However, these advantages may not be recognized by strong regimes that do not wish to relinquish control over such important agencies.

It must be acknowledged that central training institutes run by governments may suffer under excessive control. This problem develops partly because the institute has to conform to a mass of regulations and irrelevant procedures, but more seriously through the involvement of the parent department in the details of running the institute (Reilly, 1979, pp. 117-19). Another disadvantage training institutes face under governmental control is that the movement of qualified personnel between jobs is so free that there is little to choose between public service, the university, or the private sector in its ability to attract or retain employees. Some central training institutes, especially those with few graduates or professionally qualified staff, do not appear to offer as attractive a career as a university.

A training institute affiliated with a university also has various advantages and disadvantages. First, the fact that such a department can offer a degree is seen as one of its main advantages. However, it is important to note that training institutes can independently opt for granting degrees, after gaining the approval of the country and grounding themselves in the national academic tradition. Second, universities are staffed with experienced academicians who deliver in-depth training programs relevant to their expertise. Third, such training institutes have access to all the facilities of the university, including offices, classrooms, auditoriums and libraries. However, institutes within universities also face certain disadvantages, especially stemming from the lack of political and administrative support. They cope with difficulty in receiving support from various government agencies and suffer from a lack of opportunity to incorporate their training activities within a national framework.

Central Supervisory Agency

Most countries have a central government agency responsible for supervising, coordinating and regulating activities related to training in the public service. Central training agencies offer various services to their clients. They may provide simulated training activities, and technical assistance to the principal departments of the government, their administrative divisions, and to special training units throughout the public service. Some of the services offered include making training materials, books, films and other resources both centrally located and available to government departments. Central training agencies collaborate with subdivisions of the central government to establish local and departmental training units.

In addition, central agencies provide assistance to offices that are too small to maintain their own technical training units as well as to other specific governmental agencies. These services are generally delivered in the form of unique programs that are not provided by administrative divisions or the public service as a whole. They concentrate on matters of general concern related to employee skills, providing these services more economically than individual departments could. The central agencies coordinate and strengthen training efforts throughout the public services by sponsoring training, promoting an association of public officials, and providing a channel of two-way communication between top administration and the entire public service for training and career development purposes (Caldwell, 1962, pp. 18-20).

One of the ways that central agencies help coordinate a training framework is through periodic conferences on training needs, problems, or developments which bring together administrators to share their experiences. These conferences help to spread training information throughout the public services. The movement of training personnel between the centre and other administrative sub-units also serves to coordinate the role. Conferences enlarge the experience of trainers and supervisors and permit the most effective utilization of available resources by bringing trainers to the points at which they are most needed.

Central training units promote decentralization of training facilities. The majority of training in the public service, formal or informal, takes place in the government agencies where training units are established. These units can draw upon the resources of the central agencies as needed. Regional institutes represent another type of decentralized training in which trainees are brought together from a number of offices for economy of scale. This arrangement can be effectively used to implement a new training program rapidly over a large geographic area (Vadhanasindhu, 1994, p. 34).

Changing Role of Government

Since the mid-1980s, there have been changes: a redefinition of the role of government and substantial programs of reform in public administration. The key concept guiding this reform is the idea that governments should only be involved in those activities that cannot be more efficiently and effectively carried out by non-governmental bodies. Another shift taking place in the role of government concerns the tension between the public and private spheres. Any commercial enterprises retained within the public sector are now structured along the lines of private sector companies. The goals of the government, its departments, agencies and individual public servants should be stated as precisely and clearly as possible. Potentially conflicting responsibilities are, whenever possible, separated and assigned to appropriate agencies for execution. There must be a clear separation between the responsibilities of ministries and departmental chief executives. Whenever possible, publicly funded services, including the purchase of policy advice, should be made contestable and subject to competitive tendering. Furthermore, institutional arrangements must be designed to minimize the scope for provider capture, and preference given to governance structures that reduce agency and transaction costs. Finally, in the interest of administrative efficiency and consumer responsiveness, decision-making powers should be located as close as possible to the place of implementation (Boston, 1996, p. 57).

Over the years, reforms have transformed the institutional landscape, economically, socially, constitutionally or legally, and have thus paved the way for a new public service profile. Furthermore, the global transformations that are sweeping the public arena have brought with them the need for greater qualification in the field of management, and a greater rationalization of management techniques and downsizing of procedures. These reforms have also highlighted the need to make the public service more aware of and competent in the use of information technology. Such changes make it necessary to constantly revise curricula, and introduce new techniques and ideas related to management, human resources, communication and negotiation.

The roles of the government and their accompanying obligations and opportunities have also been undergoing change and reform. One can assume different constellations and different shapes of government in different countries, but no country is insulated from these changes, particularly in view of the impacts of globalization. The world in which modern governments operate is becoming increasingly uncertain and complex. The boundaries between nations, levels of government, public and private sectors, and different kinds of agencies and organizations are blurring and disappearing. Moreover, governments are facing issues that are difficult to understand and resolve, appear intractable, are difficult to define casually, and are certainly not the preserve of any one sector of government. Globalization has a corresponding impact as governments are the subject of, rather than the controlling force behind industrial, commercial and financial developments. Information technology has assisted in this shift, with improved communication and the methods of organization allowing for cooperation and collaboration at the international level. Pluralization and diversification are indicators of globalization's impact on many different societies.

Thus, changes in government and social environment demand the alteration and revision of the training packages offered by public service training institutes. Owing to changes in the working environment, those who come to such institutes for training, expect to be trained in skills and competencies related to their own sphere of operation, along with methods of work and development of good attitudes. Training institutes must anticipate these changes in order to provide public servants with the skills necessary to master and assimilate into the political, economic and technological progress of a rapidly changing society.

Internal and External Challenges

Considering the role and constantly changing nature of both government and public management, public service training institutes face a number of challenges. These are generally related to tasks performed by the institutes and the fluctuating environment in which they function and can be summarized in five categories: curriculum, transfer of experience, the conduct of research and evaluation, a balance between management and policy, and the movement of human resources.

Curricula

Training curricula need to be designed with an eye on the practical needs of the job of trainees. It is essential to be aware of and note the challenges and demands faced by those in public service. The curriculum for management education, and training and development must be relevant to the tasks and requirements of the country. Usually, the providers determine the content of the curricula but it is important that trainees identify their own needs and take part in the process as well.

Knowledge and Experience Transfer

The main responsibility of central training institutes is to promote the transfer of knowledge and experience, from one organization of government to the other or between countries which share information in order to learn from the way other countries perform administrative tasks. Training institutes that work in a variety of situations can use the experience of one national situation to raise questions and provide critiques of others. This is particularly important when similar approaches and strategies are applied in many different places. However, it should not be assumed that what works in one country is appropriate for another. In practice, it is essential to consider the extent to which the problem is unique to a country or institution, the extent to which the policy or practice has been evaluated as successful, and whether the policy and practice meet the political, ideological, and value preferences of the recipient.

Research and Evaluation

There are significant and rapid changes taking place across the globe which continue to strengthen the demand on public administration for good governance. Under these circumstances, outdated practices can no longer be justified. Consequently, there is a constant search for new methods and strategies. Training institutes have to engage in rigorous analysis of ideas and actions. A research base informs training and education activities and enables the development of forward-looking ideas. If the institutes do not engage in rigorous thinking, conceptualization and analysis, the teaching and learning will not be modern and advanced. Training institutes must encourage probing questions whether or not the answers to these questions prove useful in developing future strategies.

Policy-Management Balance

Many training institutes focus exclusively on effective management. Their role is related to efficient, effective and economical administration and management of government organizations. This approach often leads to the neglect of relevant policies. While the management element is critical, a weak policy framework can affect the performance of the government. It is essential to get the balance right between the demands of management and policy. It is essential to balance the demands of management and policy.

Movement of Human Resources

One of the key steps for getting relationships and the balance of responsibilities and opportunities right is to ensure movement of people between training institutes and the world of practice. This flow takes place, to some extent, when the practitioners undergo training. The staff of the training institute should be a mix between professional educators and practitioners among training institute staff. Secondments, exchanges, and short-term attachments have proved fruitful. If it is impossible to mix people, the next best strategy is to ensure the regular passage of practitioners through the institutes. Participants in the programs should be more than customers, they should help in constructive thinking and their involvement can import ideas from the 'real world' to the training programs.

A number of challenges arise from the changing external environment in which public administration is conducted. Among them, new skills and styles, the danger of new orthodoxies, the plurality of governance, strategic capacity, and political context are of significance. These factors influence all countries and institutes in different ways.

New Skills and Styles

There have been significant changes in the traditional skills and styles applied by public management. Public officials are now required to possess entrepreneurial skills and approaches, to adapt quickly to a changing work environment, and to exploit the potentials of information technology.

New Orthodoxies

New ideas emerge and become prominent and the advent of new public management has shifted attention to the market, customers and performance management in many countries. The new ideas do have their strong points, but several countries have embraced them without conclusive evidence of their positive impact. There is a difference of opinion as to whether the traditional values of public should be abandoned in totality. They have guided public administration over a long period of time, and there are reasons to argue that they retain their validity.

Strategic Capacity

Government organizations should have the capacity to think beyond themselves and the immediate issues that they are handling (Dror, 1986). Thus, public officials should be capable of understanding the changes taking place in the environment, their impact, and the services and skills that will be expected of public servants and organizations. These factors point to the importance of finding ways to develop the necessary skills and modes of working among public sector managers.

The Political Context

Public officials operate within the sphere of the government which reflects the immense importance of the political context. They are required to develop an understanding of, and sensitivity to, political direction. They need to be well versed in the political environment and should be able to perform their activities within the framework provided by the political system.

The Plurality of Governance

In most countries, the nature of governance is changing and the environment within which a public manager operates has now become quite different from that of the past. Governance has become more plural in nature, and the boundaries between organizations and the public and private sectors blurred. A number of organizations and agencies have been introduced and to tackle new problems and issues, leading to a demand for cooperative government. This does not mean that there should be cooperation only between the government agencies and departments, but also between government and public and private sector as well with as non-governmental organizations in this respect. Training and development needs to be sensitive to such changes.

Government Training Institutes in India and Hong Kong

Most countries of the world are responding to the challenges posed by globalization. Every country is becoming increasingly involved in international affairs, and there are continuous efforts to promote national interests abroad, in political, economic, commercial, scientific and cultural aspects. Governments are subject to such competition thus they must organize proper and adequate training for public officials in order to rise to the challenge. Rapid changes in the environment have brought new challenges, and with them new job-skill and knowledge requirements, lending credence to the idea of life-long or continuous learning for public officials.

Training of civil servants is important as it upgrades the quality of personnel in accordance with changing needs. Central training institutes are the apex organizations in the context of public service training as they occupy a key place in the administrative system. These institutes are responsible for providing strategic guidance on training and development to various departments of government. There is no substitute for on-the-job training or learning as no amount of institutional training would give a public servant the real feel of his job or teach him the best method for getting the job done. However, considering the rapid development of knowledge and its application to different areas of public administration, on-the-job training may not be the most effective strategy. Executive Development Programs and Management Development are thus instituted at different stages during the career of a public official. Generally, training activities cover the areas of management, language, information technology and other refresher courses. As globalization takes hold, training programs are now shifting emphasis towards economic, financial, social and trade issues related to sustainable development.

The LBSNAA and the CSTDI are the major government agencies providing training for public service in India and Hong Kong respectively. A brief description of the aims and objectives of each sheds light on the functions performed by these institutes. The primary functions of the training institutes—teaching, research and consultancy—are carried out by LBSNAA and CSTDI. The secondary functions of documentation and publication are also performed. Both institutes serve as information centres for various government departments. With reference to location, both serve as central training institutes and are at strategic positions within the government.

Both institutes are aware of the challenges thrown up by the changing role of public administration which has led to increased emphasis on practical issues. Trainers are invited from various branches of the public services to provide first hand experience to public officials. Another noticeable trend is the realization of the importance of imparting policy related to training in order to strengthen management. Tummala (1996) reported that the Department of Personnel and Training in the Ministry of Personnel of the government of India supervises the operation of LBSNAA (p. 167). In contrast, CSTDI functions as an independent body.

Training institutes can be viewed as job enrichment missionaries not only in the sense that they are intellectually committed to the concept, but also in relation to careers: as consultants, they try to sell job enrichment to business and management (McIntosh and Daniel, 1972, p. 50). Such institutes assess the adequacy of their training from time to time in order to review the considerable developments that take place in society, owing to changes in public demand and government policies. Constant monitoring enables training institutes to provide quality programs to meet the needs of specific departments.

Training institutes evaluate their programs with the objective of identifying and removing weaknesses as well as improving performance. They provide training in order to disseminate the vision, mission and core values of the relevant agency; enable officials to acquire knowledge and skills required to meet organizational goals and standards; improve individual performance and change attitudes and behaviour. They also prepare public officials to cope with increasing demands arising from changing political, economic and management environment.

LBSNAA, India

LBSNAA, the largest training institute for higher public service in India, was established in 1959. All government officials receive their initial training at this Academy, which aims to create a bureaucracy that commands respect by performance rather than through position (http://www.lbsnaa.ernet.in/). LBSNAA imparts induction-level training to members of the public service through a common foundation course and offers continuing professional training to regular recruits of the Indian Administrative Service (IAS). In addition, the Academy conducts in-service training courses for middle to senior ranking members of the IAS and for officers promoted to IAS from the state civil services. It attracts some of the brightest young men and women in India who are then trained as administrators for the various civil services of India. The Academy also offers a range of specialized programs for a diverse clientele. Individuals, non-governmental organizations, the corporate sector, and the government departments are offered customized courses, catering to their respective needs. The aim is to make public officials effective facilitators in promoting decentralized governance and strengthening social change and economic reforms. Its duties include:

(a) Provision of induction (foundational) training to all civil servants recruited to the All-India Services and some Central Services.
(b) Providing training to fresh IAS recruits through a Sandwich course.
(c) Providing short-term (5week) induction courses to all officers promoted/inducted into the IAS.
(d) Providing In-service/Refresher training to a large number of officers in the IAS (the 3 week courses for the 6-9 year service group, 10-16 year group and the17-20 year group; and the one week vertical integration courses).
(e) Acting as a nodal agency for developing a high degree of expertise in certain identified areas e.g. Decentralized Planning, Sustainable Development, Economic Reforms, and Co-operatives etc.
(f) Providing a platform for issues relating to the National and State training institutes.
(g) Undertaking various studies and research projects with a view to improving the training components of its activities and to carrying out studies on various governmental activities.
(h) Acting as a centre of excellence for highlighting and promoting innovations in administration.
(i) Organizing and carrying out inter-institutional activities for the development of training material in public management such as case studies, role-play, and exercises and to promote relevant action oriented research, etc. on issues and problems in public administration.
(j) Undertaking UNDP sponsored courses on topics such as Panchayati Raj institutes, Direct Trainers Skills, Communication skills, Economic liberalization, etc (LBSNAA 1996, pp. 6-8).

The Administrative Reform Commission (ARC) recommended that the central institute provide general or administrative training to civil servants, while the different ministries and departments deal with specialized training (Maheshwari, 1993, p. 123). In India, the only compulsory program is the induction, and many public officials do not receive training for a long span of time afterwards. According to one estimate, 'only one senior civil servant in five is likely to have some in-service training during his entire career' (Jain, 2001a, p. 101). The specialized institutes impart job specific training, but LBSNAA is entrusted with all round development of public officials. A Director, assisted by a Joint Director heads LBSNAA. There are eight Faculties: Management, Law, Economics, Public Administration and Social Management, Languages, Computer and Information Systems, History and Indian Culture, Political Theory and Constitutional Law (LSBNAA, 1997, p. 2). Deputy Directors are in charge of their respective units, and head the Faculties. Faculty members are deputed to reputed institutes both in the country and abroad. Besides the Faculties, there are nine operational units devoted to National Literacy; Management Training; Village Study; Training, Research and Development; Training for Administrators; Information Technology; Cooperative and Rural Development; and Sustainable Development (http://www.civilservices.gov.in/lbsnaa/academy/facilities.jsp).

In addition, LBSNAA has set up a large number of research units. They are the Centre for Cooperatives and Rural Development (CCRD), the Centre for Sustainable Development (CSD), the Centre for Micro-planning and Regional Studies (CEMPRES), the Centre for Development of Software for training of Administrators (SOFTRAIN), the Centre for Rural Studies (CRS), the National Research and Resource Centre (NRRC), the Training, Research and Development Cell (TRDC) and the Gender Studies Unit (GSU). There is also a training unit of the National Informatics Centre Training Unit (NICTU) with a well-equipped Computer Laboratory.

National Institute of Administrative Research (NIAR) is the prominent research society within the LBSNAA. The activities of the Society include research studies, consultancy services, development of training modules, and preparation of case studies. It organizes workshops and seminars along with theme-oriented training programmes. It undertakes publication of research studies for wider dissemination. Faculty members of the Society also provide their services for lectures etc. in the various training courses of LBSNAA. The registered society was set up in 1996 to undertake and co-ordinate research and development activities of LBSNAA. The society was created to become an umbrella organization for the various research units in the Academy. Due to early teething troubles, like the requirement of appropriate approvals of the various government departments and ministries, the task of unifying all the research units of LBSNAA under the umbrella of the Society could not be finished. This major task has now been completed and all the erstwhile research units of LBSNAA have come together under the support of the Society.

The Academy is spread over three campuses in Charleville, Glenmire and Indira Bhawan. Each has its specific orientation. Charleville caters to induction-level training as well as customized courses, Glenmire houses the National Research and Resource Center (NRRC) and the Indira Bhawan campus offers facilities for in-service training and other specialized courses.

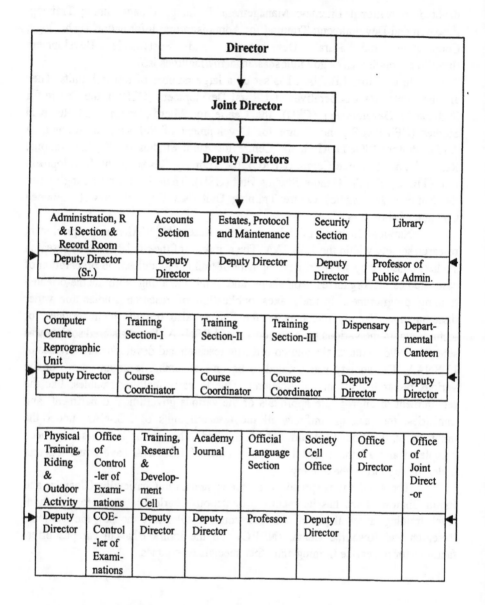

Figure 3.1 Lal Bahadur Shastri National Academy of Administration, India:
     Organization Structure

Source: Information collected at LBSNAA, 2001.

CSTDI, Hong Kong

Training and development began receiving attention and recognition in the Hong Kong public service in the late 1940s when the government's localization policy was founded on the recommendation of the then Salaries Commission which suggested that the civil service should be composed of local people, as much as possible (Scott, 1984, p. 119). To put this policy recommendation into practice, it was important that the local people be trained sufficiently in order that they could take up the job of managing the public service. Against this background, many departments began to operate training programs for their staff. In particular, induction courses were provided to local recruits in order to provide them with a general introduction to governmental machinery and basic vocational training. At that time, there was no central institute to coordinate public service training. Training programs were primitive in nature and designed only to meet specific short-term needs of departments.

The key areas of training and development covered in Hong Kong are induction training, vocational training, management development, language and communication, information technology and China studies. CSTDI, with the support of various government departments, organize training on management development, language and communication, information technology and China studies. The institute basically concentrates on centrally organized courses conducted by the CSTDI staff, commissioned staff and external invited trainers and also provides courses tailor-made for departments designed and conducted by its trainers. Apart from imparting training, the CSTDI provides other services and support through consultancy, customer service training, advice and interpretation of training regulations, compilation of service wide training statistics and production of guidebooks and self-learning packages.

In 1961, a central Training Unit was established in Hong Kong under the then Establishment Branch (now the Civil Service Bureau or CSB). The Unit was re-named Government Training Division in 1967 and was tasked to centrally provide and coordinate civil service training for the purposes of implementing the localization policy and maintaining efficiency in service (Scott, 1984, p. 120). In the following years, the demand for the services provided by the Division, increased steadily as more and more departments recognized the importance of either vocational, language or management training for their staff. The services provided by the Division were therefore expanded and diversified and its day-to-day operations became increasingly more independent, though it still looked upon the CSB for policy guidance. In recognition of its semi-autonomous status, the division was renamed the Civil Service Training Centre (CSTC) in 1980.

The main objective of training and development in Hong Kong is to enhance individual and organizational performance, leading to quality service for the public. Effective training and development contributes to organizational effectiveness by disseminating the vision, mission and core values of the organization and enabling staff to develop job competencies to meet organizational goals and standards. In addition training also contributes to organizational effectiveness by improving individual performance and changing attitude and behaviour, thereby preparing public officials to cope with the increasing demands arising from the changing internal and external environment.

The training of Hong Kong civil servants was placed under the jurisdiction of the Senior Staff Course Centre (SSCC) and the Civil Service Training Centre (CSTC) before the organization of the CSTDI in 1996. These agencies were responsible for bulk of the training-related activities in the public sector, and were combined in early 1996 to establish a centrally coordinated CSTDI (Huque, et. al., 1998, p. 59). The aim of this institute is to provide training and development programs and services for improving the performance of public servants in Hong Kong. The CSTDI has initiated various programs for preparing public officials in Hong Kong for the new environment (Huque, et. al., 1998, p. 64). It advises the government on central and departmental human resource development and organizes training activities.

The Institute is staffed by a group of professional trainers (CSTDI, 1999, p. 6). The training officers and experts assess training needs in order to develop plans and appropriate training methods. CSTDI claims that it updates itself in accordance with developments in environment and changing needs of its clients. Its mission is to assist central policy initiatives through training and development, to facilitate and tender advice on central and departmental human resource development, and to pioneer and disseminate the best in training and development (CSTDI, 1999, p. 6).

Training for the public service in Hong Kong can broadly be divided into five key areas: induction, vocational training, management development, language and communication, and computer training. Induction is aimed at familiarizing new recruits with job requirement and procedures, departmental objectives and performance standards, and the values and norms of the department or grade. All public officials are exposed to induction upon appointment. The CSTDI prepares the packages for the induction course, if requested to do so, and distributes these to the various departments of the government who, in turn, hand them over to the new recruits. Vocational training, on the other hand, aims to provide public officials with the technical knowledge and skills required in performing their daily work. As departments and grades have diverse functions and objectives, the requirements for vocational and induction training are different in each department. Thus the responsibility for planning, implementation and subsequent evaluation in the above-mentioned areas of training rests with individual grades or departments.

Management development training provides public officials with the knowledge and skills required for carrying out their tasks effectively. It widens their perspective and is provided to public officials at different stages of their career, in keeping with the concerns of resource and personnel management. Such training is either conducted by the CSTDI or by other prominent external local or overseas institutes. The CSTDI is the organizer and coordinator for all these training programs departments and grades are responsible for nominating suitable officials to attend such courses, taking into account the management development needs of their individual staff. However, with the devolution of training authorities, departments and grades can also use their own resources to arrange courses in case the central services do not meet their demands. Language and communication and computer training are provided to public officials on a need basis. However, since the change of sovereignty in 1997, officials are encouraged to enroll in Putonghua (Mandarin) and written Chinese courses. Furthermore, the officers are encouraged to acquire basic computer literacy in line with the global office trend towards automation.

The CSTDI partners with client departments to address the organizational and people issues in the pursuit of service excellence. To help departments to develop effective strategies for communicating and implementing change, the institute:

(a) facilitates strategy formulation;
(b) develops and implements change strategies;
(c) enhances communication between management and staff;
(d) identifies and meets staff's development needs;
(e) designs work-life balance initiatives and stress management;
(f) creates a supportive working environment for implementing change initiatives;
(g) disseminates good practices for managing change.

CSTDI has provided training to 60,970 trainees, which works out to approximately 168.905 trainees every day. It has also conducted 21 training surveys to identify the development needs of officials from 42 departments (10.5 per cent more than that in 1996-97) carried out 20 consultancy projects to help departments enhance their human resource management and development functions (67 per cent more than that in 1996-97); provided 28 publications on various aspects of training and development; and distributed 142,000 copies of self-learning packages on various topics (CSTDI, 1998, p. 13).

In 1998-99, special attention was given to the organization of a new high-level leadership enhancement program for senior public officials. Since the reversal of sovereignty to China in 1997, there has been a provision made for developing customized training programs on Chinese writing and Mandarin, and officials have been provided with enhanced knowledge about China. To cope with the changes in demand for forward-looking training programs, the CSTDI has strengthened its advisory services to departments formulating plans for staff training and development and establishing strategies for their implementation. With the advancement of information technology, classroom training has been supplemented with computer-based methods and increased use of the Internet.

CSTDI holds quarterly meetings to review progress and consider future plans. Training managers from all the government departments are invited to take part in these meetings. The events are useful for holding discussions on training and development issues. They help to strengthen links with departments and promote new services. At the same time, CSTDI tries to understand departmental needs and concerns. Guest speakers from both the public and private sectors are often invited to share their experience. CSTDI officials pay visits to departments to advise on the Civil Service Regulations, training and other training issues, and to discuss CSTDI's role and services. The Institute presents talks on enhancing training and development in government departments, covering about 50 departments every year. Ongoing services such as the Resource and Information Centre and the enquiry system on management education programs are under constant demand from different departments. Better understanding of training and development can lead to the improvement of the quality of the services of the departments.

A Director heads the CSTDI, assisted by an Assistant Director and an Assistant Principal Training Officer. There are seven operational units: Administration, Senior Management Development, China Studies, English and Communication, Advisory Services, Management, and General Grades (http://www.info.gov.hk/cstdi/Ehtml/engindex.htm).

The Institute has 167 officials, including 79 Training Officers, four Staff Tutors, and 16 Executive Officers. In addition, there are CSTDI Training Officers posted to other departments. At the time of writing, 33 Training Officers were posted to 11 departments. The CSTDI Advisory Board is chaired by the Secretary for the Civil Service and is comprised of heads of departments, heads of human resource sections in private enterprises, and academics with specialization in human resource and public sector management (http://www.info.gov.hk/cstdi/Ehtml/). These trainers play a very important role in the training procedures, and their understanding of the organizational context contributes to the learning process as well as organizational effectiveness.

The Institute's headquarters are located at the North Point Government Offices. There are 37 classrooms, 16 syndicate rooms, two computer-training rooms, three language laboratories, two conference rooms, one multimedia training room and one 140-seat auditorium.

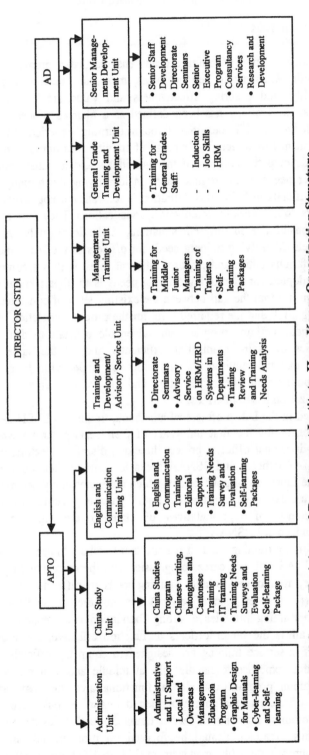

Figure 3.2 Civil Service Training and Development Institute, Hong Kong: Organization Structure

Source: CSTDI Prospectus 1999, p. 30 and Information collected at CSTDI, 2001

Training Needs Analysis

The effective identification of training needs ensures that a program can yield maximum benefit. Recognizing key outcomes, measuring success, continuously improving quality, and ensuring effectiveness and value are the products of effective evaluation. Training has been defined as a planned process to modify attitude, knowledge or skill behavior through learning experience to achieve effective performance in an activity or range of activities. Its purpose in the work situation is to develop the abilities of the individuals and to satisfy current and future manpower needs of the organization. In identifying the training needs of public service officials in India, this definition is relevant but not comprehensive. The IAS officers do not work in stereotypical organizations. They have to handle a variety of responsibilities in different situations at the local, state, and central government levels. Identifying training needs for officers of the IAS, who have to engage in multifarious duties and perform different roles, is thus a complex task. The approach adopted for identifying training needs is to impart knowledge and skills so as to ensure that the gap between the existing level of competence of an officer managing a job and the required level for the proper completion of tasks is adequately bridged. Training programs should enable officials to deal with the internal dynamics of their organization efficiently and, at the same time, to understand the external environment in order to cope with problems and contingencies, both within the organization and the external environment with which the organization has to interface.

As stated in the IAS professional handbook, training in LBSNAA aims to prepare probationers for the first ten years of their service during which they function as sub-divisional officers, project directors, district collectors, etc. Thus training of the IAS officers at LBSNAA seeks to enhance their competence in assisting with the functions of government, which are increasingly becoming more complex. There are extensive consultations both with state governments and at the bi-annual conference of representatives of state governments and central government organized at LBSNAA.

In identifying training needs it is important to take into account the stages of the individual IAS officer's career progression and the corresponding level of responsibility they are required to hold. Training needs are different for officials at the junior level (the first ten years of service) than they are for middle and senior levels. Induction training provides a strong foundation that imparts skills and knowledge that allow the junior officers to function effectively. Subsequently, various forms of in-service training are designed to equip the officials with the necessary skill and expertise to handle jobs at middle and senior levels. It is important that training programs consider the functional areas that may have to be covered by IAS officials in the course of their duties at various stages of their careers. It is important to make public service training directly relevant to the needs of the participants. Training should be focused on problem solving and the development of appropriate public management skills that can improve the delivery systems in the government. At the same time, training programs need to be grounded in current theories and concepts of public administration. In other words, theoretical input is also extremely important, although it does not seem to feature prominently in the programs offered by the LBSNAA. There is a need to strike a balance between catering to specific needs and providing a good theoretical grounding. However, it must also be noted that there is concern over the potential danger of low participation by trainees if the programs are overwhelmingly academic in nature.

Training needs are anticipated and a training and development plan is prepared at LBSNAA. The Academy provides a considerable range of training on its premises. However, LBSNAA deputes its trainers from government departments to provide in-house training. Public officials are sometimes sent to regional training centers, with the Academy taking on the responsibility for arranging these courses.

In Hong Kong, CSTDI identifies service-wide training needs, while departments and public officials are responsible for identifying training needs specific to their domains. A document entitled *Generic Competencies for Managers and Staff* lists specific skills, knowledge, abilities and attitudes that are needed to perform a job effectively at specific levels. Using the listed competencies as points of reference, the officials, their supervisors and the Institute discuss and agree upon training needs. It is important to select courses based on specific job or staff development needs. A simple training need analysis process is followed to enable trainers to make appropriate selection. Needs are assessed by means of surveys and interviews with officials of government departments and a Training and Development Plan is prepared, leading to the adoption of an appropriate method of training. CSTDI plays a role in the assessment of training and development programs for government departments.

CSTDI provides both in- house and campus training. The Institute offers training staff to conduct in-house training on site for government departments. However, usually, the trainees are sent to CSTDI campus for training. The Institute designs and organizes customized or tailor-made courses based on the specifications and requirements of the departments, which are delivered either on the premises of CSTDI or the departments.

CSTDI closely monitors changes and developments in the field of public service and conducts annual customer surveys to assess the needs of the departments of Hong Kong government. The survey allows the institute to collect suggestions on methods for improving performance. The CSTDI also keeps close contact with government departments and holds regular meetings to consider the needs of departments and their relevance to the overall needs of the public civil service.

Figure 3.3 draws out the schema of analyzing the training needs. The departments identify the competencies required for the staff to perform the job and the gap between the existing and required competencies help in identifying needs and develop the training plan. The training and development programs, depending on the requirements can be organized in-house or contracted out to training institutes.

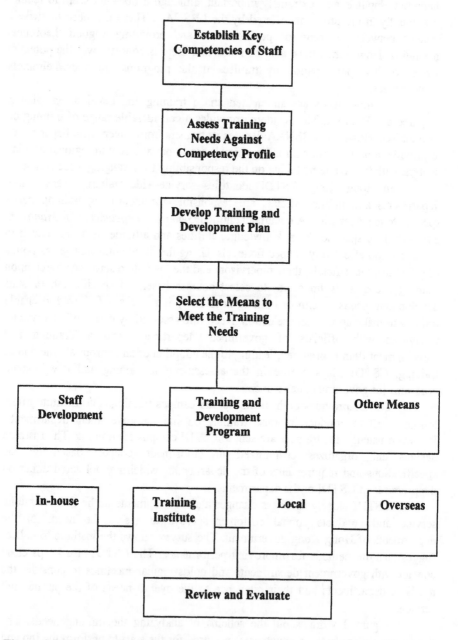

Figure 3.3 Training Needs Analysis

Source: CSTDI Prospectus 1999, p. 8.

Training Methods

At the LBSNAA, training programs are designed in accordance with the needs of the departments of the Indian government. Different courses are designed for various ranks of officials in the public services. The courses generally focus on management practices, project management, government and public order, language studies and information technology. The trainers claim to structure training and development sessions effectively; present information clearly to different audiences; select appropriate materials to support the sessions, including the use of visual aids; plan and monitor training sessions and select strategies for dealing with challenging situations (Interviews with trainers at LBSNAA, 2001).

Under the existing system of in-service training for IAS Officers, the Ministry of Personnel of the government of India requires every IAS officer to attend a one or two weeks training program in a block of two years. The first block of such training was offered from April 1990 to March 1992, the second from April 1992 to March 1994, the third from April 1994 to March 1996, the fourth from April 1996 to March 1998, the fifth from April 1998 to March 2000, the sixth from April 2000 to March 2002, and the seventh block is in progress at the time of writing (http://persmin.nic.in/iastraining.html). However, LBSNAA appears to place more emphasis on induction, in comparison to in-service training.

The skills and knowledge required by public officials are easier to impart among experienced professionals rather than the new recruits. These are measured in a number of ways. According to LBSNAA publications, correspondence is a common method of evaluation. The feedback from the trainees and their departments form a base for developing future training programs. The Academy anticipates future training needs and then submits applications for the financing of training programs to incorporate these elements. The process is assisted by public sector organizations. Collaboration with other training institutes also reveals insights about potential changes and the nature of the training required to cope with them.

In Hong Kong, the CSTDI, too, claims to develop learning objectives according to potential and perceived needs. The Institute offers a variety of courses catering to the needs of staff from directorate grade to junior rank officials. It is responsible for the organization of management studies, language and communication courses, information technology programs and China studies programs (CSB, February 1999).

The objectives, methods and techniques used in Hong Kong are not that different from those used in India. The CSTDI claims to provide training that will enhance understanding of the core values of the public service and uphold the integrity of the Hong Kong government. It assists the Civil Service Bureau in formulating and implementing training programs, advises departments on training and development matters, and designs courses with the future needs in mind. Delivering timely and high quality consultancy services to departments to support the successful implementation of Human Resource Development (HRD) and other public sector reform initiatives, such as target-based management process, is also listed as one of the objectives of the Institute. Finally, the CSTDI proposes to promote the adoption of a coordinated and systematic approach to HRD and other HRD best practices in departments to help strengthen organizational competence (CSTDI, 1999, pp. 2-3).

Since its emergence (as CSTC) in 1980, the Centre has been formulating service-wide training policies and conducting courses on management development, language and computer skills. With the devolution of training responsibilities in 1994, it was relieved of the task of training officials in the public service. Since then, more of the efforts and resources of the Institute have been devoted to expanding its advisory services on training matters for user departments. It conducts training needs surveys and reviews jointly with departments. CSTDI also helps departments strengthen their training capability by offering courses and publishing reference manuals to enhance the skills of the trainers and managers. Furthermore, the Institute provides other advisory services by participating in committees set up to select training consultants, recommending trainers and consultants for central or departmental training projects, advising on the setting up of departmental training committees, and advising on the use and purchase of training aids, equipment and training accommodation (CSTC, 1995, p. 17). In addition, the CSTDI provides training support for the implementation of central government policy programs.

Training programs are delivered either at the Institute or the workplace of the trainees. Various developmental methods are used in order to encourage and enable on-the-job training. Apart from traditional classroom instruction, skills and knowledge are facilitated through coaching, modeling, professional activities, special projects, developmental projects, and attachments. In the Prospectus, the Director of CSTDI pointed out: 'Organizations the world over are facing a dilemma these days when it comes to training and developing their staff. While it is generally agreed that learning has never been more important, organizations are finding it harder to release staff to attend courses because of overwhelming workload. Hence the rise of E-learning and workplace learning practices. CSTDI has responded with our own Cyber Learning Centre and other self-learning devices, which are described in this Prospectus. However, as revealed in the 2001 'State of the Industry' report compiled by the American Society for Training and Development, even in the United States where e-learning is most advanced, about 70-80 per cent of the training staff receive today is delivered in the classroom. Classroom training will stay in the mainstream for a long time to come' (CSTDI, 2001).

Training Evaluation

Training is not an end in itself. It can be evaluated as useful or successful only if it equips a public official to perform better on the job. Although training is accorded importance in most organizations, there is increasing demand for proof that investment in training does make a difference in the trainee as well as allowing the organization to utilize the trainee's skills.

Objective evaluation of specific training programs is necessary in order to improve future programs in the same areas and to eliminate programs that are not effective. It is also essential to update training programs and incorporate new subject areas in relation to the requirements of the public service sector and the country. Evaluation of training programs is based on various factors: i.e. the number of personnel trained, the link between training and performance, the social impact of the training, the contribution to the skills of the group, and the value for money paid out. All these aspects must be kept in view in both internal and external validations. The whole process of objective evaluation (i.e. internal and external validation) can be best considered if broken down into logical steps after considering the requirements of trainees, trainers and the organization.

In the context of India, conducting an objective evaluation of the training provided to IAS officers is extremely difficult because of the complexities involved in relating training with the post-training performance in specific jobs, considering the fact that the IAS is a multi-functional service. Nevertheless, it is necessary to try and develop methods for objective evaluation of training programs for IAS officers considering the large investments of time and finances involved in the process of training. The absence of an assessment would result in a lack of feedback to trainers, feedback which could be useful for improving the quality of programs. In addition, the trainees would not know whether they have achieved the desired outcomes. Resources would be wasted on training that does not meet its objective. Finally, without evaluation, the government would not be able to associate improved performance with training.

Internal and external validations are two methods by which to assess the impact of training programs. Internal validation has been defined as a series of tests and assessments designed to ascertain whether a training program has achieved specified behavioural objectives. Internal validation can be accomplished through a series of steps. The first step assesses the quality of training provided by questioning the trainees to find out if they found the learning satisfactory and how they feel it could be improved. In all training programs for IAS officers, feedback forms have been developed to elicit reactions immediately after the conclusion of a program. The second step assesses the quality of training by asking the trainer whether the learners have improved their knowledge/skills as a result of the training. In IAS programs, for instance, there is a continuous interaction between the trainers and trainees during the program itself, and many of the trainees are expected to make presentations during the program, allowing the trainers to make assessments on this basis.

External validation is defined as a series of tests and assessments designed to ascertain whether the behavioural objectives of an internally valid training program were based on an accurate identification of training needs in relation to the criteria of effectiveness adopted by the organization. External validation has considerable importance because training can be considered successful only if there is discernible improvement in job performance. Very often, however, such a direct link between training and job performance is difficult to establish, especially in the case of IAS officers. For instance, there are several training programs specifically directed to improving knowledge and skills in specific areas, which may or may not be directly used by the trainee in his job for a long period after the training. To take an example, consider the case of an IAS officer attending a program on Financial Management. An evaluation of the training program must first test knowledge of the officials in that particular area and then determine whether undergoing training has strengthened this knowledge. In many cases, it may take quite some time before this knowledge can be put to use in any specific responsibility.

Induction Programs

Internal validation is employed in all the four components of the induction program: Foundational course (FC), Phase-I, District Training, and Phase II. At the end of FC, and Phases I and II, the trainees are asked to assess the training from the point of view of both its achievement of objectives and relevance. However, it must be noted that neither external validation nor evaluation is undertaken for this type of training. It would be difficult to undertake these two exercises, as no systematic training needs assessment is carried out in the induction phase. Courses are designed largely on the basis of the internal validation results of past courses and on the experiential wisdom of the faculty.

In-service Courses

The Academy conducts in-service courses for officers of the IAS with 6-9 years, 10-16 years and 17-20 years of service. It also conducts an induction program for State Civil Service officers, on their being inducted to the IAS. In all such courses, only internal validation is carried out, with no external validation and evaluation (http://www.civilservices.gov.in/lbsnaa/research/trdc/rlpreport99.doc).

The outcomes of training provided by the Academy are not assessed at the performance level. It would be useful to initiate both external validation and evaluation for the programs. Evaluation is made more meaningful if it is conducted by an outside agency. However, both of these exercises require carefully designed instruments that can be administered effectively, in order to achieve optimum results. The objective of evaluation should be to upgrade, improve and modify the training programs, and their content and methodology in the light of changing requirements.

The CSTDI collects feedback from course participants as well as from the workplaces of the trainees. Evaluation and feedback are solicited to make improvements. CSTDI works closely with heads of government departments to assess training needs. Changes in public policy and demand are studied to determine future needs. Emphasis is put on changes in technology and efforts are made to upgrade the quality of personnel in the public service.

After the delivery of training programs, their outcome is evaluated by collecting feedback. There are three levels of evaluation. The end of course evaluation: i.e. the reaction level. This evaluation is merely regarded as a 'happy sheet' and is seldom treated seriously. Usually, the Institute receives very good scores on such evaluations. For courses of longer duration, three levels of evaluation are conducted. At the second level, CSTDI assesses the degree of knowledge acquired by trainees at the end of the course through tests on the knowledge, skills and attitudes the participant has learned from the training program. The second level of evaluation can sometimes be conducted immediately after the course. The trainees are subjected to skill tests and their demonstration of proficiency indicates that knowledge and skills have actually been acquired. The third level of evaluation explores the behavioral outcome of training. The Institute administers questionnaires to government departments and training participants with the objective of assessing the extent to which skills have been applied and attitudes have been improves. A subsequent set of questionnaires is used to seek the views of trainees and their supervisors. Updated feedback on performance helps in determining whether the training has been effective as well as sustainable.

Philosophy of Training

In India, the constitutional mandate for civil servants is interpreted as one that promotes empathy for the underprivileged; a commitment to the unity and integrity of the nation; a promise to uphold honor and impeccable character so that they appear as role models for the large number of subordinates working with them and for the society at large; a respect for all castes, creeds, and religions; and a dedication to the battle for the eradication of poverty, is the ultimate objective of every civil servant (LBSNAA, 1996, p. 2). The Academy includes the inculcation of a feeling of nationalism among the public officials in its mission.

The ability to work effectively for the underprivileged depends on one's professional abilities and commitment to constitutional values. The enhanced role of non-government organizations (NGOs) and an appreciation of their role are promoted by exposing trainees to such organizations in their course on Bharat Darshan (knowing India). They are also exposed to NGOs through working in the urban slums.

India is a huge country and the burden of training all of its civil servants by a single institute seems to be an impossible task. The aims of training in India are to inculcate among public officials a respect for the system of parliamentary democracy and an essentially national outlook. The Five-Year Plans play a key role in achieving India's national goals, and hence 'program orientation' has been at the heart of most training programs.

In contrast, Hong Kong is a very small unit of land and its training philosophy is different. The objectives of training are to nurture officials in order that they maximize individual performance, leading to quality service to the public in Hong Kong. The aim is to enable officials to acquire the necessary knowledge, skills and attitudes to meet operational requirements and changing circumstances; and to assist grade/departmental managers in realizing the career development plans of individual officers and the succession plans of grades/departments (CSTDI, 1996, p. 1). Successful training contributes to organizational effectiveness because: (a) it disseminates the vision, mission and core values of the organization, (b) it enables staff to acquire the knowledge and skills to meet organizational goals and standards, (c) it improves individual performance and changes attitudes and behavior, and (d) it prepares staff to cope with increasing demands arising from the changing political, economic and management environment (CSTDI, 1998).

Concluding Observations

Central training institutes require freedom and flexibility to allow their growth. In a rapidly changing environment, plans and programs require quick adjustment and governments must be prepared to support the training philosophy strongly. There is a need to recognize that training can neither be a solution to all administrative ills nor a substitute for the sound development of policies and programs. It cannot fill the gaps created by defective administrative structures, cumbersome rules and procedures and inadequate resources. Training can be regarded as one of several facets of the development process and can be seen only as a means to equip public officials with the requisite to allow them to achieve their administrative and developmental goals. The modernization of societies portrays challenges to public officials to transform themselves into agents of change. The following chapter explores the process of public service training in an age of globalization.

Chapter 4

Public Service Training in India

This chapter examines the role of central training institutes in India by reviewing their techniques and their ability to anticipate future training trends. This chapter focuses on a number of key areas as perceived by the actors involved in the training process in India. The profile of the respondents, which includes their ideas and purposes for training, provides useful insight on the issues. The following section presents the results of a survey conducted on trainees and trainers at the Lal Bahadur Shastri National Academy of Administration (LBSNAA). The survey questions concentrate on the six major factors related to training that were identified in Chapter 2.

The Respondents

Questionnaires were distributed to four hundred and fifty trainees who were identified as potential subjects in fields relevant to the study. Another set of questionnaires was sent to fifty trainers at the training institute. Two hundred and fifty two (56 per cent) questionnaires were returned by the trainees and thirty four (68 per cent) by the trainers. The group of trainers included current as well as former trainers at LBSNAA. The trainees were drawn from officials of different grades and ranks in the government who had attended training courses at the central training institute.

Later, interviews were conducted with twenty-eight trainers and forty-three trainees, as well as with two officials at the central Ministry of Personnel of the federal government. The criteria for the selection of the respondents and the actual breakdown of the response are presented in Table 4.1. The majority of trainers were in the 40 to 50 years range, while the largest number of trainees fell under the 20 to 30 age group. Many of the trainers had attained a Masters or higher degree, while most of the trainees possessed a Bachelors degree. The trainees belonged to different ranks and grades in various departments of the government of India. Some were on probation after joining the Indian Administrative Service (IAS), and thus were new recruits of the government. Other trainees included officials employed in senior positions in government departments. The latter group had received training earlier, and were able to discuss their views on the changes that took place within the government. The sample included trainers from different ranks at the Institute, and a few former trainers were approached to give their insight on the planning, implementation and outcome of training at the LBSNAA.

Table 4.1 Profile of Respondents

Trainees			Trainers	
Number of Respondents	252		**Number of Respondents**	34
Position	**Number**		**Position**	**Number**
I.A.S. Officer Probationers	163		Director of LBSNAA	1
State District Magistrates	34		Joint Director of LBSNAA	1
Additional Collectors	25		Deputy Director	13
Collector	18		Professor	4
Commissioner	4		Reader	3
Assistant Commissioner	5		Language Instructor	6
Joint Directors of various departments	1		Assistant Lecturer	3
Directors of various departments	2		Ex-trainers of LBSNAA	3
Educational Qualification	**Number**		**Educational Qualification**	**Number**
High School	0		High School	0
Bachelor degree	154		Bachelor degree	7
Master	49		Master	15
Ph.D.	5		Ph.D.	1
Specialization	44		Specialization	11
Age Group	**Number**		**Age Group**	**Number**
20-30 years	154		20-30 years	2
30-40 years	36		30-40 years	8
40-50 years	32		40-50 years	16
50-60 years	19		50-60 years	6
Above 60	11		Above 60	2

The Findings

The main purposes of training are to prepare new recruits for service in the public sector and to bring about improvements in the performance of current employees. A more general purpose of training is a comprehensive improvement of public services that would enhance, in varying degrees, the effectiveness of jobs, employees, and organizational dimensions (United Nations 1966, pp. 51-61). In the study under analysis, an effort was made to discover what areas the respondents felt were emphasized by LBSNAA. They were asked whether the Institute places emphasis on improvements in current job performance, effectiveness as an official in the public service, or skills that lead to career development. The overwhelming majority (80 per cent) of the LBSNAA trainers placed greatest priority on improving skills to perform on the present job, while only approximately 15 per cent emphasized training as a means to increase the effectiveness of the trainee as a public servant.

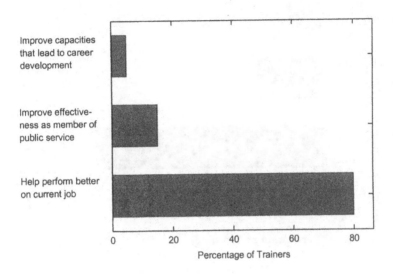

Figure 4.1 Trainers' Perception of Training

Figure 4.1 demonstrates that improving the capacity of public officials for career advancement was not perceived as important by most of the LBSNAA policy level members interviewed. A Deputy Director and Senior Trainer at LBSNAA stated that training aims to develop the employee's actual performance on the present job. Indeed, training at LBSNAA provides the employees with some knowledge to make them aware of new approaches that might be useful in performing on the job (Interview, 28th June 2000). However, another trainer supported the organizational approach to training and argued that improving employees' skills on the present job might not necessarily improve organizational effectiveness.

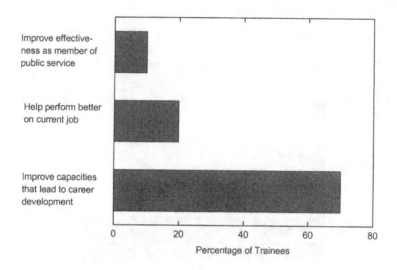

Figure 4.2 Trainees' Perception of Training

In contrast to the trainers, fewer government employees (20 per cent) placed priority on improving skills to perform their present jobs. Moreover, almost three-quarters (70 per cent) of the public service employees perceived training as a way to improve the capacity to achieve career advancement (see Figure 4.2).

This sharp difference in perception between trainers and trainees may explain a problem identified in the process for nominating trainees to LBSNAA. Trainers favour the short-term orientation that can lead to the improvement of performance on the job, while the trainees favour a long-term orientation that could have the potential for career development. LBSNAA's programs are based on the trainees' current job titles and responsibilities. Employees nominate themselves or get themselves nominated by their managers for training programs that may have little relevance to their actual job titles and responsibilities. Moreover, a large number of the trainers claim that trainees attend their programs for the purpose of promotion, instead of acquiring new job-related skills. This explains the trainees' focus on career advancement as opposed to the improvement of skills to perform on the job.

The Issue of Coordination

One of the essential elements for the success of training is coordination between training institutes and government departments. It is important for the training provided to be job specific. In the survey, a large number of trainees stated that the training provided at LBSNAA did not cater to their current requirements. One trainee added that the training seldom helped him to perform better on his current job. He elaborated that LBSNAA puts a lot of emphasis on Information Technology, although it has no practical application due to the lack of such infrastructure at the work place (Interview, 24th June 2000). The respondents rated their organizations reasonably highly in terms of supporting participation in training but added that they are not given adequate opportunity to apply the new knowledge acquired from training. Another respondent explained the problem of application by pointing to the theoretical nature of training provided at LBSNAA. He added that such teaching should be a part of the pre-entry training rather than induction or in-service training.

On this same issue, however, a Deputy Director and trainer at LBSNAA commented that training at the Academy is aimed at making trainees aware of the changing environment and national and international issues, rather than regional issues. He added that the regional/state training institutes are responsible for the more specific areas related to individual departments. Moreover, he went on to say that training programs are not designed to cater to the needs of individual departments, but focus on the training needs of the government as a whole (Interview, 1st July, 2000).

Most of the trainees thought that there was a lack of coordination and support between LBSNAA and their respective government department. Some felt that the Institute held an outdated perception of bureaucratic training needs. Interestingly, most policy level members and trainers agreed that the current communication and coordination between the LBSNAA and departments was not ideal, but was adequate for the present administrative needs of the country. Another Deputy Director at LBSNAA does not consider the current approach to be the best, but found it acceptable under existing circumstances. Government departments vary with regard to function, although their position titles may be similar. Thus, job activities are not the only criteria and each department should be treated as a unique case. It would be helpful if departments identified their requirements and informed the LBSNAA of them. However, one constraint that limits this practice is the lack of qualified training specialists in individual departments, aside from those who merely collect training nomination forms and submit them to LBSNAA (Interview, 1st July 2000).

Effectiveness of Training Programs

Generally, the evaluation of training programs is conducted by asking questions such as 'Has learning taken place?', 'If so in which areas?' and 'Will the new knowledge be applicable to the job of the trainee?'. Evaluation aims to improve training packages, provide feedback to trainers, assess the skill levels of the trainees, and determine how effective training has been. Many training providers are sceptical of the validation process but it remains an extremely important element for improvement of training. The effectiveness of training at LBSNAA is measured in relation to three training objectives: the evaluation of trainees, their performance in the course, and the transfer of techniques.

A key area of concern in public service organizations is the ability of employees to perform in a rapidly changing environment. It is interesting to note that only one trainer strongly agreed that training at the Academy helps trainees adjust to the changes in the environment as a result from occasional changes within the department (Table 4.3). However, 13 trainers agreed that the trainees are prepared for the changing environment, while 10 respondents neither agreed nor disagreed, and 8 disagreed. It is also interesting to note that 2 trainers strongly disagreed on this point. Most of the trainees did not support this point. Furthermore, most of the trainees also did not feel that preparation for a changing environment was vital to training programs. Only 13 trainees strongly agreed with this point in the survey. A large number of trainees (44.8 per cent) strongly disagreed that the training at LBSNAA helps trainees to adjust to the changing environment in their departments (Table 4.2). One of these trainees commented: 'The main purpose for attending in-service training is to upgrade and update the knowledge, but we are often disappointed. We have to acquaint ourselves with the changes in the job environment during our day-to-day work and hence there is sluggishness within the departments after changes are introduced' (Interview, 20th June 2000). In addition, most of the interviewees felt that the Academy still focuses on the traditional training format and makes only superficial efforts to keep pace with change. Reform appears only in the documents of the Academy. However, some respondents felt that training programs do try to keep up with the changing environment by making them aware of new problems and challenges and providing them with skills to deal with them. In addition, some respondents recommended that LBSNAA should consider both the present and future scenario when planning training programs.

A large number of trainees also strongly disagreed with the statement that training programs are designed to fulfil the requirements of present jobs. The participants (trainees) did not agree that the training keeps them informed of the latest developments in their specific fields (see Table 4.2). However, the main reason for sending employees for training is to develop human resources and achieve the mission and goals of the government. Furthermore, the trainees did not think that LBSNAA provides adequate training for their work.

Most of the trainers had similar views to the trainees. The trainers felt that the Academy trains public officials to perform their jobs, and also helps them become aware of the latest developments in their specific areas of work. A Deputy Director of LBSNAA pointed to the fact that the Academy has a monopoly in providing training services and there is no competition. It can make them disinterested in the needs of the customer, i.e. the organization sending officials for training (Interview, 21st June 2000). These comments from a trainer confirm the view held by trainees that they do not receive the kind of training they require.

It is interesting to note that trainers neither strongly agree nor strongly disagree that LBSNAA constantly reviews and updates their training needs. In fact, the majority of trainers are non-committal on this point (see Table 4.3). Most trainers stated that regular meetings are held at the LBSNAA to update the training programs, and that changes are constantly monitored. It is, however, pertinent to note that there is no evidence of the Academy's method for monitoring changes and revising training packages on that basis. Such responses from both trainers and trainees do not reflect positively on the training offered at LBSNAA.

Table 4.2 Evaluation of Training Effectiveness by Trainees

	Statements	Strongly Agree 1	2	3	4	Strongly Disagree 5	No Comment 6
1	Training programs are designed to fulfil the present job requirements	32	34	35	50	88	13
2	The programs provide adequate training as required for work	19	24	27	61	104	17
3	LBSNAA establishes a positive training environment and motivation to work	12	28	30	79	101	2
4	Trainees are informed of latest developments in specialized areas	11	35	26	78	92	10
5	The training helps adjust to the changing environment and reforms	13	33	32	51	113	10
6	LBSNAA provides quality service and training	12	25	28	161	25	1
7	Knowledge/skill acquired from training is applicable to present job	24	25	74	62	57	10
8	LBSNAA uses evaluation results to improve performance	26	119	49	24	18	16
9	Training programs are modified on the basis of evaluation	24	36	26	39	80	47
	TOTAL	173	359	327	605	678	126

Table 4.2 demonstrates that the majority of trainees strongly disagree with the statement that training programs at LBSNAA are effective. This is not the level of satisfaction expected of a central training institute. LBSNAA provides

foundational training and skills to all government officials and if it is not strong and efficient, the entire structure of the government would be affected.

Table 4.3 Evaluation of Training Effectiveness by Trainers

	Statements	Strongly Agree 1	2	3	4	Strongly Disagree 5	No Comment 6
1	Training leads to career advancement	12	4	5	1	7	5
2	Training programs are designed to fulfil the present job requirements	2	5	6	5	15	1
3	The programs provide adequate training as required for work	9	4	12	1	4	4
4	Training is provided for work enrichment	11	4	12	6	1	
5	LBSNAA establishes a positive training environment and motivation to work	2	5	15	10	1	1
6	The training helps adjust to the changing environment in government departments and reforms	1	13	10	8	2	
7	Training programs are designed to prepare public officials for the changing environment	3	8	6	14	3	
8	LBSNAA assesses the adequacy of their programs regularly	7	1	10	14	1	1
9	LBSNAA provides quality service and training	2	3	12	7	8	2
10	Knowledge/skill acquired from training is applicable to present job	2	16	4	5	6	1
11	LBSNAA uses evaluation results to improve performance	3	10	16	4	1	
12	Training programs are modified on the basis of evaluation	2	15	10	5	1	1
	TOTAL	56	88	118	80	50	16

Most trainers are hesitant to confirm that the training programs at LBSNAA are highly effective. It is commonplace for providers to rate their services highly, but this is not the case in LBSNAA. It is through evaluation that a department learns whether training programs can achieve the objectives set, whether the programs require updating or modification and whether the programs should be continued in the future. Tables 4.2 and 4.3 show that trainers and trainees at LBSNAA agree that the institute employs evaluation techniques to improve performance. However, the majority of the trainees disagreed, while, in contrast, most of the trainers agreed, that training programs are modified on the basis of the evaluation. A trainee complained that feedback are collected, but not acted upon (Interview, 20th June, 2000). In a slightly different assessment, a language trainer at LBSNAA informed that 'only valid suggestions' from the trainees are considered (Interview, 26th June 2000). However, another Deputy Director of LBSNAA remarked that the trainers obtain feedback through informal conversations with the participants during breaks in sessions. The trainees can, therefore, give comments on the specific session and the feedback can be considered for revising and adjusting the content of the program (Interview, 1st July 2000). One trainee stated that feedback was collected regularly, giving the example of an Academy-organized 'Course Review Meeting', where the trainees were given an opportunity to express their views and comment critically on the training provided (Interview, 23rd June 2000). Counsellor Group Meetings are organised every month. According to most of the trainees, these meetings could be more flexible and provide scope for generation of innovative ideas.

Even in cases of efficient and effective training delivery, evaluation seems somewhat incomplete. In theory, training has a follow-up (a brief discussion on the training delivered) to gauge the extent to which trainees apply the new knowledge and skills gained from training. But in practice, this follow-up is not always efficiently carried out. Moreover, LBSNAA practices one level of evaluation, i.e., end of course evaluation. In this exercise, participants comment on what they think and feel about the training programs. This is the least expensive and most immediate level of evaluation, but it only reveals the participants' subjective views and does not reflect what has actually been learned. Such evaluation can be considered a 'happy sheet' as it seldom specifies the real impact of training on trainees. In the survey, a large number of trainees agreed that the programs are highly flexible and are altered during the training sessions based on the needs and demands of specific groups of trainees.

It can be said that investment in training does not yield tangible results due to deficiencies in design and evaluation. Thus, external validation is essential. Further, evaluation becomes more meaningful if conducted by an outside agency. It must be noted that most trainers stated that there were plans being made to send trainers out randomly to various government departments in order to monitor the practical impact of training. This method seems quite attractive though its practicality is open to question. The trainers obviously know what impact the training can be expected to have realistically, and they would be the best judges to measure the practical implications of training.

A former Deputy Director at LBSNAA remarked that standardized training packages are required and that they should not be very flexible (Interview, 7th July

2000). Training at LBSNAA appears to be flexible i.e. it can be changed on the basis of the participants' requirement. However, it is possible that the trainer might not have expertise in the areas identified for concentration. Thus there is a possibility that the quality of training provided would not be adequate.

A Deputy Director currently serving at LBSNAA commented on the difficulties involved in assessing the impact of training. 'In the kind of training we give, it is very difficult to measure the impact because it is so broad based and long. We take feedback from our trainees on whether they found the training session relevant but it is unfair to us as the trainees are not in a position to assess. They can only judge the relevance after they utilize the training on-the-job' (Interview, 21st June 2000). There is a need to initiate different levels of evaluation, instead of just end of course evaluation. The trainees should be sent evaluation forms in order to comment on how they are utilizing the training on their jobs. At the same time, the heads of their departments or their supervisors should be requested to comment on their job performance after receiving training.

If an evaluation shows that the training program has fallen short of achieving its intended objectives, some modification in the program content and/or methods are usually recommended in order to make the training more effective. The Director of LBSNAA commented: 'At the end of training sessions, we conduct evaluation, which often hears the voice of the immediate customers, i.e. the organizations directly related with the training activities. However, we do not consult the ultimate customers i.e. the citizens of India. When we are criticised that the government does not perform well and is not delivering, I am tempted to say, unless our per capita income and net economic growth are improved, change would be unseen. We are doing a good job.' He added that in spite of their best efforts to make the programs effective, there remains a gap between the perceptions of the trainees and their organizations as well as the needs of the country (Interview, 25th June 2000).

The reasons for attending training courses were found to influence motivation and effectiveness significantly. Attending the training to learn new knowledge had a positive influence on the trainees' motivation to learn, their reaction to the training programs, and their transfer of learning. However, attending training as an obligation or in order to get a break from the job was found to influence the trainee in a negative way. According to some trainers, the performance of the trainees indicated that they attended the programs as an obligation or a requirement, and that they were not interested or committed to learning. The trainees defended their position by pointing out that much of the training provided at LBSNAA was not relevant to their work and that they are actually trained on-job to meet their job requirements. Most of the trainees admitted that they attended training programs because they had no choice. Such attitudes affect the effectiveness of training. A language trainer found that some of the trainees who have prior plans of transferring to a different state (province) show little interest in learning when they attend language training programs. 'On the contrary, they disturb the work atmosphere of the entire group and at the end give a negative evaluation for the program' (Interview, June 2000). In terms of course evaluation, these participants often assign contrasting or varied grades and feedback on the evaluation sheets.

One trainee commented that the institute should depart from its focus on law and order issues and instead emphasize developmental issues (Interview, 24th June 2000). The role of the civil service has changed along with the world scenario, and the Academy should train public officials to deal with these changes. A field-level official of the Government of India detected an excessive emphasis on changing attitude, but not enough on knowledge of various facets of the tasks performed in public organizations. He felt that the focus of training should be on immediate challenges confronting public officials, rather than on long-term goals (Interview, 10th July 2000). One of the trainees suggested that more practical issues, such as crisis management, should be included in the content of training.

Table 4.2 reflects the diverse views held by trainees on whether or not the knowledge and skills acquired by training can be applied to their present jobs. Although the trend shows an inclination towards a negative response among trainees, the trainers support the fact that the training at LBSNAA does provide the trainees with the skills required in their present jobs. The table shows that the participant trainees were not highly motivated for training. Although the participants did not find the training to be applicable to their jobs, they did not provide any specific reasons for this decision. Furthermore, after receiving training and returning to work, all trainees reported that they could apply the knowledge and skills gained from training either directly or directly, although it did not meet their expectations. Some participants appreciated the training, and claimed that they learned a lot from training. When asked about the practical usage of training, the answers varied: some were certain that the new knowledge could be applied, some were unsure and others predicted difficulties in practical application. Some respondents admitted that they had not learned much from training because they usually lost interest when the trainers started talking about theory or cited examples from other countries.

Reliable and specific informational feedback would help the Academy to improve the design, organization and implementation of current and future training programmes. Giving serious consideration to evaluation results and thereby making the training package worthwhile to consumers could improve the quality of training. This in turn could also assist in creating a positive attitude among trainees towards learning, training, education and development.

Improvement of Ability

As seen in Tables 4.2 and 4.3, the respondents did not make positive comments on the effectiveness of training provided at LBSNAA. Both trainers and trainees identified problems that needed to be addressed. The views and needs of the trainees and the departments sending them for training are very important, since they are the customers of the Academy. Some trainees noted that the results of training evaluation tended to be positive all the time and this raised doubts about their reliability. The most significant performance indicator of LBSNAA is the outcome of training. The Director of the Academy argued in favour of reforming the entire government structure rather than the training programs only (Interview, 25th June 2000). A former Deputy Director of LBSNAA suggested continuous training impact evaluation instead of simple evaluation of programs (Interview, 7th July 2000).

After a span of time the various department heads should be sent an evaluation form to evaluate the performance of the attendees after training. One trainee expressed dissatisfaction with the program and recommended obtaining feedback and suggestions from the trainees before designing programs (Interview, 23rd June 2000). Most of the trainees held the government responsible for not monitoring the performance of LBSNAA. Admittedly, the Academy is an agency of the government, but regular inspection could be an impediment to its smooth operation by way of disruption and interference.

Trainees expressed concern over the extended length of training. As can be gathered from the interviews, the officials receive actual training at their respective work sites, and to make the training at the institute more meaningful, they suggest that training programs focus more on practical issues. At present, after the completion of 'Phase-I Training' every official returns to his/her post for on-the-job training. Later, they come back to LBSNAA to finish the two-year long training package. The trainees complained that they felt lost and disoriented when they go back to their work sites for training, as the institute provides them with only the basic training or guidelines to commence the on-job-training.

Identification of Training Needs

'In today's context, "Knowledge is Power". Considering the fact that some of the brightest young people available in the country today are recruited to the civil services through a stiff competitive examination, the basic objective of the training of IAS Officers, should be to stimulate young and creative minds and provide them opportunities during their entire career span for personal growth, freedom for creativity, and to develop leadership potential in order that they are in a position to discharge the multifarious responsibilities awaiting them in the field with greater efficiency. No training programme, in order to be effective could afford to place less emphasis on the development of the mind and the intellect leading to the actualisation of the latent potential of each officer. LBSNAA has finally decided to develop its training to deal with the widely recognized problems in the administrative system, instead of waiting for the government agencies to provide their own training need assessment information' (Interview with a Deputy Director of LBSNAA, 27th June 2000). This statement indicates that most of the government departments do not receive training services based on their specific requirements.

Training is a planned process to modify attitudes, knowledge, skills and behaviours through a learning experience, in order to achieve effective performance in an activity or range of activities. Its purpose is to develop the abilities of the individual employee and to satisfy the current and future manpower needs of the organization. In identifying the training needs of government officers, this definition might be considered relevant, but is not comprehensive enough. Government officials do not work in a stereotypical organization. They have to shoulder a variety of responsibilities in different situations. Identifying training needs for government officials, who have to perform multifarious duties and act in different roles, is thus a complex task. For the effective and efficient performance of the duties and responsibilities of any position in an organization, a certain level of competence in terms of knowledge, skills and attitudes is required. An individual holding the position should normally have this level of competence, or otherwise he would not be able to do his/her job and contribute to the achievement the organization's goals. Thus in identifying training needs, it should be ensured that the gap between the existing level of competence of an officer manning a job and the required level for the proper completion of functions is adequately bridged.

Identifying training needs involves the collection of data on the job, and from employees and organizational sources. Although training needs assessment data sources may complement one another, they are different from each other. For example, job training needs assessment data sources may include, but are not limited to, job descriptions and specifications. Employee training need assessment data sources may include attitude surveys, rating scales, and critical incidents. Organizational needs assessment data sources may include the analysis of organizational goals and objectives, organizational climate incidents, and changes in system or sub system (Moore and Dutton 1978; Camp, Blanchard and Huszczo, 1986; McGehee and Thayer 1961; Hall and Goodale, 1986). LBSNAA uses seven main sources of data in designing training programs: (a) Ministry of Personnel of the Government of India; (b) trainers; (c) a team of experts from LBSNAA and the managers of the various departments where the trainees are employed; (d) responses on questionnaires administered to a sample of employees; (e) training nomination forms; (f) results of evaluation by trainees; and (g) the five-year plans of the government.

Training needs assessment data normally includes data on: (a) training already received, and (b) new training needed (United Nations, 1966, p. 204). Such information usually contributes to decisions on the kind of training to be provided. In assessing training needs, information is obtained from a variety of sources in different format for the design, development, and refinement of training programs.

A number of steps are taken by trainers in designing new training programs or improving existing ones. Job specifications help identify the abilities and skills required to perform a job effectively. Trainers collect data from a sample of the trainees' job descriptions and from questionnaires sent to their supervisors, in order to learn about the actual tasks they perform and to see whether these tasks vary from or are similar to those identified by the training provider. The trainers add behavioural aspects which they think might increase the trainees' effectiveness in performing the job. A large number of training needs are identified by reviewing the collected data. These needs are considered to see which could be addressed by existing LBSNAA training programs. Finally, the existing training programs are readjusted and improved through information about new training needs derived from the evaluation results.

Additionally, a team of experts from LBSNAA are involved with developing and incorporating new material to meet the changing needs of public service in India. It is claimed that the 'academic curriculum is constantly reviewed and updated to keep it relevant. This is done on the basis of extensive consultations with the State Governments through the State counsellors, and the bi-annual conference of representatives of the State Governments and the Central Government' (LBSNAA, 1999). However, the interviews revealed that most of the trainees and their departments were not aware of this process in training needs assessment. Heads of various departments commented that they would welcome an opportunity to participate in the needs assessment process, but were given no opportunity to do so.

Most of the senior officials at LBSNAA claimed that they are satisfied with the current needs assessment process and would not do anything differently. Nevertheless, it is the responsibility of policy level members and trainers to identify new training needs through interaction with trainees, government officials and the trainers of departmental/state training institutes. The LBSNAA trainers are responsible for identifying new training needs in their respective areas of specialization and assigning the design and development unit to further investigate the need and develop a training package.

The annual training plan, prepared by the Ministry of Personnel, should be constantly upgraded and presented to LBSNAA as a foundation for its training program development. It should also be dovetailed with the Academy's annual plans. A Deputy Director agreed that the LBSNAA's annual plans should ideally be based on the departments' training plans. But only a few departments submit their training plans, and the Academy has to predict their training needs (Interview, 25th June, 2000). Furthermore, the training program should be designed to train officials to deal with the internal dynamics of an organization efficiently and, at the same time, to develop a good understanding of the external environment. This dual approach will allow trainees to develop strategies for coping with problems and contingencies relating to factors both within the organization and outside of it.

An organization has to interface with the external environment on a continuing basis. A trainer elaborated: 'An important dimension to be taken into account, in identifying training needs, is the stages of career progression of an officer trainee and the levels of responsibility he is required to discharge at the different stages of his career. Thus we have different training needs for officers at the junior level (say up to first 10 years of their service), than middle and senior levels. Induction training, besides providing a strong foundation, which will stand the officer in good stead throughout his career also specifically, caters to meeting the requirements of imparting skills and knowledge to equip the officer to function effectively at the junior level. Subsequently, the various types of in-service training are designed to provide the officer with the necessary skills and expertise to handle the jobs at the middle and senior levels' (Interview, 28th June 2000).

Table 4.4 Trainees' Views on Identification of Training Needs

Statements	Strongly Agree 1	2	3	4	Strongly Disagree 5	No Comment 6
1 I determine the training needs	30	64	15	26	17	100
2 My manager determines the training needs	50	26	32	37	93	14
3 Our training department determines the training needs	17	19	33	79	85	19
4 LBSNAA determines the training needs	20	74	24	52	55	27
5 Trainees should complete questionnaires on their training needs	107	49	40	19	23	14
6 LBSNAA establishes training objectives based on identified needs	52	39	28	26	87	20
7 LBSNAA constantly reviews and updates training needs	26	32	22	29	128	15
8 Available information on jobs and the organization should be used to gain insight on training needs	113	56	27	18	29	9
TOTAL	415	359	221	286	517	218

Most of the trainees are ambivalent about their role in determining the training needs and they expressed no opinion on this matter (Table 4.4). There were mixed responses regarding the role of trainers, departmental training units, and LBSNAA in identifying training needs. This suggests that the trainees (public service employees) do not have a clear idea about the process of training needs assessment.

Most trainers described their role in identifying training needs as stemming from their interaction with trainees: asking the trainees about their expectations, the degree to which the training meets their needs, and their actual job tasks and activities. The trainers then compare this data to the training program goals, objectives, and requirements. However, trainees felt that the needs assessment process would be more successful if they were asked to fill in questionnaires on their training needs. The trainees expressed a desire for greater involvement in the process. They suggested that the training managers of individual departments should encourage employees to identify and discuss their needs with supervisors. They believed that the employees are in the best position to identify the skills they need to learn, and would attend training programs that correspond to their needs.

A language trainer at LBSNAA gave more information on the issue. He found language to be of great importance in a country like India where many languages are in use. Public officials are frequently posted outside the region of their origin, and need to learn new languages to be able to communicate with people in serving them. All entrants to the public service have to go on village visits to interact with the villagers and understand their problems (Interview, 26th June 2000).

Table 4.5 Trainers' Views on Identification of Training Needs

	Statements	Strongly Agree 1	2	3	4	Strongly Disagree 5	No Comment 6
1	Trainees should complete questionnaires to help identify training needs	4	5	16	2	7	
2	LBSNAA establishes training objectives based on required needs	2	3	5	18	4	2
3	LBSNAA constantly reviews and updates training needs	6	1	11	8	7	1
4	LBSNAA focuses on future training needs	3	1	7	13	9	1
5	Employee and organizational records should be used to gain insight on training needs	5	16	4	9		
	TOTAL	20	26	43	50	27	4
6	For training need assessment, LBSNAA uses						
a)	job/task analysis	19					
b)	personal analysis	7					
c)	organizational analysis	3					
d)	demographic analysis	3					
e)	no comments	2					

The trainers seemed to think that the identification of future training needs at LBSNAA lacked focus (Table 4.5), but most accepted that as an on-going process. The Director of the Academy admitted that all future training needs cannot be identified, and constant updating of the programs is helpful (Interview, 25th June

2000). The trainers also drew attention to the flexible approach adopted in the training sessions. A Deputy Director described the process: 'There is a syllabus committee which is required to review the syllabus every ten years. But by the time they publish it, it gets outdated. Course design is a very detailed exercise and a lot of freedom is given to the course team and they use this freedom to update and impart appropriate training to the trainees' (Interview, 21st June 2000). While an overview of the syllabi gives an impression of outdated training approaches and methods at LBSNAA, it should also be pointed out that there are modifications in discrete subject areas, which allow trainees to get some exposure to new developments.

Obviously, the training programs cannot follow the syllabi to the letter, as every cohort of trainees enter the Academy with new problems and issues. For in-service courses, LBSNAA consults client departments in order to understand their requirements and expectations. Thus, training needs analysis and evaluation helps in the understanding, planning and implementation of programs that are relevant and practical.

Training Techniques and Mechanisms

LBSNAA is responsible for coordinating and conducting activities concerning the development and training of civil servants. The annual report states: 'The effort of the Academy as a training institute is to help in creating a bureaucracy that commands respect by performance rather than through position. The Constitutional mandate for civil servants is interpreted as one that promotes empathy for the unprivileged, commitment to the unity and integrity of the nation; a promise to uphold integrity and impeccable character in a manner that they appear as role models for the large number of subordinates working with them and for the society at large; a respect for all castes, creeds, religions; and a professional competence that makes the battle against poverty eradication the ultimate objective of every civil servant' (LBSNAA, 1999).

LBSNAA develops and delivers training curricula, courses, techniques and materials in areas common to employees in several ministries and departments. The Academy also conducts training courses in subject areas that fall under their responsibility and for organizations that do not have their own internal training facilities and/or capacity. The Academy develops training objectives to guarantee identifiable outputs, against which training effectiveness can be evaluated. They capitalize on the use of new training methods that reduce the labour intensity of teaching and the classroom time of participants. This includes the use of audio-visual media and programmed learning. One objective they have is to have people associated at work attend training together, so that skills learned will be practiced when participants return to their jobs at the same place.

'It was clear to us that the conventional classroom lecture method would be the most inappropriate to impact on attitudes and values. We have therefore innovated with several new methodologies, and achieved significant successes. Most of the courses operate on a modular structure. According to this, relevant themes are chosen and dealt with in a consolidated fashion so that all aspects relating to them are dealt with comprehensively' (LBSNAA, 1999). However, in contradiction with this mandate, the Director informed that the lecture method is most common at LBSNAA because it is economical. But the Academy has introduced group work syndicate, case studies, audio visual and video conferencing (Interview, 25th June 2000).

The following discussion explores the various methods employed by LBSNAA in the training programs. The annual reports point out that lectures are used by both in-house and guest faculty, and panel discussions are organized to promote a diversity of opinions and views. Case studies and discussions are helpful in developing critique on social values. Group discussions, simulation exercises, seminars, moot courts, mock trial, order-and judgement, writing practices, practical demonstrations, problem solving exercises, paper writing (term paper, syndicate paper), group activity, and field visits complete the range of methods and mechanisms for training at LBSNAA.

Table 4.6 Trainees' Views on Techniques and Mechanisms

Statements	Strongly Agree 1	2	3	4	Strongly Disagree 5	No Comment 6
1 LBSNAA performs well in anticipating future training needs	22	22	25	29	123	31
2 LBSNAA provides strategic guidance on training and development to your department	23	27	21	45	15	121
3 LBSNAA modifies training programs based on the results of the training evaluation	24	36	26	39	80	47
4 Modern training methods are used	4	46	36	39	80	47
5 LBSNAA focuses more on practical issues	20	30	87		106	9
TOTAL	93	161	195	152	404	255

As central training institutes do not aim at providing specific services for various departments, some course contents are rudimentary and do not appeal to trainees who have different levels of ability, perform a variety of tasks, and work in different types of organizations. However, the existing system of evaluation of training programmes is not adequate in assessing the ways in which the current programs are falling short. The system of evaluation for induction and in-service programmes can be taken as an example.

There are four components in the induction programme: Foundation Course (FC), Phase-I, District Training and Phase-II. An internal validation process is followed in each of these courses. At the end of FC, Phase I and II, officer-trainees are asked to assess the training in terms of its relevance and whether or not it has achieved its objectives. However, it must be noted that neither external validation nor evaluation is undertaken. It would be difficult to undertake these two exercises in the absence of a systematic training needs assessment program. As a result of the current evaluative system, course design largely depends upon the internal validation results of past courses and the experiential wisdom of the faculty.

The Academy also conducts in-service courses for officers of the IAS with 6-9 years, 10-16 years and 17-20 years of service. In addition, it conducts an induction programme for State Civil Service officers on their initiation into the Indian Administrative Service. In all such courses, only internal validation is carried out. External validation and evaluation are not undertaken. Hence, the outcomes of training imparted at LBSNAA are not assessed at the performance level.

Most of the trainees did not make any comment on whether LBSNAA provides strategic guidance on training and development to their respective departments (Table 4.6). This indicates that they are not aware of the internal working of their departments or have no interest to know about the same. The responses are ambivalent, and reflect lack of interest and confusion on the part of the trainees.

The trainers, on the other hand, claimed they were alert to future training needs. However, this task is made difficult by the rapid and continuous changes affecting most tasks and responsibilities as a result of new technologies. Additionally, the Academy did not seem to be informed about the nature, direction and pace of changes. Thus, trainers at LBSNAA try to anticipate changes, but cannot always act to deal with new needs or keep pace with the changes.

It is fascinating to note that none of the trainers strongly agreed that the Academy attaches importance to modern training techniques (Table 4.7). The Director claimed that the lecture method was most commonly used as it was the most economical. But with the large amount of funds allocated for training, with frequent surrender of surplus back to the government, economy should not be essential in designing training programs. LBSNAA has the means to develop and implement modern training techniques with extensive use of technology and innovative teaching methods. Over the years, there has been a gradual shift in emphasis from the lecture mode of training to a more participative approach. This has made it easier for probationers to digest the essence of training, understand the process and develop skills.[1]

Table 4.7 Trainers' Views on Techniques and Mechanisms

Statements	Strongly Agree 1	2	3	4	Strongly Disagree 5	No Comment 6
1 LBSNAA modifies training programs based on the results of the training evaluation	2	5	10	15	1	1
2 Instructional techniques are appropriate to learning objectives	6	17	8	1	1	1
3 Selection of training format and content is appropriate to type of training required	7	10	12	5		
4 LBSNAA emphasizes modern training techniques		11	7	9	6	1
5 LBSNAA focuses more on practical issues	11	2	9	7	3	2
TOTAL	26	45	46	37	11	5

A large number of trainers stated strongly that the Academy focuses more on practical rather than theoretical issues. The district experience presentation session is an example of the emphasis on the practical aspect of administration. It helps familiarise trainees with the actual conditions in the field and they learn strategies for dealing with similar situations at their respective work places. Case studies help trainees learn about situations faced on the field. Moreover, the trainers deputed from government departments bring examples and explain links between the training and the real world.

Direction of Public Service Training

Future needs are created by changes in work and workplace, and are an essential element of planning for every department. Most of the respondents focused on changes emanating from technology and modernisation throughout the world. New issues such as information technology and e-governance are increasingly becoming evident in the government of India. Administrative reforms have rattled the customers of training institutes, as government departments are required to redefine their needs and demands. For their part, training institutes must generate new training programs to cater to new demands. Numerous reforms—economic, social, constitutional or legal—are transforming the institutional landscape and have underlined the need for a new profile of public service. Furthermore, the global transformations that are sweeping the public arena have brought with them the need for competence in management, a greater rationalization of techniques, and a streamlining of procedures. It has also become important to adapt public service to the demands of information technology. These changes make it necessary to constantly revise curricula and introduce new contents.

The structural adjustment program launched by the government of India in 1991 has added to the urgency for change. The liberalization of import policies had to be accompanied by a relaxation of administrative control. Basic changes had to be made in macro economic, fiscal, trade and industrial policies. The licensing system was overhauled, and most sectors were opened to foreign investment. The process for generating and the extent of regulation were reduced and streamlined.

The Director of LBSNAA stated: 'New changes and developments like globalisation, liberalization, privatisation, etc have negative effects. People are uncomfortable with it and for valid reasons. The politicians, bureaucrats, businessmen, trade unions are all unhappy with liberalization and competition as they begin to loose power and the capital market. Customers are not exposed to changes for quality goods and service. The sooner the change is accepted, the better, as society, consumer and the country as a whole will benefit. New and uncomfortable things have to be accepted. Decentralization has to be introduced. However, the politicians and bureaucrats are unwilling to share power' (Interview, 25th June 2000). He believes that the priority is to expose the officials to the changes and try to influence the mindsets which are not responding to them. The obvious reference was toward more emphasis on a participatory approach and well as distant learning.

These changes have implications for the role and function of the public service. At the administrative level, a number of issues needed attention. These included the management of information, the analysis of policy alternatives, performance improvement, investment analysis, financial planning, and human resource development. There was more demand for training on facilitating faster growth, development and equity. There was a need to achieve a greater degree of social cohesion to resolve problems of ethnicity and strengthen the process of governance.

Major changes are taking place in the world economy and states are striving to keep up with them. 'At a time when nations are going global in the processes of liberalisation and economic reforms, it is our endeavour to make young civil servants realise the need for upholding enlightened national interest in their interface with the world at large. We also try to learn from the experiences of bureaucracies that have helped in the achievement of economic progress, growth with equity, and human well being in other nations' (LBSNAA, 1999). In addition, the trainers stated that the different faculties of the Academy have been networking with other leading institutes to update and upgrade the contents of their courses. The Director added that there is a conscious attempt in the Academy to attract faculty from various services to provide a perspective on the latest development in their fields of work.

The pressure to change and upgrade the level of the existing work force has many positive impacts. Information technology can be a tool for ensuring transparency, a means for altering the existing mindset of people in dealing with the public services, and a link between the government and the citizens. With more communication between citizens and public officials corruption can be reduced, to a certain extent. However, the lack of understanding of and knowledge about information technology creates a generation gap at the different levels of government. It is difficult for the fresh public officials to communicate with the seniors, who have not been equally steeped in the technological tradition.

Proficiency in information technology can make substantial contribution toward the enhancement of capability in the public service. A Deputy Director of LBSNAA views the immense potential of Information Technology in the government and its use as a tool for training. He believes in focusing on both theoretical and practical aspects for improving the efficiency of the public services. Information technology can ensure transparency and facilitate access to the government (Interview, 21 June, 2000).

Computer training is one of the main inputs given to the trainees in the Academy, and it is included in most of the induction and in-service courses. The trainees come from various backgrounds; some with a deep insight into computers and others with no or only rudimentary knowledge of the same and thus training officials with different levels of computer proficiency presents a challenge. In view of the importance of IT and computer-literacy, public officials are exposed to computers and their operation, and encouraged to promote e-governance.

Most trainers considered identifying future training needs a very sensitive issue at LBSNAA. They remarked that trainers try to find information on change and keep themselves abreast of developments. They are sent for training and development overseas as well as within India. The trainers recognized that it is important to interact with other advanced countries in order to understand and deal with change. The experience of developed Western countries can be helpful in devising plans for India, but caution must be exercised in adopting the same strategies because each country has its unique problems and circumstances.

A large number of trainees strongly disagreed that LBSNAA successfully anticipates future training needs. Table 4.8 shows that there are varying preferences on different issues related to the anticipation of future training needs. Many trainees admitted having acquired knowledge about issues concerning personal growth and advancement from the training provided. They discovered aspects of their jobs that they were previously not aware of. However, a large number of trainees rejected the idea that LBSNAA aims at upgrading human ability to meet with the changing times. They felt that the Academy is not keen on reform, and simply alters and modifies the existing training programs. These efforts were not adequate to prepare public officials for the challenges confronting them. There is a need to reform the entire structure of training if future training needs are to be adequately addressed.

Table 4.8 Trainees' Views on Anticipation of Future Training Needs

Statements	Strongly Agree 1	2	3	4	Strongly Disagree 5	No Comment 6
1 Programs are oriented toward future needs	27	27	18	59	99	22
2 LBSNAA updates programs with changes in society, public demand and government policies	24	39	28	78	70	13
3 The programs help understand issues concerning personal growth and advancement	31	69	37	35	51	29
4 LBSNAA identifies future training needs	27	19	28	19	137	22
5 LBSNAA aims at upgrading ability to meet with demands of changing times	24	32	21	45	118	12
TOTAL	133	186	132	236	475	98

According to Table 4.8, only 11 per cent of the trainees strongly agreed that the training at the LBSNAA is oriented toward the future (11 per cent agree, 7 per cent neither agree nor disagree, 23 per cent disagree, 39 per cent strongly disagree and 9 per cent have no comments). However, the respondents qualified their assessments by adding that it was not easy to identify future training needs. To make things worse, the public agencies are not making any contribution in making their needs and priorities known to the Academy.

Based on the totals for the responses to the various questions focusing on the capability of LBSNAA to anticipate future training needs (Table 4.9), a maximum number of the trainers neither agree nor disagree that the Academy anticipates future training needs. The varied responses from the trainers suggest that the trainers are either not willing to disclose their actual position or do not have an adequate understanding of the concept of future training needs. Three kinds of training are usually organised at LBSNAA, i.e. training for fresh recruits, in-service training, and induction training for state services to be inducted into IAS. Another Deputy Director and senior trainer found it easy to identify future training needs for new entrants to public service, but considered it difficult to do so for senior officials (Interview, June 2000). In an effort to overcome this difficulty, trainees are asked to identify changes as observed or experienced by them. Their observations are used as case studies for in-service courses.

Public Service in a Globalized World

Table 4.9 Trainers' Views on Anticipation of Future Training Needs

Statements	Strongly Agree 1	2	3	4	Strongly Disagree 5	No Comment 6
1 Programs are oriented toward future needs	14	4	3	7	5	1
2 LBSNAA updates programs with changes in society, public demand and government policies	13	3	9	3	2	4
3 LBSNAA conducts organizational analysis	2	2	14	10	3	3
4 LBSNAA considers changing functions of the government	1	7	12	10	4	
5 LBSNAA conducts analysis of social and economic change	2	1	14	11	3	3
6 LBSNAA considers technological change	14	1	7	2	7	3
7 LBSNAA identifies future training needs	6	14	1	3	9	1
TOTAL	49	32	60	46	33	15

The trainers claimed that '*meeting with constant changes*' is the motto of LBSNAA. Change is constantly monitored and responded to, although the content of the courses does not change, there are some adjustments in training programs to accommodate the changing needs. This is done through the insertion of a few topical and current items in the syllabi, while most of the course content remains the same.

Changes in government require the alteration and revision of training packages offered by public service training agencies. Since there are frequent changes in the work environment, trainees prefer to receive help developing specific sets of skills and competencies in order to help them deal with these changes. The changes have thus compelled training agencies to prepare for or even to anticipate changes in order to provide public officials with the skills necessary to understand and react to the political, economic and technological progress of a rapidly changing society.

Trends in Training

There are various visible changes and challenges faced by the governments of many different countries, which have led to reforms and innovations. In some countries, there have been fundamental structural changes, such as the privatisation of railroads, airlines, and telephone companies. In other countries, there have been profound process changes made to the form of customer service and improvements made in the public procurement system. These changes have taken place against a backdrop of fundamental social and political change. Governments in almost all countries have downsized, privatised, reengineered, and sought improved customer service with the objective of improving performance and reducing costs. There have been Parallel developments in the enhancement of the skill of government workers and the accountability of public organizations. The reform movement has spread throughout the world and a set of common characteristics has become apparent. There is a demand for 'smaller' government, through efficiency gains (doing more with less), rather than through cutting programs; the development of new processes—reengineering of service systems, contracting out, performance management, and accrual accounting to promote efficiency gains, transparent government operations and strong emphasis on customer service.

India embarked on the road to liberalisation in the early 1990s and has followed the global trend. At the LBSNAA, several trainees referred to the impact of colonial influences on public service training in India, but the Director of LBSNAA takes a different view: 'We got our independence 53 years ago, the curriculum has very little in common with the colonial set-up. In those days, the only subjects taught were law and political science, and there was no emphasis on public administration, management, economics, information technology, issues of rural development including working with local governments, communities and NGOs, as we have now, and the trainees have a lot of fieldwork to do' (Interview, June 2000).

India has experienced substantial changes and continues to move rapidly along the road of transition and reform. It is important for the training agencies to prepare programs with these changes in mind. Public service officials have to work to ensure continuity, stability and leadership to the public services. Information technology has changed the foundation and methods of governing, and recruits to the public service are advised to discard the traditional approach of treating citizens as passive recipients of service with no voice. The elite core of administrators in India is undergoing a significant phase of transition and role definition.

Government organizations need to have the capacity to think beyond themselves and the immediate issues that confront them (Dror, 1994). Public service officials should now be capable of understanding the changes taking place in the environment, the impact of these changes and the new demands they generate. It is important to find ways of developing the necessary skills and methods of working among public managers in India, in order that they are properly equipped to deal with broad and changing issues. As in many countries, public sector reform in India has consisted of five main components: efficiency, decentralisation, accountability, resource management, and marketization. 'In the face of continuing challenges of globalization and corporatization, the Government of India's Department of Administrative Reforms organized in 1997 a national debate on the issue of making administration responsive, accountable and effective, and assuring its adherence to constitutional principles. On the basis of responses received from officials, experts, voluntary agencies, citizen's groups, media, etc., an Action Plan was evolved which was discussed in the Conference of Chief Ministers convened by the then Prime Minister on 24th May 1997. The Conference resolved that the central and state governments would work together to concretise the Action Plan dealing with: (i) accountable and citizen friendly government; (ii) transparency and right to information; and (iii) improving the performance and integrity of public services. As a follow up, several measures have been taken to make the administration accountable. For instance, in order to make public agencies more responsive to citizen needs, a number of Citizen's Charters have been instituted by a number of central departments/agencies and state governments' (Jain, 2001b, p. 1322). Effective training programs can enhance competence of public service officials in these areas.

Modern training courses encourage meaningful participation by the trainees, and they are provided with appropriate material and opportunities for that purpose. Participation and absorption remain unsatisfactory in courses where lectures are the sole medium of instruction. A large number of trainees at LBSNAA have suggested doing away with lectures and substituting them with participative instruction through tutorials, seminars, workshops and group discussions. However, it is recognized that the lecture method cannot be completely eliminated, and hence, there should be a mixture of different methods.

Recent developments at the Academy include the use of audio-visual media. LBSNAA is developing CD Rom based training and hopes to shift basic training away from classrooms. The CD Rom project has been initiated, but will require some time to reach completion. These innovative approaches keep the trainees alert and involved in the training. The content of training courses has also changed following recent developments in the government and the country. Trainees are exposed to real examples, which give them a sense of situations likely to be encountered at work.

Although it is almost impossible to demonstrate concrete evidence of change, the impact of which is hardly visible in the Academy's prospectus and course manuals, some transformation has definitely taken place. For example, information technology and computers were not included in the training documents in India even a decade ago.[2] Previously, public officials were trained on the basis of theoretical input and followed the training programs designed by the founders of LBSNAA for years. Earlier, history featured prominently in the content, but the importance of contemporary and emerging issues has now been recognized. Thus, the Academy has shifted attention towards the comprehensive development of public officials.

However, the respondent trainees did not notice positive developments in the trends followed by training at LBSNAA in the past five years (Table 4.10). Most of them have neutral views on this issue, which can be explained by the fact that most of the respondents had just entered public service and were not in a position to discern developments. However, a large number of in-service trainees commented positively on this point. Furthermore, since many of the trainers are government officials on deputation as training providers at LBSNAA, they were able to comment effectively on this issue. They claimed that major changes had taken place in the training structure of the Academy. Theoretical input still constituted the main thrust of the training programs, but increasingly content was being introduced based on recent changes and developments in the government and international arena. A Deputy Director felt that the current programs helped trainees learn a much larger repertoire of skills compared to the past. He acknowledged that public officials in India require new and professional skills, and was optimistic that LBSNAA is moving in the right direction (Interview, 21st June, 2000). Trainers are aware of the knowledge gap and work on ways to bridge it. The Academy is developing web-based and distance learning to emphasize training and learning as a continuous process.

Table 4.10 Trainees' Views on Trends of Training

Statements	Strongly Agree 1	2	3	4	Strongly Disagree 5	No Comment 6
1 Public service training has responded to government policies and objectives	21	27	22	55	115	12
2 There have been positive developments in the training trends of LBSNAA	17	18	84	67	65	1
3 LBSNAA follows traditional syllabi and training methods.	12	36	22	75	94	13
TOTAL	50	81	128	197	274	26

Most of the trainees appeared to agree with the claim of the Academy in saying that it tries to move away from the traditional pattern of syllabi and training methods (Table 4.10). However, some respondents complained that the contents of some courses, such as law, are too theoretical in nature. They suggested that these courses should be taught with the aid of case studies and mute courts should be conducted to generate interest among the learners. While most trainers claim that the academy is moving away from traditional syllabi it is interesting to note, as seen in Table 4.11, that 7 trainers strongly agreed and only 3 strongly disagreed with the statement that traditional civil service-type of syllabi and training methods are used at LBSNAA. They commented that some of the trainers still adhere to the lecture method and use mostly theoretical input. New recruits felt time was wasted on some course content which they had already covered before entering the public service. In some cases, the syllabi were not consistent with the training provided and so the customers (the departments sending them for training) were often misinformed about the available programs. It is difficult to determine the reasons for a large number of trainers non-committal position on the use of traditional training methods.

Table 4.11 Trainers' Views on Trends of Training

Statement	Strongly Agree 1	2	3	4	Strongly Disagree 5	No Comment 6
1 Public service training has responded to government policies and objectives	6	4	12	5	5	2
2 There have been positive developments in the training trends of LBSNAA	14	11	2	1	5	1
3 LBSNAA follows traditional syllabi and training methods	7	1	10	10	3	3
TOTAL	27	16	24	16	13	6

Priorities in Training

LBSNAA is limited in the amount of training it can provide. Thus it tries to concentrate its programs on areas that are considered the most important and that can have the maximum impact, such as language, IT, and management. Care must be exercised in establishing training priorities to achieve the stated goals of the Academy. This calls for closely following the stated programs and course objectives, identifying training audiences, establishing criteria for participation, preparing training courses and materials that meet the most significant needs and rigorously evaluating outputs against realistic objectives.

The Academy identified three new knowledge areas to be developed in the training programs. Negotiation and coordination, scientific management and personal productivity were chosen as the areas on which training will concentrate in the future. In addition, LBSNAA will strongly emphasize conceptual skills and knowledge of policy areas. Policy input, which has been largely ignored in the past, has been identified as an important element that can help in developing government plans (http://www.civilservices.gov.in).

Among the various training priorities of LBSNAA, the trainers identified developing and conducting induction training for new entrants into the public service as the most prominent. They considered the period of entry into public service as extremely important because the trainees are left with strong impressions of what is expected from public officials during this period. They also develop deep-seated attitudes about the importance of their role as public service employees. In addition, in this period, civil servants make themselves familiar with the objectives of the government and develop work habits that influence their behaviour patterns in their career. At the same time, LBSNAA should establish itself as a major provider of training to those employed as trainers in various public organizations in India, and assist the government in developing training technology.

The Academy strives to make the system more efficient, effective, transparent, responsive and accountable. In recent years, the importance of ethical issues in administrative matters has been emphasized, and course contents are aimed at inculcating moral standards in making and implementing decisions. Institutional arrangements are being devised for training the trainers and training managers in the techniques allowing for the identification of training needs, design of courses, and management and evaluation of trainees and training programs.

At the administrative level, the issues of: the management of information, the analysis of policy alternatives, performance improvement, investment analysis, financial planning, human resource development, and knowledge about international experience in economic reform and liberalization merit attention. India is also trying to resolve a variety of problems such as violent crime, drugs, slow economic growth, child abuse, budgetary constraints, pollution, etc. Behind all of these, one of the most formidable problems is the inadequacy of the institutional mechanism in making public decisions. The government generally fails to generate effective responses to the problems confronting the country. Citizens are excluded from the decision-making process, and believe that public officials—who are out of touch with the concerns of ordinary citizens and who respond only to the persistent demands of organized interests—do not always act in the public interest. The distance between the government and citizens continue to grow, and there is little trust placed in public institutions. LBSNAA needs to keep these factors in mind and develop plans to train public service officials to be more responsive and accessible to the citizens.

The Director suggested that the main tasks of LBSNAA were to make projections on the future role of administrators and 'reinvent government' before totally reforming its training programs. Public management is characterised by a high level of public awareness and expectation as well as a high degree of public intolerance, expediency in public life and technical skills of the highest order. Thus it is essential to set the right priorities and adhere to them in formulating training programs (Interview, 25th June 2000).

Other Relevant Observations

In addition to the six major factors discussed above, a number of other points deserve acknowledgement. The trainees were emphatic in stating that LBSNAA is staffed by a group of highly dedicated and professional trainers (Table 4.12). Most of the trainers are public officials deputed to the Academy. They are qualified and can share their experience with the trainees and also draw upon their own experience as trainees at the same institute earlier in life. However, their capability and experience as public officials are not enough to ensure their effectiveness as trainers. These public officials may have performed extremely well in the execution of projects and programs, but this does not mean that they possess the qualities and skills to serve as trainers. To overcome this potential handicap, officials deputed to LBSNAA are refreshed with courses on 'training for trainers'.

Table 4.12 Trainees' Views on Training at LBSNAA

Statements	Strongly Agree 1	2	3	4	Strongly Disagree 5	No Comment 6
1 LBSNAA is staffed by dedicated and professional trainers	115	11	40	48	28	10
2 Training programs prepare public officials for the changing environment	22	25	53	69	72	11
3 LBSNAA assesses the adequacy of training on a regular basis	34	27	105	44	32	10
TOTAL	171	63	198	161	132	31

A large number of trainees felt that the training programs at LBSNAA are not aimed at preparing the public officials for the changing environment. They reported experiencing a knowledge gap at their workplace in spite of receiving training at the Academy. Most of the trainees strongly disagree that the LBSNAA has made progress with time. In contrast, most of the trainers claimed that the training programs did prepare public officials for the changing environment (Table 4.13). The trainees reported that they were humiliated by their supervisors who expected them to perform their duties efficiently after training, but they were unable to do so because they do not receive comprehensive training. They cited examples such as office administration and report writing which are neglected.

A large number of trainers agree that the institute develops the human ability to adapt to the changing times. The trainers claimed that trainees are informed of current developments and are trained with the purpose of adapting to changing environment in mind. Interestingly, one trainer strongly disagreed with this statement, and commented that the Academy does not possess the infrastructure to collect and disseminate information on the latest developments. He added that, in reality, negligible changes have taken place in this respect. There is no external higher authority monitoring the training delivered, thus there is lethargy within the institute (Interview, 23rd June 2000). On the contrary, LBSNAA is an attached office of the Ministry of Personnel of the central government of India, and the Director reports to the Secretary of the Ministry. A summary of the Academy's annual report is merged with the Ministry's report, which is tabled at both Houses of the Parliament.

Table 4.13 Trainers' Views on Training at LBSNAA

	Statements	Strongly Agree 1	2	3	4	Strongly Disagree 5	No Comment 6
1	LBSNAA is staffed by dedicated and professional trainers	10	11	8	3	2	
2	LBSNAA provides strategic guidance to government departments	2	5	8	6	12	1
3	LBSNAA helps with job enrichment	8	17		4	5	
4	LBSNAA aims to develop human ability to adapt to changing times	7	13	8	5	1	
	TOTAL	27	46	24	18	20	1

The trainees remained non-committal on the statement that LBSNAA assesses the adequacy of its programs on a regular basis. It seems that the trainees do not have the access to such information. They are unable to view records from the past as the Academy does not have a systematic process for documentation.

A large number of trainees strongly believed that relevant training would lead to career advancement. This factor led to the expression of anxiety. Trainees wished that LBSNAA would concentrate on efforts to familiarize them with changes in the workplace, and develop programs accordingly.

Trainees believed that they are sent to receive training in order to enrich their jobs and most expected to benefit from the experience. The trainers agreed with this point. Training could turn into a process of mutual benefit, since the experiences of both the trainers and trainees can contribute to the formulation of case studies, which in turn provide first hand experience and information to the trainees about the demands and requirements of their work. Moreover, the trainees are exposed to field visits and practical sessions. Since trainees are not formally in charge of the administrative units, where they train, during training, they are not under constraints, and can afford to make mistakes while they learn.

Concluding Remarks

LBSNAA basically organizes three types of training—for fresh recruits, in-service officials, and induction training for state service officials joining the IAS. Despite some changes in content and methods, LBSNAA faces new challenges in conducting training that will equip public officials to meet with the changes taking place within and outside the government. Training services in India are virtually monopolised by the government. Private training agencies have been suffocated by the state sector, and public service training is provided within the confines of the state.

Trainees regard training as a process for improving their capacity to secure career advancement, whereas the trainers consider it a means for improving the skills of the trainees to perform better on their present jobs. Due to lack of adequate and regular contact and interaction between government departments and LBSNAA, the trainees' needs are not properly addressed. The Academy does not undertake intensive evaluation of its programs and relies on simply an 'end of course' evaluation for the training packages.

A proper and systematic method of needs assessment is not followed, and public service officials are unaware of the process of needs assessment. The Academy relies on informal contact with the trainees to assess their needs, resulting in ad-hoc changes to the content of training. Trainers and trainees realize that it is not easy to identify future training needs, although the trainers and the administrators at LBSNAA are determined to satisfy the needs of their clients. The forces of globalization have released a series of liberalisation and economic reforms, and it is important to make public officials sensitive to the need of upholding national interest in their interface with the other nations and international organizations. LBSNAA is keen to learn from the experiences of bureaucracies that have helped in the achievement of economic progress, growth with equity, and human well being in other nations (LBSNAA, 1999). Thus the training programs have to adjust to the demands of globalization, and their scope widened to equip public officials to understand the world order and work to protect the national interest while participating in the activities of the globalized world. LBSNAA has been working towards meeting the demands of their clients, and it entails a long and arduous journey towards excellence.

Notes

[1] The probationers, during the interviews, strongly supported the participative approach.
[2] During the interviews, most of the deputed trainers indicated that about two decade earlier when they themselves received training at the institute, there was no IT and computer related training imparted to them.

Chapter 5

Public Service Training in Hong Kong

This chapter presents the findings of a survey conducted among trainers and trainees at the Civil Service Training and Development Institute (CSTDI) in Hong Kong. As a centralized training agency, the CSTDI is autonomous and is responsible for monitoring matters relating to the training of personnel in government departments. The respondents to the survey provided their views and opinions on various issues related to training, following the same framework outlined in the previous chapter. The profiles of the respondents, their perception of training objectives and their comments and observations provide interesting insights on key areas of concern in public service training.

The Respondents

Five hundred trainees were requested to return questionnaires in an effort to obtain information on their experience with training at CSTDI. Fifty trainers were also invited to respond to a set of questions. A total of two hundred and eighty seven (57.4 per cent) questionnaires were returned by the trainees and thirty (60 per cent) were returned by the trainers. The trainers included full time as well as part time trainers, along with some guest trainers who were available for consultation. The trainees included government officials of different grades and ranks. They represented a number of government departments in the government.

Full and part-time trainers were subsequently interviewed both to follow up on the questionnaire responses and to explore specific issues. In addition, twenty-one interviews were conducted with the trainees to obtain similar information. Several of the target interviewees expressed a reluctance to be interviewed, and a number of external trainers who had provided training services to the CSTDI were interviewed. This arrangement helped to gain an unbiased perspective on the activities of the Institute. The other reason for interviewing these external trainers was the limited quantity of information provided by the full-time trainers who did not wish to elaborate on specific matters. The full-time trainers' responses consisted mostly of standard information found in the brochures of CSTDI, and resembled a publicity campaign to promote the Institute, rather than critical insight on its activities. Also, in order to compensate for this drawback, trainees were subjected to intensive interviews and information was also collected from them through informal meetings.

Table 5.1 Profile of Respondents

Trainees			Trainers	
Number of Respondents	287		Number of Respondents	30
Position	Number		Position	Number
Administrative Officers	5		Chief Training Officer	13
Executive Officers	110		Training Officer	11
Junior Staff	85		Manager	2
Clerical Grade Staff	35		Executive Officer	2
Land Registration Officer	4		Invited Part-Time Trainers	2
Assistants	25			
Accounts Officer	21			
Manager	2			
Educational Qualification	Number		Educational Qualification	Number
High School	55		High School	0
Bachelor degree	129		Bachelor degree	6
Master	49		Master	11
Ph.D.	0		Ph.D.	0
Specialization	54		Specialization	13
Age Group	Number		Age Group	Number
20-30 years	103		20-30 years	0
30-40 years	136		30-40 years	8
40-50 years	32		40-50 years	20
50-60 years	16		50-60 years	2
Above 60	0		Above 60	0

Table 5.1 presents the profile of the respondents and the actual breakdown of responses. The range in age of both the trainees and trainers was between 20 and 50 years, with the majority of trainers falling in the 40 to 50-age bracket. Most of the trainees were in the 30 to 40 year age group. A large number of the trainers had attained a Masters degree or specialization in their fields, while most of the trainees possessed a Bachelors degree.

The Findings

Pre-entry training allows potential employees to prepare themselves for service in the public sector, while post-entry training helps existing employees to obtain or develop the knowledge, skills and attitudes they need to make an effective contribution to the Service (Hong Kong Government, 1978, para. 109). The main objectives of training in the Hong Kong public service are: to enable officials to meet operational requirements and respond to changing circumstances and to assist grade/departmental managers in realizing career development plans for individual officers and succession plans for grades/departments (CSB, June 1998 Newsletter). The trainers at CSTDI identified the primary purpose of training as a means to prepare civil servants for government jobs and provide them with practical training on issues related to their work environment and culture.

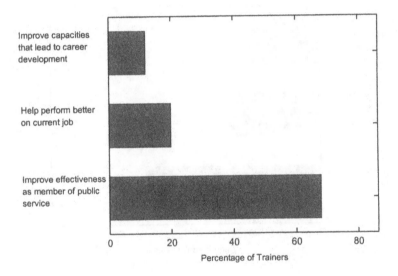

Figure 5.1 Trainers' Perception of Training

    The respondent trainers were asked to indicate their views on the purpose of training at CSTDI. A substantial majority (68 per cent) of the trainers considered the improved effectiveness of public officials to be CSTDI's most important purpose. About 20 per cent chose the enhancement of trainees' ability to perform in their current job, and the remaining 12 per cent believed the main purpose of CSTDI was to improve trainees' capability leading to career development. One of the trainers commented: 'CSTDI focuses on all round development of the trainees. However, maximum priority is laid on improving the effectiveness of the employees as a member of the government. Training is mainly focused on the areas related to changes in the government and government policies' (Interview, 5th September 2000). A different view was expressed by another trainer: 'It is essential to provide employees with training related to their current job so that application of training provided is guaranteed. Training on subjects beyond the areas related to work could be regarded as useless input. There are various different departments and grades in the government and each individual has different work requirements depending on the nature of work performed. Hence, he/she should be trained in areas directly focusing on his/her work requirements' (Interview, 23rd October 2000). In spite of these differences of opinion, most CSTDI trainers felt that all training programs at the Institute directly or indirectly lead to the career advancement of all attendees.

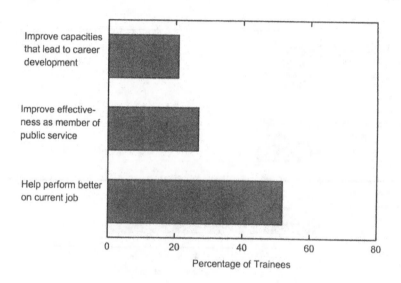

Figure 5.2 Trainees' Perception of Training

The trainees' perception differed from the trainers' in several respects. Fifty-two per cent of the trainees ranked better performance in the current job as the main purpose of training. Twenty-seven per cent of the trainees thought that the main purpose was to improve the effectiveness of public officials. Surprisingly, only 21 per cent of the respondents saw training as a tool to enhance their capabilities, leading to career development and advancement.

The difference between the trainers' and trainees' perceptions about training may explain a certain level of dissatisfaction expressed by the attendees of training programs. The principal aim of the CSTDI is to organize training programs aimed at improving the effectiveness of the government, while the trainees expect training input to improve their performance in the current job. However, seemingly in agreement with the trainees, a large majority of the CSTDI trainers recognized the fact that public officials attended training programs to acquire new job-related skills. The discrepancy between the aims of CSTDI and the expectations of trainees could be a major factor affecting the satisfaction of the trainees.

The Issue of Coordination

Training upgrades and updates the skills and attitudes of public officials according to the changing needs of society, government and individuals. Training agencies are responsible for providing strategic guidance on training and development to various government departments. It is important that training takes into account the practical aspect of the job being trained for, since institutional or theoretical training alone does not provide a public official with real work experience or a sense of the best methods for getting the job done. However, considering the rapid pace of institutional knowledge development and its application to different sectors of administration, theoretical training must complement on-the-job training.

CSTDI provides training to public officials from many different departments and agencies within the government of Hong Kong. The mandates and responsibilities of these various departments are very diverse, as they are required to provide services to different sections of the community. It is critically important to identify the specific needs of the different departments based on their mandates.

However, each department has job requirements and needs that are not adequately addressed by the training provided by the Institute, which is more inclined towards programs that are more general in nature. For instance, while the titles of various grades in the public service may be similar in different government departments, the natures of these jobs may differ significantly. But training programs are formulated with mainly the titles and listed tasks of a specific level in mind, and hence many trainees find the skills and knowledge acquired to be irrelevant to their particular jobs. Some respondents felt that sometimes this type of training was inappropriate and inadequate in meeting the requirements of the trainees.

To address this problem, the CSTDI tries to provide more customized and tailor-made courses for the attendees. Such as, the trainers at CSTDI claim that they are careful in grouping public officials from different departments together, considering their backgrounds and work experience in the process. This problem could be further addressed by treating each department as a unique case, and developing programs to meet their needs.

Effectiveness of Training Programs

The objective of public service training in Hong Kong is to enable civil servants to acquire the necessary knowledge, skills and attitude to meet operational requirements and changing circumstances and to assist grade/departmental managers in realizing career development plans of individual officers and succession plans of grades/departments. At the operational level, departments have to supplement the above-mentioned general training policy with their own policies, suited to their specific needs and operational requirements. Hence, the ownership of human resource training and development rests with the individual departments and grades, while the Civil Service Bureau (CSB) and its executive branch, CSTDI, advise departments on the implementation and execution of their training programs. The Institute provides both regular and customized courses, advisory services, and other services and products, including: self-learning packages, a Learning Resource Centre and a Cyber Learning Centre.

A training effectiveness evaluation system enhances the likelihood that the contents of the training have been useful and allows for the modification of existing programs, in order to increase their effectiveness. The evaluation process can help develop programs that produce observable changes in the behaviour and attitude of trainees. Training effectiveness is measured on the basis of a number of factors: evaluation by trainees, course performance and the transfer of techniques. A four-tier measure is used to assess the level of satisfaction in customized courses provided by CSTDI: fulfilment of agreed objectives; elevation of skill level; enhancement of performance; and contribution to organizational development.

The trainers and trainees identified a few areas in which the CSTDI excels. These included the variety of training programs and packages on offer, their customized courses for clients, the cost-effectiveness of self-learning packages such as Cyber learning and a good learning environment, both within and outside of classrooms. They also positively commented on the quality of training programs and their format, such as the sharing of knowledge among public service officials from different departments and guest speakers from the private sector.

At the same time, the respondents identified some areas that could be improved. Recent entrants to the public service felt the range of courses offered was insufficient for trainees at their level. One trainee said: 'Training at CSTDI is mainly focused on people of senior ranks. However, sometimes it is irrelevant to them. They might attend for just half a day, sign in and leave after lunch. This is a waste of training resources' (Interview, 7th September, 2000). There was concern over the level at which some courses are pitched, as some respondents felt the level was too difficult for them. They also felt that topics such as training administration, nomination, re-scheduling, training records, and charging systems required more attention and revision. Another area of concern was the inadequate allocation of self-learning packages.

It is also necessary to measure the effectiveness of training. An invited trainer for CSTDI commented: 'It is very difficult to identify an effective way of measuring the effectiveness of training. The 'feel good' factor is quite misleading, as, if the trainees have enjoyed the training, they will rate it positively, but is it really having an impact on the people's behaviour or attitude when they go back into their departments? We have to accept a lot of that on faith' (Interview, 6th August 2001). This requires the full commitment and investment of public agencies and government.

Table 5.2 Evaluation of Training Effectiveness by Trainees

Statements	Strongly Agree 1	2	3	4	Strongly Disagree 5	No Comment 6
1 Training leads to career advancement	41	157	60	16	2	11
2 Training at CSTDI is beneficial	6	178	77	10	8	8
3 Training programs are designed to fulfil the present requirements	20	41	213	12		1
4 The programs provide adequate training as required for work	2	27	41	205	6	6
5 Training assists with job enrichment	4	223	31	22	3	4
6 CSTDI establishes a positive training environment and motivation to work	15	144	119	4		5
7 Trainees are informed of latest developments in specialized areas	7	29	223	17	6	5
8 The training helps adjust to the changing environment and reforms	8	25	120	121	2	11
9 CSTDI provides quality service and training	4	100	168	10		5
10 Knowledge/skill acquired from training is applicable to present job	3	28	188	35	30	3
TOTAL	110	952	1240	452	57	59

The Annual Reports and documents viewed during field visits and interviews indicate that the CSTDI has always received positive evaluation and, at times, the results of the evaluation were far better than that expected by the trainers. This gives rise to questions over the reliability of the evaluations. Multi-level evaluations, however, can yield more useful information.

The CSTDI employs different levels of training evaluation. One method used by CSTDI is the end of course evaluation. This is hardly an adequate tool. The result of this type of evaluation is generally positive if the trainees are impressed with the trainers. It seems that trainees are either naïve or try to be nice in evaluating training programs, and they usually award good ratings to the trainers.

For courses of longer duration, three levels of evaluation are conducted. At the second level, CSTDI assesses the acquisition of knowledge at the end of the course by testing to determine the knowledge, skills or attitudes the participants have learned from the training program. The second level of evaluation can sometimes be done immediately after the course, within the classroom. The trainees are given skill tests and their success on these tests indicates whether knowledge has been acquired. The third level of evaluation assesses the behavioural aspect of training outcome. The departments and the trainees respond to questionnaires in order to assess the application of skills and change in the attitude after training. After a suitable span of time, the CSTDI requests trainees and their supervisors to provide feedback on the performance of the trainees to assess the sustainability and the effectiveness of training. However, the information obtained should be used with caution because it may be ambiguous and incomplete due to subjective reporting from the respondents.

A trainer admitted: 'A few years ago, we had not been concerned about whether the training acquired within the classroom can be transferred to the workplace. But now we have already started to conduct second and third levels of evaluation' (Interview, 23rd October, 2000). The CSTDI sends out evaluation forms to the supervisors of the trainees and the trainees themselves, to assess their performance after returning from training, and changes are made on the existing programs on the bases of feedback from the different departments. Over the years, increased attention has been devoted to the evaluation of training programs.

Many trainees remained neutral while commenting on the effectiveness of training at CSTDI. This can be seen as a reflection of their inability to assess the effectiveness of training. It should be pointed out that a large number of trainees agreed that training at CSTDI is effective, but only a small number of trainees strongly agreed or disagreed on the effectiveness of training at CSTDI. Most of the respondents chose a safe option while ranking the effectiveness of training, and gave non-committal responses on this issue.

A large number of the respondents disagreed that the CSTDI provide trainees with adequate training as required by their work. A trainee commented: 'It depends. Work is so diversified that the training programs can by no means be 100 per cent adequate. Anyway, there are some essential training courses such as how to conduct performance appraisal interview, how to write performance appraisal reports, and some other job-related courses held regularly for us to apply on voluntary basis' (Interview, 5th September 2000). The CSTDI offers courses related to public service, but cannot meet individual expectations of the trainees.

Most of the trainees agreed that they attend training to obtain benefits, although eight respondents strongly disagreed with this statement. These eight could belong to the group who attend training to get a break from their daily work routine and are least interested in training. A large number of respondents remained non-committal on the suggestion that training keeps them informed of the latest developments in their specific fields. Furthermore, six trainees strongly disagreed with this statement, reflecting a lack of awareness of the purpose and outcome of the programs. It is obvious that the CSTDI cannot keep pace with the rapid change taking place in the Hong Kong public service. The Institute develops training packages based on requests from specific government departments, but new demands soon render these packages obsolete. Staying up-to-date with changes is a major challenge faced by the CSTDI.

Many of the trainees perceive training institutes as centres for job enrichment. Some of the respondents felt that training at CSTDI did not meet their expectations. Nevertheless, they consider it as a suitable venue for assisting with bridging the knowledge gap arising as the public sector faces constant changes and new problems.

There was mixed response to the statement related to the applicability of knowledge and skills acquired from training to the public officials' present jobs. On a scale from 1 (strongly agree) to 5 (strongly disagree), most of the respondents chose 3, which suggests that they are unsure of the utility of the programs. Only three respondents strongly agreed to this suggestion, while 30 strongly disagreed. A respondent trainee stated: 'I have experienced that the objectives of the courses are sometimes misleading and the training provided does not directly prepare us for the change in the work style' (Interview, 13th August, 2000). However, the CSTDI finds it almost impossible to address individual or departmental needs, as the Institute offers training to a diverse population of trainees from different departments. The trainers, for their part, claimed that they try to address individual needs in the training sessions.

Most of the trainers agreed that the Institute provides adequate training, as required by the jobs of public officials. A trainer who recognized the problem of specificity explained: 'It varies from level to level, for really junior levels like front line staff and people doing manual work, there is not much opportunity available. An officer at that rank is not that keen on learning and they feel that learning or going for training should be sometime when they are much younger or still at school. However, some of these people complain that adequate opportunity is not available to them. For the middle level and top level staff we have adequate training' (Interview, 23rd October, 2000). Sometimes, officials cannot be released to attend relevant training programs due to heavy workload and the need to remain at their post.

The majority of the trainers agreed that the training programs at CSTDI are effective. A training officer explained: 'We put in the best resources and appoint the most competent person to train for us. If we feel that an expert or professional can better deliver a particular training, we invite a guest trainer to train. Our programs are highly relevant and competent' (Interview, 23rd October 2000). Another trainer claimed the courses at CSTDI are highly effective because they are based on the needs of the clients, and are not offered on the whims of the Institute (Interview, 17th November 2000).

As seen in Table 5.3, only one trainer strongly supported the statement that CSTDI's programs are designed to fulfil the requirements of trainees' present jobs. Six trainers disagreed on the same point. During the interviews, the trainers reiterated the relevance of training programs to the clients' needs. However, in response to the questionnaires, many of the trainers did not agree strongly with this claim. Their support was more subdued, many choosing to merely 'agree'. An equal number of trainers agreed and disagreed with the suggestion that the knowledge and skills acquired at CSTDI are directly applicable to trainees' jobs. Only one respondent strongly agreed with this statement, while the others opted to remain neutral.

Table 5.3 Evaluation of Training Effectiveness by Trainers

	Statements	Strongly Agree 1	2	3	4	Strongly Disagree 5	No Comment 6
1	Training leads to career advancement	3	15	6	6		
2	Training programs are designed to fulfil the present job requirements	1	14	8	6		1
3	The programs provide adequate training as required for work		13	6	6	3	2
4	Training is provided for job enrichment	1	16	8	4		1
5	CSTDI establishes a positive training environment and motivation to work	4	13	4	8	1	
6	The training helps adjust to the changing environment in government departments and reforms	2	9	9	5	2	3
7	Training programs are designed to prepare public officials for the changing environment		16	4	6	2	2
8	CSTDI assess the adequacy of their programs regularly	1	12	7	8		2
9	CSTDI provides quality service and training	1	15	6	4	4	
10	Knowledge/skill acquired from training is applicable to present job	1	10	8	10		1
	TOTAL	14	133	66	63	12	12

A large number of the trainers agreed, and seven strongly agreed, that CSTDI constantly reviews and updates training packages. Only one trainer did not support this claim (see Table 5.5). However, during an interview, a trainer stated that the review of programs takes place annually. At a time when changes take place at a rapid pace, annual reviews cannot be considered adequate. Thus the discrepancy between the interview response and the questionnaire responses should be noted.

The CSTDI provides training services to the government of Hong Kong which is responsible for a dynamic and international city. Public service officials are constantly facing new challenges emanating from the changing environment across the globe. While it may be one of the aims of the CSTDI, none of the trainers strongly support the statement that training programs at CSTDI are initiated in order to prepare civil servants for the changing environment. Most agreed only unenthusiastically with this statement. Six trainers disagreed and two trainers even strongly disagreed that the institute is preparing the trainees for change.

Most trainers felt that the CSTDI provides quality service and training to the trainees. The Chief Training Officer claimed, 'Quality service is our top agenda. All the same, sometimes the quality of our service is questioned. However, there is no mechanism to relate or co-relate training provided by our department to different services provided by individual departments because there are a whole lot of factors that affect the quality rather than just training we provide. We are just trying to provide people with the necessary skills and how they can improve their own existing skills' (Interview, 15th November 2000). But it should be borne in mind that service providers are usually confident of the quality of their output.

The different reasons cited by trainees for attending training courses were found to influence their motivation and effectiveness significantly. A trainee stated: 'I feel that some civil servants are not eager to attend the courses. They attend the courses either because their supervisors instruct them or else they want to take a break from work by attending the courses. Therefore, they learn nothing at the end and evaluate the courses negatively. Sometimes, as their learning attitude is not good, some group work or role-play cannot achieve the estimated objectives. CSTDI should review such situations' (Interview, 14th September 2000). These comments reflect a lack of direction and motivation in public service training.

At the interviews, full-time trainers responded with regular usage of terms like 'maybe', 'trying', and 'I suppose', and thus appeared to be unsure about the performance of the Institute. They admitted that there were shortcomings like inadequate training packages, shortage of space and competent manpower, and inability to forecast the future. The tentative position of the trainers raises questions about the steps taken to rectify the problems identified by the trainers.

Improvement of Training

The Chief Training Officer of the CSTDI presented a positive picture of the training activities and commented that the mode of the training should be more diversified. 'Essentially, there will still be classroom training but that would be complemented by a whole lot of other self-learning tools either in paper form or CD-ROMs or even internet web based training. In fact we are developing in a lot of directions' (Interview, 15th November, 2000). But the respondents did not speak convincingly in assessing the effectiveness of training at CSTDI. The trainees generally chose the safe option of ranking the questions on this topic neutrally, but some of the perceived weaknesses became evident at informal meetings. A middle management officer commented: 'I often have to consult a native English speaker to check the minutes of meetings prepared by me. I no doubt attend the courses at CSTDI and have relevant reference material, but I do not have the confidence. After all, it is a question of my career and at this time of recession and retention I want to take no chances' (Informal Meeting, 23rd December, 2000). A trainee complained that the civil servants who taught many management courses are not trainers by profession and therefore lacked the necessary skills, and recommended the employment of professional trainers from the private sector (Interview, 13th September, 2000). The lack of confidence over the expertise of trainers can affect the perception of trainees adversely.

A trainer admitted that it was difficult to foresee future needs, and thus planning with this objective in mind is not an easy task. However, the institute maintains close contact with their customers and major clients and can provide courses at short notice to meet their needs. Usually, such courses are designed instantaneously, without careful planning. These courses are often criticized on grounds of quality and relevance.

Identification of Training Needs

Training helps trainees acquire job-related skills, along with offering opportunities for advancement, increasing morale and improving individual performance. For the organization, it is an important means by which to enhance employee's capabilities and efficiency (Scott, 1984, p. 118). The training needs assessment process is extremely important, as it is critical to the success of the entire training effort. Yet, effective needs assessment will not guarantee the desired outcome, as success is dependent on a number of factors. Some of these factors include training design, implementation and evaluation and the commitment to the training function, both on the part of the training provider and the client organization. Kaufman and English, (1979) have defined need assessment 'as a tool for determining valid and useful problems which are philosophically as well as practically sound. It keeps us from running down more blind educational (training) alleys, from using time, dollars and people in attempted solutions, which do not work. It is a tool for proper identification and justification. Needs assessment is a humanizing process to help make sure that we are using our time and the learner's time in most effective and efficient manner possible' (p. 31).

Training deals with modifying attitudes, skills and knowledge of individuals in order to better cope with changes. Public service officials perform multifaceted and complex duties, and are required to play different roles effectively and efficiently. These tasks call for a high level of proficiency, especially in Hong Kong, where the government is becoming increasingly involved in activities that can no longer be carried out by non-governmental bodies. Thus the identification of training needs must be geared towards bridging the gap between the existing level of an official's capability and the required level for the proper discharge of functions. In order to accomplish this, training needs identification that involves collecting data from various sources such as job descriptions, individual employees and the organization.

The CSTDI identifies service-wide training needs; government departments are required to assist by informing CSTDI of their specific training needs. A document entitled *Generic Competencies for Managers and Staff* suggests the skills, knowledge, abilities and attitudes needed to perform a job effectively at specific levels. By referring to these listed competencies, the staff, supervisors and the Institute discuss and agree upon training needs that should be given preference (CSTDI, Prospectus 2000, p. 7).

The Institute monitors developments within and outside of the public service and considers designing programs to respond to the changing needs it perceives. An annual customer survey helps CSTDI assess the needs of the different government departments. The survey collects suggestions from the different departments on strategies for improving performance. Regular meetings and communication with the client departments allows CSTDI to understand their training needs and incorporate them into their programs. There is an attempt to compliment the needs of the public service with the operational needs of the government. Thus, both consultation with government and the results of the three levels of evaluation are useful in identifying training needs.

An invited trainer for CSTDI stated that good strategic planning for the Institute entailed identifying the changing needs and responding to them. However, he thought that the process used in identifying training needs was not as broadly based as it should be and added: 'The training institutes have to scan the environment extensively and very frequently to determine the most recent changes and developments and identify the most up-to-date requirements, and, I think, to be on the cutting edge they have to do that in an international context. It is not sufficient for the training institutes in Hong Kong to look at what's happening in Hong Kong. Beyond that they need to have a much wider perspective on what's happening in other places in Asia, what's happening basically across the world and much more, kind of an international perspective' (Interview, 6th August, 2001). It is possible to obtain such information and use the services of consultants to develop programs to adjust to the changing circumstances.

A senior trainer agreed that there are times when trainers find an incompatibility between the real needs of the trainees and the needs that are actually addressed. She stated: 'Sometimes we ask the trainees what they expect to get from the training at the very beginning. However, when some people enrol for a particular program, they do not spend time to study the objectives and simply enrol. When we know that there are some people who shouldn't be there, then we just put a kind of bridging in the training program. What we try to do is to align their expectation to what we meant to achieve and, in the case of very experienced trainers, when they find out that the majority of the participants are not expecting what he has already planned, they just put aside what they had already planned and discuss what is demanded' (Interview, 23rd October, 2000).

The trainers also indicated that the selection of training candidates is done with great care and the Institute seeks information on the background of trainees and their job requirements before they are selected. Often, the trainees are unable to secure release from their departments to attend specific training programs. When they are finally able to come to CSTDI for training, it could lead to the difficult choice of taking or leaving it. Complete satisfaction is extremely difficult to achieve, as the courses are not tailor-made to suit individual choice. But they should be able to generate some level of satisfaction.

CSTDI seldom consults front line staff in order to identify their training needs. Ideas are collected from public service officials who go through the training process and then provide feedback on the program. But the trainees are often unable to provide helpful specific suggestions for improvements that could help officials to perform better on the job, and these questions are often ignored. Feedback on the programs gives an indication of the level of satisfaction in the existing programs, but the issue of changes required for the future and better performance remains neglected.

Seven main sources of data used to design CSTDI training programs can be identified: (a) the Civil Service Bureau (CSB); (b) assessment of training needs by trainers; (c) the identification of training needs by government departments; (d) communication and the monitoring of changes within and outside the government; (e) training nomination forms; (f) the three level of training evaluation; and (g) the annual training needs survey conducted by the CSTDI. The needs of Hong Kong government are of prime importance and they are communicated through the CSB. The other sources are utilised with varying degrees of emphasis.

The trainees had mixed views on the identification of what factors determine their training needs (see Table 5.4). Most of the respondents agreed on all three options: that they themselves, their managers and their training departments each determine the training needs. This can be interpreted in two ways; either the trainees are not aware of the process of needs identification, or the departments have entrusted the responsibility of determining training needs to different people or groups of people without informing the public officials. The individuals identify their own needs based on the nature of their jobs and/or work style, while the manager assesses the needs of the department as a whole and is supported by the training institute in monitoring changes and eventually preparing a needs-based training package. This is relatively easy with tailor-made courses.

CSTDI provides consultancy services to different departments and helps them identify areas that need more attention. A majority of the trainees were neutral in response to the suggestion that the CSTDI constantly reviews and updates training needs. This choice probably reflects a lack of knowledge in this area. It is, however, interesting to note that that none of the respondents strongly disagreed on this issue. Most of the trainees agreed that the needs assessment process would be helped by making greater use of available employee and organizational records as a means of gaining greater insight into their training needs. The trainers were satisfied with their work in assessing the needs of the trainees through extensive evaluation and close contact with the clients.

Table 5.4 Trainees' Views on Identification of Training Needs

Statements	Strongly Agree 1	2	3	4	Strongly Disagree 5	No Comment 5
1 I determine the training needs	10	220	33	16	3	5
2 My manager determines the training needs	2	153	29	61	7	35
3 Our training department determines the training needs	4	123	50	62	12	36
4 CSTDI determines the training needs	7	24	29	69	45	113
5 Trainees should complete questionnaires on their training needs	63	176	31	6	7	4
6 CSTDI establishes training objectives based on identified needs	6	125	103	49		4
7 CSTDI constantly reviews and updates training needs	11	86	165	10		15
8 Available information on jobs and the organization should be used to gain insight on training needs	6	183	83	8	1	6
TOTAL	109	1090	523	281	75	218

However, a large number of trainees (61 per cent) supported the idea that the needs assessment process would be more successful if the employees were asked to complete questionnaires on their training needs (Table 5.4). The trainees expressed a desire for greater involvement in the needs assessment process. As they are the recipients of training and are responsible for service delivery, they should have greater autonomy in identifying and voicing their needs. They suggested that departments should give each employee an opportunity to indicate their needs. The department should review these preferences and incorporate them in a final plan before forwarding it to the training agency. Trainees were concerned that the department may sometimes overlook the gaps in skills/knowledge that are felt by the individuals.

In practice, identification of needs is a top-down exercise and the departments control the process, with little attempt to get the stakeholders involved in the decision-making process. Information and ideas are collected from the employees, but these are treated with minimal importance. Austin, Brannon and Pecora (1984) argued that in order for training to be effective in achieving the organization's mission and objectives, an employee development plan, which recognizes both organization and employee perspectives, must be developed. In order for the plan to incorporate both perspectives, a negotiation process must take place (p. 53). The negotiation process should include (a) knowing the organization's mission, its status in achieving that mission, and the current implications of training; (b) knowing the employees' interpretation of their operational goals and their training needs; and assessing how other factors contribute to the agreement or disagreement between the two perspectives (p. 55). The concept of empowering the consumer and client is still at the early stages of recognition in the Hong Kong public service. The situation is changing and the government is becoming sensitive to the need to consult the clients, but the idea of sharing power has yet to be fully developed.

Table 5.5 Trainers' Views on Identification of Training Needs

	Statement	Strongly Agree 1	2	3	4	Strongly Disagree 5	No Comment 6
1	Trainees should complete questionnaires to help identify training needs	12	6	8	3	1	
2	CSTDI establishes training objectives based on required needs	5	13	10	2		
3	CSTDI constantly reviews and updates training needs	7	11	9	2	1	
4	CSTDI focuses on future training needs	9	13	3	2		3
5	Employee and organizational records should be used to gain insight on training needs	2	14	10	2		2
	TOTAL	35	57	40	11	2	5
6	For training need assessment, CSTDI uses						
a)	job/task analysis	18					
b)	personal analysis	3					
c)	organizational analysis	7					
d)	demographic analysis	1					
e)	no comments	1					

As seen in Table 5.5, the majority of the trainers agree with the trainees that it necessary to seek the opinions of public officials about their training needs by asking them to complete questionnaires, although one trainer strongly disagreed and three others disagreed. However, it should be pointed out that this procedure can be cumbersome and impractical because the civil service is huge with large numbers and diverse groups of members.

Most trainers and trainees agreed that better use be made of available employee and organizational records in order to gain insight on training needs. They suggested that departments should consider the background of the trainees and communicate their needs to the Institute accordingly. While CSTDI does consider the records of the trainees in grouping them for different training programs, these records are not consulted for the purpose of assessing needs at present. It is interesting to note that the trainers believe that CSTDI identifies future training needs in advance. Thirty per cent of the trainers strongly agree and 43 per cent agree that training needs are anticipated in advance at the institute. However, during the interviews, they pointed out that it was difficult to identify training priorities for the future. They also felt that changes were happening so rapidly that it was impossible to plan in advance. A trainer summed this up: 'Although we cannot identify the priorities well in advance, due to various constrains, we are responsive to the needs of the government and the departments' (Interview, 23rd October 2000). Some trainers expressed concern over the diversity of the needs of the different departments and said that this factor made added to the difficulty of anticipating future needs. The Chief Training Officer felt that the departments have different needs and changes take place in the individual context but the civil service as a whole has very broad goals, such as transparency, accountability, and better service (Interview, 15th November 2000). While the overarching goals and their general nature is a formidable problem, public service training could benefit from an efficient system of record-keeping that can be drawn upon for ready reference in preparing officials to perform in a changing environment.

Training Techniques and Mechanisms

A variety of methods are used by the CSTDI to conduct training. Generalised training programs consider the basic requirements of the government. The Institute also caters to the specific requirements of government departments by developing customised training packages. These training programs 'support departmental reform initiatives, change management programmes, or meet job-specific requirements' (CSTDI, http://www.info.gov.hk/cstdi/outline.htm).

CSTDI has different training units. One unit deals with general administration, while others are given specific responsibilities: the Training Schemes Section monitors regulations on public service training and external management education programmes. The Information Technology Training Section organizes training on the use of information technology. The English and Communication Unit offers training aimed at the improvement of English language and communication skills. The Chinese Language Section is responsible for providing training in Putonghua, Cantonese and written Chinese. The China Studies Section 'organises training aimed at familiarising civil servants with the political, social and economic systems of China. In addition, three other units offer training for public officials who perform managerial and supervisory functions (Management Training Unit), for general-grade staff (General Grade Training and Development Unit) and for senior civil servants (Senior Management Development Unit)' (Huque et. al, 1998, p. 65).

Table 5.6 Trainees' Views on Techniques and Mechanisms

Statements	Strongly Agree 1	2	3	4	Strongly Disagree 5	No Comment 6
1 CSTDI performs well in anticipating future training needs	7	20	179	65	1	15
2 CSTDI provides strategic guidance on training and development to your department	3	19	121	19	3	122
3 CSTDI modifies training programs based on the results of the training evaluation	2	27	182	4		72
4 Modern training methods are used	212	74	1			
5 CSTDI focuses more on practical issues	186	26		73	2	
TOTAL	410	166	483	161	6	209

CSTDI sends circulars to all government departments informing them about the regular or ad hoc courses at least four to six weeks ahead of the deadline for nomination. Generally, a trainee is required to fill in an enrolment form, obtain approval from the head of the department/grade or supervisor and send the form directly to the Institute for enrolment. For standard courses, the minimum class size is 6 and the charges range between HK$190 to HK$330 per trainee. For custom-made courses, the charge normally varies between HK$2,700 to HK$4,000 for each trainer per day, and an additional charge is paid on a daily basis ranging from HK$500 to HK$1,200 for each trainer's assistant. For on-site courses, the charges range between HK$2,200 to HK$3,000 per trainer per day, and from HK$500 to HK$1,200 for the training assistant per day. The CSTDI operates on a self-financing basis within the government.

Customised courses are designed and conducted for a department in order to cater to its specific needs. A Senior Training Officer stated that various government departments submit requests for customised courses and most of the requests are entertained. However, some proposals are rejected, mainly because of insufficient resources to meet the client departments' requirements within the short time frame (Interview, 15th August 2000).

CSTDI also provides advisory/consultancy services to government departments in a wide range of human resource development areas, in order to support central and departmental policies, programmes and initiatives, and promote best practices in management (http://www.info.gov.hk/cstdi/Ehtml/engindex.htm).

CSTDI uses a variety of training methods. The regular training programs are related to service-wide areas and deal with topics such as financial and human resource management. 'Customized programs are available to meet specific requirements of departments, and are frequently used to support departmental reform initiatives, change management programs or meet job specific requirements' (Huque, et. al, 1998, p. 65).

The Director of CSTDI cited the advent of e-learning and workplace training as examples of efforts to deal with the problem of releasing officials to attend programs in view of their overwhelming workload. But the American Society for Training and Development reported that, even in the United States where E-learning is most advanced, about 70–80 per cent of the training is delivered in classrooms, and this trend will continue. CSTDI has established a Cyber Learning Centre and developed other self-learning devices to take training outside the classrooms, although the programs delivered at the Institute will continue as usual (CSTDI, 2001).

Table 5.7 Trainers' Views on Techniques and Mechanisms

	Statements	Strongly Agree 1	2	3	4	Strongly Disagree 5	No Comment 6
1	CSTDI modifies training programs based on the results of training evaluation	1	11	12	2	2	2
2	Instructional techniques are appropriate to learning objectives	3	12	10	1	1	3
3	Selection of training format and content is appropriate to type of training required	6	14	7	2		1
4	CSTDI emphasizes modern training techniques	16	5	6	3		
5	CSTDI focuses more on practical issues	18	2	7	1	2	
	TOTAL	44	44	42	9	5	6

Evaluation of training programs must be followed up with action to remedy problems and/or strengthen potentially successful activities. Both the trainers and the trainees agreed that CSTDI employs evaluation techniques to improve performance (Tables 5.6 and 5.7). However, 40 per cent of the trainers were neutral to the suggestion that programs are modified on the basis of the results of evaluation. In addition, 36.7 per cent of the trainers believed that training evaluations are seriously considered in modifying training packages. But only 3.3 per cent of the trainers strongly agreed on this claim, while 6.6 per cent disagreed and an equal number strongly disagreed. Training evaluation at the CSTDI is considered a means of anticipating training needs and soliciting the opinions of the clients. The trainees were unsure about the utility of their feedback to the Institute. The main purpose of evaluation appears to be lost due to an absence of follow-up action.

Direction of Public Service Training

The Hong Kong Special Administrative Region (HKSAR) government faced unique challenges in the context of the change of sovereignty in 1997 and subsequent reforms. Public officials were trained prior to 1997, and the training programs were based on values predominant in Western liberal democratic systems, thus their knowledge and appreciation of Chinese society and style of administration were never tested. In view of the reintegration, it was felt necessary to educate the Hong Kong civil service in these areas as well as to develop their language proficiency to complement this task (Huque, et. al, 1998, p. 55).

Technical analysis might once have sufficed in policy development, but public officials are now required to adopt a more strategic approach in which advocacy, persuasion, and negotiation skills are needed to serve a wider array of constituents. The Director of CSTDI put it succinctly, 'Changes continue unabated as we enter the new millennium. Changes bring new opportunities but also uncertainties. Training and development has been widely regarded as the answer to tackling these uncertainties. The belief is that it is only through continuous learning that we can acquire the skills and knowledge to deal with change' (CSTDI, 2000, p. 4).

A related issue is the importance of anticipating the needs of public service training under the changed circumstances prevailing in Hong Kong. A trainer explained that there are efforts to identify future needs. 'It is usually through Chief Training Officers, who represent the institute in a strategic planning group, which meets once in six months. They have some sort of a retreat or meeting with the directors and assistant directors on what the future trends should be, which are identified with the aid of the type of information available. The feedback received and the voices of the clients are taken into consideration. Finally they determine how the institute would move forward in the coming few years. However, there are areas that are beyond our knowledge' (Interview, 23rd October 2000).

A trainee favoured the methods used by the CSTDI to identify future training priorities. She remarked: 'As far as I know, the staff/experts in CSTDI try to identify the future training priorities by:

(a) Asking the students / participants to write job evaluation questionnaires.
(b) Attending local and international conference on training-related subjects.
(c) Familiarising themselves with the training trends by reading magazines, newspaper, liaising with local academic/training institutes'.

A Senior Training Officer noted that CSTDI annually reviews and updates its training programs, but expressed doubts in it doing it successfully in advance in the face of rapid changes (Interview, 15th November, 2000). But an invited trainer for CSTDI identified comparative and China studies to be the main training priorities for Hong Kong in the future. 'All training institutes in this globalising world must prepare for challenges. For these reasons, they should take external changes into consideration when they design courses. Hong Kong Civil Servants, being a part of an international city, need to know what happened in other parts of the world and thus comparative study is important' (Interview, June 2001). Another invited trainer commented that training agencies in Hong Kong take a very narrow approach by focusing on what is happening locally and what the government is doing, and recommended the adoption of a wider perspective to acquire ideas from developments in Asia and the world (Interview, 6th August 2001). Comments from these external trainers expose the narrow scope of programs at the CSTDI.

Table 5.8 Trainees' Views on Anticipation of Future Training Needs

Statements	Strongly Agree 1	2	3	4	Strongly Disagree 5	No Comment 6
1 Programs are oriented toward future needs	4	23	179	67	2	12
2 CSTDI updates programs with changes in society, public demand and government policies	5	157	105	11	2	7
3 The programs help understand issues concerning personal growth and advancement	5	28	30	213	9	2
4 CSTDI identifies future training needs	1	27	221	15	5	18
5 CSTDI aims at upgrading ability to meet with demands of changing times	9	182	78	11		7
TOTAL	24	417	613	317	18	46

A large number of trainees were unsure of the suggestion that CSTDI successfully anticipates future training needs. Table 5.8 shows that there were varying responses on different issues related to the anticipation of future training needs. Some trainees agreed that they learned about many new issues at the Institute, allowing them to upgrade their ability to deal with the challenge of changing times. However, a large number of trainees disagreed that CSTDI aims to enhance officials' capability to face the new circumstances. Similarly, most of the trainees were non-committal with regard to the future direction of programs at CSTDI. Both the trainers and the trainees agreed that the future is difficult to predict, and thus were unable to make emphatic statements on this issue. Nevertheless, 23 per cent of the respondent trainees disagreed with the statement that the Institute's programs are oriented towards future needs and demands. However, it may be fair to conjecture that the process of future needs identification could be helped if the departments informed the CSTDI of their specific needs. The Institute, on its part, tries to meet the common needs of the various departments.

Table 5.9 Trainers' Views on Anticipation of Future Training Needs

	Statements	Strongly Agree 1	2	3	4	Strongly Disagree 5	No Comment 6
1	Programs are oriented toward future needs		9	16	3		2
2	CSTDI updates programs with changes in society, public demand and government policies	4	9	10	3	2	2
3	CSTDI conducts organizational analysis		6	10	2		12
4	CSTDI considers changing functions of the government	1	4	6	3	1	15
5	CSTDI conducts analysis of social and economic change		5	4	4	2	15
6	CSTDI considers technological change	5	6	6	2	1	10
7	CSTDI identifies future training needs	2	5	13	3		7
	TOTAL	12	44	65	20	6	63

A large number of trainers did not take a clear stand on the issue of whether or not CSTDI anticipates future training needs and designs training programs oriented toward the future (Table 5.9). The trainers did not clearly state the factors taken into consideration in anticipating future training needs. Rather, there were a range of responses, suggesting that all of these factors are important. The responses included: changes in society, public demand and government policy, as well as, social, economic and technological changes. Only two trainers strongly agreed (five also agreed) that the CSTDI performs well in anticipating future training needs, while a large number neither agreed nor disagreed. None of the trainers strongly disagreed and only three disagreed on this issue. Generally, the trainers felt that CSTDI tried to keep pace with the developments and changes faced in the public sector. However, this attitude is not shared by the trainees. For example, a trainee suggested that new courses should be developed within short periods of time in order to keep pace with changes in the public service and society (Interview, 13th September, 2000).

A Senior Training officer noted that CSTDI has recently introduced a three-year Training and Development package for public officials. She added that as the Government aims at modernising the civil service and helping government officials face the challenges in both the external and internal environments, a new program of continuous learning which targets all government officials has been introduced. The Programme helps civil servants develop both a self-learning culture and the skills and knowledge needed to meet the latest service requirements (Interview, 17th July, 2000). The main focus of this training package is the development of a continuous learning culture, support for the voluntary retirement scheme, and civil service reform initiatives.

Trends in Training

Governments face constant changes and challenges, which are usually addressed through reforms. In many countries, reform strategies have included streamlining, privatisation, re-engineering, and emphasis on customer service. The most common pattern has been to improve performance and reduce cost, which has led to a greater demand for skilled government workers and an increased level of accountability.

The expansion of social services, the opening up of opportunities for education, the increased exposure to external influence due to large scale emigration and the return of former residents, and economic growth have helped reshape the image and ideals of the civil service in Hong Kong (Huque, et. al, 1998, p. 9). Other noticeable recent developments in Hong Kong include the change of sovereignty, the introduction of a voluntary retirement scheme and public sector reform. The CSTDI has had to respond to these changes and has developed and altered training packages in order to prepare the government officials for dealing with them.

The CSTDI was established with the objective of streamlining training programs and bringing them under the umbrella of one overarching unit. As it has been in operation for a relatively short period of time, it is difficult to discern trends at CSTDI. During its existence, the CSTDI has initiated a number of training programs designed to prepare Hong Kong public officials to face the new environment. CSTDI assists the Civil Service Bureau in formulating and implementing 'training policies and regulations; supporting initiatives launched by the Government; providing advisory services on human resource development to departments; and providing general training to meet job and departmental needs of civil servants' (Huque, et. al, 1998, p. 64).

The Chief Training Officer listed the changes taking place in the CSTDI since its designation as an independent body. The most noticeable development has been a move away from broad and general programs to tailor-made courses for individual departments based on their specific needs. The Institute has also started to provide training outside its premises. Another development worth mentioning has been the introduction of consultancy services to the departments and leadership training for senior public officials (Interview, 15th November 2000).

A trainer pointed out one recent development under which the CSTDI is piloting a plan to train employees of Non-Governmental Organizations (NGOs). Thus, the NGOs would send their employees for training at full cost (Interview, 15th November 2000), thereby generating more revenue for the Institute. This would also allow CSTDI to offer its services to a wider section of the society. However, the initiative is still at the preliminary stages and several issues, including the limited number of trainers and facilities, need to be addressed.

Trainers identified other areas in which they had witnessed changes in the past few years. A trainer recognized a constant pressure to scale down operations because there is a conscious effort to ensure operation on limited resources and maintaining an image that does not give the impression of expansion and high expenditure (Interview, 23rd October, 2000). This is a consequence of the Asian economic crisis of the late 1990s and creates tension in view of the need to develop and implement new training programs while maintaining a strict limit on expenditure.

More examples of change have already been documented. The emphasis on making people multi skilled is worth noticing, because public officials must be capable of performing different tasks. Officials require competence in the use of Chinese language and a large number of courses in this area were introduced prior to the handover in 1997. New training programs were designed for public officials to familiarise them with the state, government and social system in China, and the scope of training programs was expanded to adjust to the wider environment (Huque, et. al, 1998, p. 163). The expansionist approach of the 1990s had to be reigned in as the state of the economy declined.

One trainer found developments in the public service to be quite similar to those in the private sector, and commented that the civil service strives to be at par in terms of efficiency and customer orientation with the private sector organizations. Thus, there are increasing evidence of private sector practices in the in the civil service (Interview, 23rd October, 2000). As the distinction between the public and private sectors become blurred, the management of huge multinational corporations have opened up a new source of inspiration for governments to draw upon.

Table 5.10 shows that most of the trainees noticed positive developments in the training trends of CSTDI. The Institute monitors changing trends within the government and modifies training packages accordingly. Unlike other older and established central training institutes, CSTDI is still evolving. So far, it has helped to streamline training programmes for the Hong Kong public service by making it possible to coordinate various programmes under the umbrella of a single agency.

The CSTDI strives to maintain a forward-looking approach to training, and has developed training packages aimed at continuous improvement of the tasks performed by civil services and preparation for new challenges as Hong Kong enters a new phase (Huque, et. al, 1998, p. 65). However, it is interesting to note that 10 trainees disagreed and 33 strongly disagreed that they had witnessed positive training trends (i.e. training coordinated with needs) at the CSTDI. An interviewee complained that he had not had a chance to receive training at the Institute during the last four years, highlighting the inadequacy, in places, of the training programs.

Table 5.10 Trainees' Views on Trends of Training

Statements	Strongly Agree 1	2	3	4	Strongly Disagree 5	No Comment 6
1 Public service training has responded to government policies and objectives	6	37	227	4	4	9
2 There have been positive developments in the training trends of CSTDI	70	122	30	10	33	22
3 CSTDI follows traditional syllabi and training methods	2	22	22	222	7	12
TOTAL	78	181	279	236	44	43

A large majority of the trainees disagreed that CSTDI follows traditional syllabi and training methods. Some of respondents complained that the duration of training was too short, and failed to generate interest among the trainees because the sessions ended before the participants could warm up to new ideas. It is also interesting to note that a large majority of trainees remained neutral to the suggestion that the content of public service training has responded proactively to government policies and objectives in the past five years. Only six respondents strongly agreed and 37 agreed to this suggestion, while four each disagreed and strongly disagreed to this suggestion. It seems from this response that the CSTDI is not in a position to coordinate the content and direction of training with the objectives of the government.

Table 5.11 Trainers' Views on Trends of Training

Statements	Strongly Agree 1	2	3	4	Strongly Disagree 5	No Comment 6
1 Public service training has responded to government policies and objectives	2	14	6	7	1	
2 There have been positive developments in the training trends of CSTDI	2	22	2	1	1	2
3 CSTDI follows traditional syllabi and training methods	2	7	5	12	4	
TOTAL	6	43	13	20	6	2

Most of the trainers agreed that there have been changes in the training trends of the CSTDI in the past five years (Table 5.11). A large number of trainers believed that the Institute has a tendency to follow the traditional syllabi and training methods. In practice, CSTDI still adheres to traditional classroom training, but this is increasingly being complemented by self-learning tools and also Internet based training. There are signs of changes in the training methods.

Priorities in Training

CSTDI encounters limitations and constraints on the amount and variety of training it can provide to the public servants of Hong Kong. Owing to limited resources, the Institute attempts to concentrate on areas that could provide multitudinous outcomes. In establishing training priorities, it is necessary to assess the outcome of existing programs against required needs. This calls for careful consideration of the requirements of the clients, changes in local and international environment, clients' expectations, and a systematic preparation of training courses and materials that meet the most significant needs. The final step involves an evaluation of outputs against realistic objectives.

The challenges facing CSTDI involve developing the ability to provide the new skills and strategies required throughout the public services, helping departments identify needs specific to themselves, designing training programs to fulfil new training needs, expanding the mode of delivery beyond classroom training, and facilitating the development of a learning culture in government departments (CSTDI, 2000, p. 6). The items on this long list apparently remain unattended to, as the Institute's efforts are restricted due to the complexities related tom jurisdiction and the rapid pace of changes in the public sector.

Most of the trainers named areas like information technology, public sector reform, managerial responsibility, performance management, comparative studies, productivity, and coping with rapid changes and new challenges as issues at the top of the Institute's agenda. In addition to these areas of interest, there is considerable demand for products/services based on self-directed learning. CSTDI is expected to take advantage of development in IT to further enhance its services/products, such as electronic access to self-learning packages and resources, and tutorials/training conducted through the Internet (i.e. web-based training). Another acknowledged the development of information technology related programs as a major priority, and commented that it could have an impact on service delivery, as well as policy development and management in the public sector (Interview, 6th August, 2001). A full-time trainer remarked: 'Teaching people how to learn and retain the knowledge provided is our main priority. There are a lot of changes and challenges faced by the employees' as the world is moving very fast. What we have to do is really enhance the capability to learn better and faster' (Interview, 23rd October, 2000).

In addition to the task of developing skills required to perform on the job, there are some non-traditional tasks confronting the CSTDI. The institute gives priority to developing training packages relating to recent changes in Hong Kong, and must organize training programs to help officials deal with various aspects of the reform initiatives in the civil service (Interview with a full-time trainer, 5th September, 2000). An external trainer felt that issues related to public sector reforms will continue to remain a major concern of CSTDI (Interview, 6 August, 2000). The wide scope and range of reforms are affecting an increasing number of public officials, and training programs must adjust to accommodate their needs.

The CSTDI launched a three-year Training and Development Program in 2001-02 at a cost of HK$ 50 million dollars. The program targeted three major areas, including training to facilitate staff of the 59 voluntary retirement designated grades in redeployment and job transition. The plan allowed public officials of certain grades and years of service to receive attractive compensation packages if they volunteered to retire before their scheduled dates of retirement. The other objectives were to provide training to public officials who have chosen to remain in the civil service and may need to be redeployed either within or across departments. CSTDI aims to provide them with the necessary skills to take on new challenges and advance their careers by organizing programs for training and vocational skills, stress management and handling job transition. Promoting a life-long learning culture in the civil service is also on the agenda of the three-year training program. The focus is on encouraging public officials to develop a self-learning culture and upgrade themselves. A number of seminars, sponsorship to attend courses intended to broaden their perspective and knowledge, enrichment of the content of the Cyber Learning Centre of the CSTDI, and promotion of on-line learning were expected to help in this respect (http://www.info.gov.hk/cstdi/).

The priority of CSTDI, as identified by the trainers, is to help public officials cope with changes. They declared that it is essential for public officials to be sensitive to the needs of the departments, who are facing major changes in the nature of business, public mindset and culture as the Hong Kong public service transforms itself from that of a British colony to that of an autonomous region of the People's Republic of China.

CSTDI faces an uphill task as a result of the changes it has encountered and continues to encounter. A trainer pointed out that the Institute tries to provide as many services as possible with the limited resources at its disposal. Efforts are made to use less costly modes to deliver training programs (Interview, 23rd October, 2000). The inadequacy of the training programs is another problem faced by CSTDI. Most of the training packages are over-subscribed and trainees complain that they are unable to secure place in programs that could be useful to them. Releasing public officials from their departments in order that they can attend training programs is another sensitive area. But this situation has improved as CSTDI has shortened the length of quite a number of programs or has split them into separate modules.

The trainers accepted professionalism and expertise as basic requirements for all training staff in the training institute. Knowledge management is one of the greatest challenges faced by CSTDI trainers. A trainer commented that the Institute has to stay ahead of the departments and remain updated to offer service of value to the clients (Interview, 23rd October, 2000). There is a need to have a sound understanding of the business and operations of departments in order to provide better service.

A trainer noted that requirements and needs as assessed by departments were sometimes inappropriate and did not always match their actual demands. She added that when a department says that they are not doing well in a particular area, there is always a possibility that the knowledge gap does not exist in the specified area but in another. In other words, departments do not always do a good job of recognizing their needs. She suggested that the departments should make a request to CSTDI for consultancy services in order to help identify their needs accurately.

A senior trainer complained that the CSB sometimes pushes the CSTDI towards activities preferred by the bureau. Theses drives happen when central initiatives are taken, and the CSB seeks to promote them through the Institute, which has to develop plans for implementing them. Since the CSTDI is not involved at the policy formulation stage, its training plans can be disrupted by such imposition of priorities by the CSB (Interview, 23rd October 2000). But most trainers agree that the CSTDI has to take into consideration the demands of the CSB and, at times, are required to shift their priorities on the basis of ad hoc requests from the bureau.

Rapid increase in workload was another area of concern. The trainers felt overworked, as they had to deal with numerous requests. They felt dissatisfied due to the lack of time for preparation, which, in turn, affects the quality of the programs. This becomes a difficult challenge, as it demands for immediate demonstration of results and cost effectiveness.

The trainees and their respective departments also pointed out problems and emphasized the need for developing effective alternatives to classroom training. A trainer reported that public service employees feel great stress from training but do not get tangible rewards. Promotion prospects are slim and thus officials lose the incentive to work, leading to a lack of commitment to their jobs.

Other Relevant Observations

A number of other findings deserve mention. A majority of the trainees agreed (3.8 per cent of the trainees strongly agreed) that CSTDI has dedicated and professional trainers (Table 5.12). However, 33.8 per cent of the respondents refrained from taking a position on this issue and a small group did not rate the trainers highly. It appears that a significant number of trainees were not satisfied with the performance of the trainers. Not surprisingly, none of the trainers strongly disagreed with the suggestion that CSTDI employs competent trainers. The

Institute closely monitors the performance of the trainers and looks for opportunities to train the trainers. The invited trainers are also chosen carefully so the best use can be made of their expertise. The monitoring system of the Institute helps ensure that the trainers measure up to the benchmark. A trainer confidently commented: 'Since the institute takes good care while formulating the training packages and also while allotting them to the most suited trainer, the question of incompetency and lack of ability of the deliverers can never be felt' (Interview, 23rd October, 2000).

Table 5.12 Trainees' Views on Training at CSTDI

Statements	Strongly Agree 1	2	3	4	Strongly Disagree 5	No Comment 6
1 CSTDI is staffed by dedicated and professional trainers	11	157	97	6		16
2 Training programs prepare public officials for the changing environment	25	96	84	56	24	2
3 CSTDI assesses the adequacy of training on a regular basis	15	47	182	23		20
TOTAL	51	300	363	85	24	38

The trainees' perception of the performance of the Institute is presented in Table 5.12. A large number of trainees felt that the training programs at CSTDI are aimed at preparing public service officials for the changing times. However, some trainees felt that they were unable to receive training at suitable intervals. A trainee complained that he could apply for training only after being posted to a new job. The process takes up to one month or more, and there seems to be no coordination (Interview, 8th September 2000). There was a long waiting period to get access to the training and it leads to a knowledge gap at work.

Fifty-six trainees disagreed, while 24 strongly disagreed, on the issue of the capability of the Institute to enable trainees to cope with changes. CSTDI is not in a position to cater to all needs, owing to its size and the existing diversification in the training provided. However, training is a continuous process and the institute has to meet with the challenges of providing learning opportunities. In this regard, CSTDI provides a large number of self-learning packages to help trainees adapt to changes. On the other hand, some of the trainees disliked the concept of self-learning, as there is not much opportunity to receive answers to questions that may arise in the process of learning. One trainee criticised the fact that the institute takes a long time to register the applicants and provide them with their passwords for using the self-learning packages (Informal Interview, 10th February, 2001). Problems with minor administrative procedures followed by the Institute can affect the perception of the trainees about its programs.

The trainees appeared unsure in commenting on whether or not CSTDI assesses the adequacy of its training programs on a regular basis. It seems that the trainees do not have access to such information. The CSTDI claims to maintain regular contact with its clients and provide custom-made training packages to cater to the needs and demands rather than generalized courses. Apparently, the Institute has arrangements in place for soliciting the views of their customers, but these are not utilised in the best possible way.

A large number of trainees believed that relevant training would lead to career advancement. Training was regarded an important means by which to upgrade skills, making employees more inclined towards accepting changes. They were keen in suggesting that the departments should accord more importance to training and release employees regularly to attend programs at the Institute. They also expressed their preference for CSTDI to provide more customized courses. Trainees attend programs for job enrichment and expected to benefit from appropriate on-the-job training.

Table 5.13 Trainers' Views on Training at CSTDI

	Statements	Strongly Agree 1	2	3	4	Strongly Disagree 5	No Comment 6
1	CSTDI is staffed by dedicated and professional trainers	10	13	4	2		1
2	CSTDI provides strategic guidance to government departments	4	7	11	3	4	1
3	CSTDI helps with job enrichment	1	13	11	2		3
4	CSTDI aims to develop human ability to adapt to changing times	7	18	4	1		
	TOTAL	22	51	30	8	4	5

Only two trainers disagreed that the CSTDI staff are dedicated and professional trainers, while most of them felt the opposite. Like the trainees, a large number of trainers were neutral to the suggestion that the CSTDI provides strategic guidance on training and development to various departments of the government.

As seen in Table 5.13, a large majority of the trainers agreed that CSTDI aims at upgrading human ability to meet and cope with changes. The trainers claim to monitor changes in the environment of the public sector, and they respond by providing trainees with updated information and skills necessary to perform. Rapid changes in the environment have brought new challenges, along with skill and knowledge requirements. Ironically, these changes impose additional burdens on the public service employees and their time that often affect their ability to attend training programs at CSTDI.

Concluding Remarks

CSTDI offers mostly general training programs, with an eye on the basic requirements of the government. The institute provides various central training programs, tailor-made training programs and consultancy services for various departments. The trainers place priority on improving the effectiveness of public officials as members of the government, while the trainees emphasize better performance on the job. CSTDI identifies service-wide training needs and the departments facilitate the process with information on their own specific training needs. CSTDI uses three levels of evaluation, and they are useful in identifying training needs.

The trainers as well as the administrators realise the difficulty in assessing the future training needs. Some of the government departments do not give training due importance and often easily release staff for training. The hindrance to training lies in the fact that training is assigned only a remedial function and is seldom used as an instrument to achieve more lofty aims and goals, such as upgrading and development of civil servants on a regular basis.

Chapter 6

The Challenge of Training in a Globalized World

After reviewing the programs, roles, responsibilities and performance of the central training institutes in India and Hong Kong, this chapter explores the challenges faced in anticipating and assessing needs, designing training programs and implementing them to cater to the needs of diverse demands from the public service in a globalized world. The discussion draws upon prescriptive models and conceptual ideas, and seeks to explain the causes for the success or otherwise of the LBSNAA and CSTDI. The ultimate objective of this chapter is to suggest ways and means of improving public service training to better cope with the challenges created by globalization.

Needs assessment exercises ensure that training output is and priorities are properly addressed. Needs assessment also allows consideration of past and present trends along with the anticipation of emerging trends. The employment of appropriate training techniques enables the effective planning and delivery of training, and influences the process of identifying and assessing training needs. Central training agencies not only organize and deliver training programs, but also have to perform other activities that are directly linked with the development of human resources in a country. Therefore, effective training programs, trends, priorities, need identification processes, techniques, mechanisms, and the direction of future civil service training programs are intertwined and interdependent.

Training at LBSNAA and CSTDI

Two different systems were studied in chapters four and five to illustrate the complexities, elements and concepts of central training agencies in diverse settings. India is a huge country, and has existed independently for over half a century, while Hong Kong is a small autonomous unit of the People's Republic of China. There are noticeable differences between the two in terms of size, level of economic development, political system and social composition. LBSNAA has a large inflow of trainees from the different states and services of the government of India. CSTDI caters to an extremely small number of clients, mainly from the different departments of the government of Hong Kong. Nevertheless, some common elements can be identified in order to understand the challenges faced by central training agencies in developing human resources in a globalized world.

Common Tasks and Challenges

It is common to find central training agencies employing a mix of both centralized and decentralized approaches to training. Under this dual approach, the central training institute offers general courses that cater to the majority of personnel in the public service, while departmental training units address job specific needs. Beyond this, the CSTDI in Hong Kong also addresses individual departmental needs by designing customized training courses based on requests from the departments. It also deputes training officers to departments that require or and request certain kinds of expertise.[1]

The rapid changes resulting from globalization as well as local and international development make the task of identifying needs and responding to changes more complex. But India and Hong Kong seem anxious to strengthen public service training in areas related to technology which they both see as the best approach for developing training programs oriented to the future. Our survey of trainers and trainees at these institutes revealed a number of interesting points. While respondents saw technology and modern training techniques as the most appropriate tools to face the new challenges, there appeared to be declining interest in other areas such as knowledge building, skills development, and the ethical aspects of public service.[2] Trainees were apparently satisfied with the Institutes' emphases on technology, regardless of its applicability in their workplace. Both LBSNAA and CSTDI may be pursuing a misleading path in concentrating on information technology and emulating the programs of other training agencies abroad. It is most important for both India and Hong Kong to cater to the needs of the public service in order to enable public sector officials cope with new challenges. The needs are not concentrated exclusively in the area of information technology and are relevant to other areas including the culture and approach to work.

Adequate financing is an important element for the effective training of public officials, and many training institutes suffer from lack of finances that can hinder progressive development. LBSNAA and CSTDI appear to be the exception rather than the rule in terms of financial support because, unlike training institutes in many other countries, both receive adequate allocations from their governments. In fact, LBSNAA has to surrender unutilised funds at the end of each financial year.[3] CSTDI's financial position allows it to invite experts from different areas to share their expertise with the trainees.[4] The Institute is equipped with state-of-the art technology and facilities. However, adequate finance and access to technological gadgets do not ensure the efficient and satisfactory performance of training agencies.

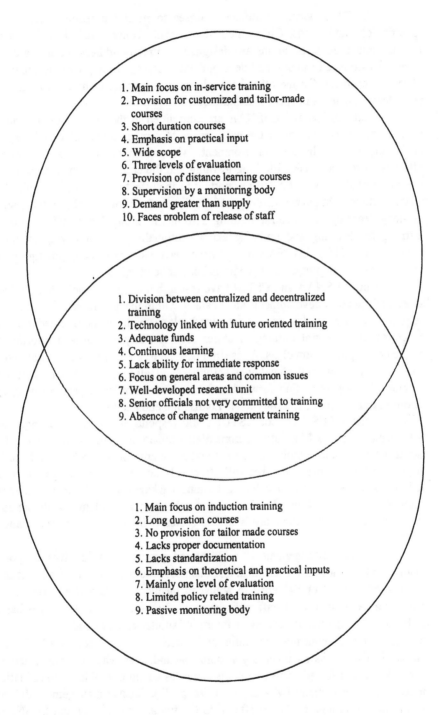

1. Main focus on in-service training
2. Provision for customized and tailor-made courses
3. Short duration courses
4. Emphasis on practical input
5. Wide scope
6. Three levels of evaluation
7. Provision of distance learning courses
8. Supervision by a monitoring body
9. Demand greater than supply
10. Faces problem of release of staff

1. Division between centralized and decentralized training
2. Technology linked with future oriented training
3. Adequate funds
4. Continuous learning
5. Lack ability for immediate response
6. Focus on general areas and common issues
7. Well-developed research unit
8. Senior officials not very committed to training
9. Absence of change management training

1. Main focus on induction training
2. Long duration courses
3. No provision for tailor made courses
4. Lacks proper documentation
5. Lacks standardization
6. Emphasis on theoretical and practical inputs
7. Mainly one level of evaluation
8. Limited policy related training
9. Passive monitoring body

Figure 6.1 Public Service Training in India and Hong Kong

CSTDI provides customized courses to meet the requirements of the specific jobs and needs. Government departments convey their requests to the Institute and training programs are designed to directly address the needs of the clients. Customized training and development courses help improve the capability of the government. On the other hand, the central training institute in India does not cater to the needs of specific departments.

Both CSTDI and LBSNAA are committed to the concept of continuous learning and development as the only means to remain competitive and respond effectively to the changing environment. Along with the need to train public officials on relevant tasks, life-long learning and the continuous enhancement of a repertoire of skills is particularly important to the effective performance of public service officials (http://www.info.gov.hk/cstdi/). In an effort to achieve the goal of life-long learning, the central training institute in Hong Kong offers distance learning for learning and updating skills continually, without having to attend programs at CSTDI. LBSNAA does not yet have such provision, although plans are afoot for developing similar programs for public officials.[5]

Both LBSNAA and CSTDI have research units, which help them to keep abreast of the latest developments and changes within the government.[6] These units help to organise workshops and seminars along with theme-oriented training programs. Both central training institutes seek to analyse ideas and information before developing action plans. A research base helps an institute understand issues related to training and educational activities and also enables the trainers and program developers to find forward-looking ideas. In order to perform well, the institutes must exercise rigorous conceptualisation and analysis.

Neither LBSNAA nor CSTDI could respond efficiently to change, and both displayed a lack of ability for immediate adaptation.[7] This could be due to the fact that the agencies require more time and more appropriate techniques in order to prepare training programs that will effectively address the challenges. Hurried actions for amending and developing training packages are not suitable in these circumstances. Ironically, the clients exacerbate this problem by demanding immediate response to their needs as the scenario in the public sector changes rapidly.

'Change management is a structured process that involves proposed changes to be reviewed for technical and business readiness in a consistent manner that can be relaxed or tightened to adjust to business needs and experiences. It involves a database to help staff make better decisions about future changes based on historical data such as success or failure of similar changes and is a structured process that communicates the status and existence of changes to all affected parties. It also yields an inventory system that indicates what and when actions were taken that affected status of key resources, as an aid in problem determination or resource management' (McCalman, 1992, p. 23). Change management did not feature in the training packages offered to the trainees by CSTDI and LBSNAA. This reflected a lack of interest in this important area of public sector management. Strengthening the skills of public officials, the management of change could lead to a reduction of the demand for the instant design of new courses. These kinds of courses are not of the highest standard, given the lack of time allowed for planning and designing them. The training institutes could provide better courses with more time at their disposal.

Senior officials attending training at both the institutes did not seem to be committed to training.[8] As the operations and emphases of governments can change at short notice, it is important that public officials at various levels within the hierarchy are aware of and remain prepared to cope with such situations. If officials at the middle level receive training and those at higher levels are not similarly prepared to manage change, the issue of compatibility becomes a serious problem. Senior public officials need to convey and secure commitment in support of changes and developments taking place within their respective departments.

Other Issues of Concern

LBSNAA mainly focuses on induction training for new recruits, coming from all the departments of the government of India. The content of this training includes history, public administration, law, management, language, and information technology. The Academy aims to arm new recruits with the knowledge of the operation of public administration in the country before they actually start work in the public service. At this stage, training tends to be more theoretical than practical. Although there are elements of real life experience, role-playing and case studies, the emphasis is toward theoretical issues in training. Later in the induction period, there is scope for on-the-job training as well as visits to different departments. This experience allows a view of the actual working procedures of government departments. Such courses are extremely long in duration, and can stretch over almost two years. Although the trainees are provided accommodation at the LBSNAA, they intensely dislike spending such a long period of time there.

On the other hand, CSTDI concentrates on in-service training for public officials from different levels in the government of Hong Kong. The training courses offered at the Institute are mainly related to management, language studies and information technology. The trainees comprise mostly of middle or senior level officials in the public service. The duration of most of the courses is short, which has attracted criticism on the grounds of inadequacy. CSTDI appears to be more inclined toward practical issues in training, although there is a fair amount of theoretical input as well.

Training at LBSNAA suffers from lack of a sound system of standardization and documentation. Consistency, evenness and regularity are important in maintaining training standards. The training programs at LBSNAA are very flexible, which allows deviation from a planned approach. Appropriate documentation, supported by a suitable mechanism for quick retrieval, can prove beneficial for updating and storing information at frequent intervals. Development of institutional memory can be improved through proper documentation.

It has been said that the CSTDI is incapable of providing training to the entire civil service.[9] Trainees find it difficult to get nominated for training, as the numbers of nominees for all training packages are limited. Thus, over subscription is a big issue, and there is an imbalance in the demand-supply equilibrium at CSTDI.

Another issue facing both CSTDI and LBSNAA is related to the training on policy-related skills. Public officials are agents for implementing policies and must have a thorough understanding of the processes and implications of the adoption of specific policies. Regardless of high quality training, the work of the government will suffer if the substance of a particular policy is weak or inappropriate. Thus, both management and policy elements need to be incorporated in training programs. A general view is that the training institutes concentrate on the management skills, while little is offered by way of strengthening the policy capacity of the public service officials.

The Civil Service Bureau (CSB) monitors the work of the CSTDI and supervises its operation and management. Thus, a high degree of accountability contributes to the efficiency of this public organization. The Ministry of Personnel of the Government of India is responsible for managing the operation of LBSNAA but, in practice, the monitoring body is passive.[10] We could not find any evidence of the Ministry of Personnel's supervision over the LBSNAA. The Director of LBSNAA is responsible for all the business of the Institute. An annual report on the work of LBSNAA is submitted to the Ministry of Personnel; however, these reports have been accepted without any question being raised about the operation of LBSNAA.

Identification of Training Needs

The first step in identifying training needs is to recognize problems and determine if training will provide a solution. Effective training is generally a response to a real need or a specific problem, and not to passing fashion. LBSNAA and CSTDI have different ways of assessing needs, but no specific and pre-determined processes. This study has identified the different sources influencing and affecting the identification of training needs at LBSNAA and CSTDI (see chapters 4 and 5). It was noticed that all the potential sources are not tapped in order to identify training needs.

In India, the Ministry of Personnel is passive towards the workings of LBSNAA and seldom contributes to the process of need assessment.[11] The main source in assessing the training needs in India is the team of experts who frequently meet to discuss changes within the government and various departments. Furthermore, few public service employees respond to questionnaires sent out by LBSNAA to help in assessing training needs. LBSNAA faces another issue in the fact that it seldom receives assistance from its client departments. The problem can be attributed to the fact that LBSNAA is a central training institution serving a huge country, which renders coordination and regular contact with the departments extremely difficult. Thus, the trainers seek to identify needs through interactions with the resident trainees. The process involves asking questions about the trainees' expectation from the programs, the degree to which training meets their needs, and the requirements of their job tasks and activities. The trainers then compare these data to the training program goals, objectives, and requirements. The long duration of courses gives adequate time to the trainers to develop new programs or modify the existing ones based these findings.

In Hong Kong, the needs assessment process is comparatively easier, partly due to the small size of the region. CSTDI receives support from government departments in assessing training needs. The Institute closely monitors the changes and developments within the civil service and formulates training programs based on the perceived needs. An annual customer survey helps the Institute assess the needs of the different departments and collect suggestions for improving performance. Contact is maintained with the departments through regular meetings. But even the apparently simple structure and tasks in the training institutes do not lead to an effective system of needs assessment due to rapid changes and uncertainty in the environment.

Influencing the Needs Assessment Process

Needs assessment is systematic exploration of the way things are and the way they should be. The first step in conducting needs analysis is to check the actual performance of the trainees against existing standards. The current state of skills, knowledge, and the abilities of current and/or future employees considered. This analysis should aim at examining organizational goals and climate and internal and external constraints. Further, the training institute must recognize the desired or necessary conditions for organizational success. The process focuses on the required job tasks/standards, as well as the skills, knowledge, and abilities needed to accomplish these successfully. The training institute must be in a position to distinguish actual needs from perceived needs. The 'gap' (the difference) between the current and the required levels will identify needs, purposes, and objectives of training. However, the data collected from India indicates that only 20 per cent of the respondent trainees strongly agree while 35 per cent strongly disagree that training at LBSNAA establishes training objectives based on required needs. In Hong Kong, 43.5 per cent of the trainees strongly agreed that the training objectives directly address needs.

Needs assessment must consider the level of training required for employees at different levels, the best learning sequence for conducting the training, and the most effective methods and techniques of presenting the training (Shafritz, 2001, p. 322). Training should provide civil servants with the necessary knowledge and skills as well as proper attitudes, important for the efficient and effective performance of their functions and responsibilities. Training packages must be relevant and realistic, and based on proper diagnosis and analysis of the kind and amount of training required by the client. Systematic and continuous assessment of training requirements is also important for its success.

A number of sources influence the outcome of the needs assessment process, and these should be carefully considered in determining the requirements of the various government departments (see Figure 6.2). Information is gleaned from: job analysis, discussion meetings, questionnaires, reviews of performance appraisal data, interviews of employees, supervisors and experts, departmental training divisions, feedback on different levels of evaluation, forecasts and predictions by trainers, international contacts, conferences, trends in demographic changes in the workforce, local academic and training institutes, changes in government, contact with departments and experience of other countries.

Job analysis involves a detailed analysis of functions, activities and tasks performed by the different levels of government officials receiving training (Shafritz, 2001, p. 332). This requires extensive surveys, which allow the job to be analyzed on a continual basis. Cooperation from client departments is very important for this purpose. The CSTDI has adopted job analysis as one of its strategies in assessing the training needs of public services. The Institute carries out a detailed search of the component tasks and responsibilities so that training may be directed to specific ends. The annual customer is helpful in assessing needs, collecting suggestions from the client departments for improving performance.[12]

Questionnaires seek information related to an estimation of the skill levels of public officials, in order to match training needs and interests. A review of performance appraisal reports helps to identify areas of 'skill gap' and thus can form a basis for the formulation of training packages to bridge such gaps. LBSNAA sends out questionnaires to focus groups but seldom receives an adequate number of responses. There is a need to carefully identify and monitor the focus groups in order to improve the process. Focus groups can be a valuable source of information, as they are made up of groups of public officials, supervisors or experts within a specific department or job category, and thus they can be used to secure information on training needs. Extensive interviews with such groups can help identify problems that might be overlooked by trainers.

Information obtained from departmental training divisions directly indicates the needs of each department, and collective information from all agencies can assist in identifying the needs of the public service in general. This approach can prepare the way for training programs designed to meet the common needs of various departments which require similar training or the more general training that addresses the needs of the entire government. CSTDI maintains close ties with the various departmental training divisions. Besides, trainers from the Institute have been deputed as training officers in the Department of Housing and Department of Health (http://www.info.gov.hk/cstdi/Ehtml/engindex.htm). LBSNAA, too, maintains contact with various state and departmental training institutes and trainers are often rotated between them.

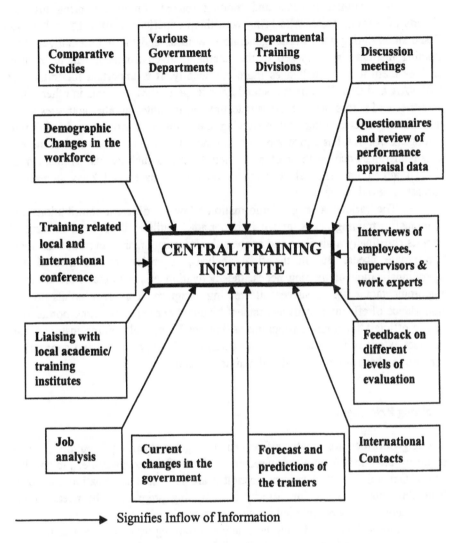

——————▶ Signifies Inflow of Information

Figure 6.2 Sources Influencing Assessment of Training Needs

Evaluation helps in measuring the adequacy of training, and feedback at different levels of evaluation helps training institutes to measure their performance based on the customers' perspective. The process is helpful in assessing the actual needs of clients, adjusting existing training packages, or designing new programs to meet the needs of clients. Evaluation and feedback on training programs provide information on the clients' level of satisfaction with existing programs, but do not suggest ways for dealing with future needs. The CSTDI tries to address this issue by consulting the public sector and agencies.

International contacts and training related conferences bring together experts on various areas, who bring with them experiences from the real world. Discussions during such events generate new ideas and the representatives from training institutes are exposed to the international environment which, in turn, enables them to face challenges more confidently. It is important for trainers at LBSNAA and CSTDI to have a sound knowledge of developments in other Asian countries and across the globe. Visits to training institutes in other countries assist trainers in understanding and observing the training environment in different settings. LBSNAA has a provision for sending trainers to conferences, but there is a general reluctance on the part of trainers to attend such events. Trainers from CSTDI attend international conferences on regular bases and keep themselves abreast of new developments.

The various sources of information allow for different contributions and opinions on training needs, and it is important to utilise all of them. A team of experts can finally assimilate and analyse the information and determine the most appropriate needs. But in the final analysis, regardless of the method and operationalization of training needs, the motivation of the trainee remains most important factor for a successful training program. This fact points to the importance of effective needs assessment by client departments before nominating public officials for training programs. Additionally, central training institutes can conduct extensive needs assessment to determine the types of training appropriate for meeting both organizational and individual needs.

Training Priorities

Training priorities are greatly influenced by a government's perception of areas requiring attention. Administrative agencies have their recognizable, job-specific needs. Generally, central training institutes are fed these information and ideas from this source receive top priority in designing programs. The needs of the government are always accorded prime importance.

International trends and the practice of training institutes overseas serve as models in determining training priorities. The institutes identify training priorities on the basis of the expertise of their trainers. They claim to exercise utmost care in deciding training priorities. Importance is attached to the requirements of the clients, which are determined through the identification of training needs and the evaluation of existing training packages against the criteria of rational objectives.

Generally, training priorities are established with an eye on the requirements of a country, based on an analysis of the demands of the government, the needs of public sector organizations, and international trends. The practice of establishing priorities is strongly influenced by the capability of training institutes to anticipate needs and deploy adequate resources for meeting them.

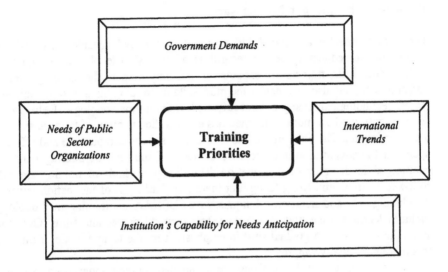

Figure 6.3 Factors Shaping Training Priorities

LBSNAA is currently developing three new areas—negotiation and coordination, scientific management, and personal productivity—to be incorporated in their training programs. The Academy also emphasizes conceptual skills and knowledge on policy related issues, which have been largely ignored in the past. The CSTDI gives priority to skills that will overcome the challenges faced by the training institute. Being able to tackle new training needs required service-wide cooperation and entailed the tasks of helping departments identify needs specific to their jurisdiction, designing new training programs to meet new needs, expanding the mode of delivery beyond classroom training, and facilitating the development of a learning culture in the departments (CSTDI, 2000, p. 6).

Training priorities are determined on the basis of needs and demands and, therefore, must be addressed effectively. Training institutes often advertise their most popular programs, and are ultimately unable to provide the expected level of quality and substance. LBSNAA has a group of experts who attempt to identify and fill needs, yet the Academy has been described as 'outdated' and 'traditional' by the trainees. Thus not many government employees opt to go there for on-job-training.[13] CSTDI is endowed with modern facilities operated by capable trainers. Still, some of the trainees complain that they can seldom apply the skills and knowledge obtained from training to their jobs. In Hong Kong, only one per cent strongly agreed, while 65.5 per cent of the respondent trainees neither agreed nor disagreed, that the outcome of training was applicable to their jobs. In India, 41.3 per cent of the trainees strongly disagreed that adequate training is provided in order to meet demands at work. Thus, the training institutes need to develop ways and means to establish better linkages between changes within the government and the skills needed to deliver the necessary changes.

Training Techniques and Mechanisms

The word 'trainer' is associated with an intelligent, knowledgeable person who is responsible for educating people regardless of their skill levels. Being equipped with certain skills, trainers are expected to not only prepare the teaching content and approach, but also to consider the most suitable training manifesto for trainees. Rapid technological changes have affected training methodology. Delivery of training with modern multimedia methods attracts the attention of trainees and has a greater impact. The only problem is that, at times, considerable time and effort is spent on the preparation and the core element of the area of training may get submerged in the glitz of presentation. Traditional methods of training are still followed in India and Hong Kong, but there are clear signs of inclination towards developing new and modern techniques.[14] At LBSNAA the training methodology includes lectures, case-studies, tutorials, management games and films. Over the years there has been a gradual shift in emphasis from the lecture mode of training to a more participative approach.

The trainees in Hong Kong are nominated by their supervisors to attend programs at CSTDI. There are some interesting points to note in this process. Officials with a heavy workload were seldom nominated to attend training even if it could be beneficial to them and the organization. Sometimes, the nominations were influenced by personal considerations, and officials considered them to be biased.[15]

The induction course at LBSNAA is mandatory for public officials in India, although many would prefer to attend specialized training at other training institutes in the country. The objective is to familiarize the new entrants to the public service with the structure and operations of the government, and explain the complex interrelationships between the various units.

The concept of compulsory training hours for officials does not exist both in either India or Hong Kong, this affects the development and up-gradation of public officials.[16] There is no stipulation regarding the minimum number hours of training that public officials must receive before they could be entrusted with certain responsibilities or promoted through the ranks.

The syllabi of training programs in India are revised every ten years and quickly become outdated.[17] This factor often causes potential trainees to withdraw. Regular revision of syllabi and inclusion of relevant content is extremely important. If these are undertaken at too long intervals, there is a risk of the content being outdated as well of losing the advantage of crucial new initiatives.

Centralized and Decentralized Training Institutes

Centralized training for public service makes sense in terms of the common areas related to the entire service. For example, public sector reform is an area that needs to be understood and implemented throughout the service. In addition, centralized training exposes trainees to new ideas and experiences and facilitates cross-organizational exchanges. However, this is not an effective approach for training courses that have a narrow area of coverage.[18] Central training institutes are responsible for training the entire public service, but it is inappropriate and impractical to provide every kind of training from one central source. First of all, most of the areas in which the employees need training are directly related to their jobs. Such training can be best accomplished through supervisory efforts at the worksite or in training courses organized by the department, under the direction of those who are acquainted with the immediate requirements of the job. Second, some areas in which employees need training are of a technical nature, such as engineering, forestry, health care, etc. These skills are relevant to the functions of particular agencies/departments, and can be imparted more efficiently by experts at the field level. Third, the areas in which there is demand for training are often specific to the departments' need. Therefore, those departments are best qualified to organize such training. Finally, both India and Hong Kong have a diverse group of employees in the public sector, a factor that must also be taken into consideration.

It may be argued that central training institutes are not really significant as all departments have their own training departments.[19] Only a few initiatives may be centrally undertaken, usually on general issues such as language, management, and information technology. However, centralized training has its benefits in bringing together people from different organizations and having them interact with one another. This approach can also have a positive impact on areas such as strategic and disaster planning and management. On the other hand, departments are better equipped to manage the areas for which they have a better appreciation of the requirements and can adjust the curriculum in terms of the changing scenario of the department. Centralized training agencies cannot always respond quickly and adequately to demands from departments due to the complexity of the system. Thus, both in India and Hong Kong, decentralized training is suitable for specific areas while centralized training is necessary for more strategic or cross-sectoral undertakings.

Effectiveness of Training Programs

The effectiveness of training is difficult to measure, but it is essential to identify and measure the relevance and importance of training. Both LBSNAA and CSTDI regard evaluation as a means to measure the effectiveness of training programs.

Evaluation refers to the assessment of the total value of a training program, i.e. its costs as well as the outcomes that benefit both the organizations and the individuals who have received training. Training evaluation is not an isolated process. Training needs identified at an earlier stage set training objectives and these objectives, in turn, serve as the basis for program design and implementation. These identified needs and objectives provide further criteria for evaluation.

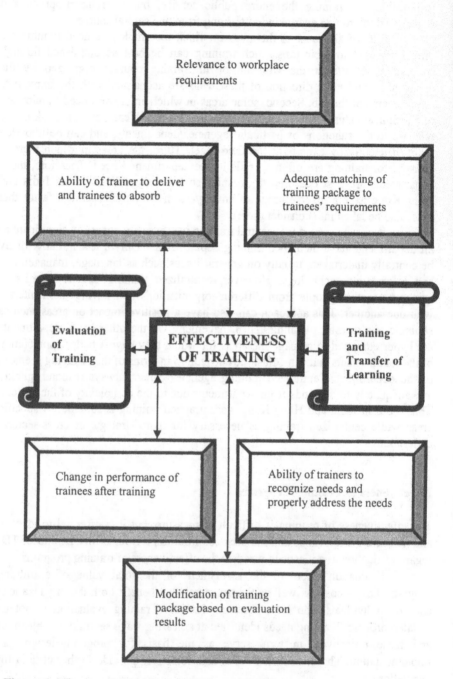

Figure 6.4 Factors Influencing Effectiveness of Training

Evaluation is the most important way of measuring the effectiveness of any training program. Other factors linked to the evaluation procedure must also be considered but they are often overlooked. Transfer of learning, the ability of the trainer to deliver and trainees to absorb information, the ability of the institute and the trainers to recognize needs and properly address them, and the adequate matching of training packages to trainees' requirements have an impact on the effectiveness of training. A proper assessment of the effectiveness of training packages aids in decisions made about the continuation of the program, the improvement of existing programs and the allocation of resources for training. All training agencies conduct some form of evaluation, but their approaches and levels of evaluation vary. The validity and accuracy of the evaluation process is usually uncertain. Changes based on evaluation results are not disclosed to trainees or client departments. Consequently, the evaluator rarely takes the process seriously and is often influenced by the personality of the trainers and the methods and techniques they use. The third and fourth levels of evaluation—relating to behaviour and results respectively—receive limited response from the clients, thus an actual measure of the effectiveness of such training institutes, relying solely on the evaluation, cannot be concluded. Hence, it is necessary to consider additional methods and factors that influence the effectiveness of training.

Evaluation of Training

Kirkpatrick suggests four logical steps in evaluation (see Chapter 2). An ideal training evaluation allows all four levels of assessment to be included, but limited resources—both financial and personnel—often makes this difficult. As more resources become available, the evaluation utilizes trainees' reactions, learning measure, behavioural measure and results measure, in that order. Evaluation is often added to implementation processes at the end, and is not offered as an integral part of the operation. But evaluation is critical, as it provides trainers with an opportunity to understand the impact and consequences of training.

The LBSNAA practices just the first level of evaluation at the end of a training course. In other words, only the immediate reaction to training is considered through the participants' comments on the training programs. This is an inexpensive system, but it only reveals the participants' subjective views and does not reflect what has been learned. Such evaluations seldom indicate the actual impact of training on trainees. Evaluation at LBSNAA seems to receive minimal importance and the agency claims to use informal feedback channels to compensate for the absence of detailed evaluation techniques. The trainers stated that their close contact with trainees during the training course facilitated the process of evaluation. The validity of such evaluation may be open to question. Although LBSNAA appears to have adequate resources at its disposal, a critical aspect of public service training—evaluation—is neglected.

Evaluation can be broadly divided into two types: 'process' 'outcome'. The first level of evaluation falls under the former category, in which the trainee focuses on the trainer's performance, teaching and learning environment, content, and schedule. This type of evaluation hardly leads to better performance. The outcome of training programs is measured with the aid of the second, third and fourth levels of evaluation. The second level of evaluation considers the immediate outcome of training. The third level of evaluation assesses whether or not the on the job behavior of trainees has changed. Finally, the fourth level of evaluation examines the effects of training on organizational effectiveness. The third and fourth levels of evaluation can be considered post-training evaluation. It would be best to evaluate training programs directly in terms of expected results. But there are complicating factors that make this task extremely difficult and most training providers overlook the higher levels of evaluation.

Information obtained through the evaluation carries the risk of being ambiguous and incomplete because it is based on subjective perception and reportage by the trainees. This problem can be addressed by conducting follow-up interviews with the participants or their supervisors so that more detailed information can be collected. Such a strategy may have a higher cost, but it ensures the collection of important information. It may be wise to select some participants and their supervisors at random and interview them to seek their opinions on training packages.

The CSTDI practices the first three levels of evaluation.[20] Normally the Institute receives very positive feedback in the end of course evaluation, although some of the trainees disclosed efforts by the trainers to gain sympathy by telling the trainees about the importance of evaluation to their future careers. At the second level, CSTDI assesses the acquisition of knowledge at the end of the course by determining the knowledge, skills or attitudes the participants have learned from the training program. The second level of evaluation can be accomplished in the classroom immediately after the conclusion of a course. The trainees are given skill tests to demonstrate that knowledge has really been acquired. For courses of longer duration, three levels of evaluation are conducted. The third level of evaluation assesses post-training behaviour by considering the applicability of knowledge, skills and change in attitude. After a suitable interval, CSTDI sends out questionnaires to the trainees and/or their supervisors seeking feedback on the performance of the trainees. This exercise helps assess the long-term impact of training. It should be noted that only a few trainees among those interviewed had experienced the second level of evaluation and none had experienced the third level of evaluation.

Both LBSNAA and CSTDI organize training programs in order to enhance the capacity and efficiency of the public service. Their clientele includes public officials from all levels of government, although CSTDI pays more attention to senior officials. In Hong Kong, there is a provision for customized training that can lead to higher effectiveness, as the package is prepared with specific needs in view. The positive features of CSTDI include the variety of training programs offered, their provision for customized courses, and the cost-effective measures they employ, such as self-learning packages. The quality of training programs at CSTDI is enhanced by strategies such as the sharing of experience by public officials from different departments and guest speakers from the public and private sectors. At the same time, there are some areas that require attention. Junior-level public officials complained of an insufficient number of courses, mainly in the area of language. This reflects poorly on the central training institute in a modern polity like Hong Kong. On the other hand, LBSNAA trains public officials from the central and regional governments, and there is no provision for organizing special courses based on clients' requests. The principle objectives of training in both cases are to ensure that public officials acquire knowledge and skills and to develop appropriate attitudes and standards of ethical conduct, in order to enhance efficiency and effectiveness. Our research found that neither institute is achieving these objectives to the satisfaction of all parties concerned.

In assessing the effectiveness of central training institutes, trainees in both India and Hong Kong appeared to be unsure. Trainers in India were largely non-committal, while those in Hong Kong considered it to be effective. Opinions differed among trainees and trainers regarding the various aspects of effectiveness of training packages.

Training and Transfer of Learning

Training is an expensive process and its effectiveness must be carefully weighed in order to be ensured. The financial cost can be calculated by adding up all the expenses involved in delivering training and the cost of the absence of the trainees from their workplaces. The benefits from training are more difficult to calculate. Training does not simply consist of attendance courses and programs; rather, it is a multifarious activity that includes on-the-job training, study visits, management consultancy exercise and action research. The transition from 'learning' to 'execution' and 'application' is one of the most critical segments of the process, and thus, training is viewed as a means to an end, and should be judged on the basis of its outcome rather than process.

Generally, the issue of effective transfer of learning to the client departments is not adequately considered by the providers and receivers of training. 'Positive transfer is often expected to happen automatically, as an inevitable consequence of formal training processes' (Analoui, 1996, p. 1). Training remained unsatisfactory because many providers ignore the realities of the workplaces to which the trainee returns after training, where the social, cultural and managerial aspects of an organization may assist or obstruct the transfer of learning.

Transferring learning is one of the problems faced by trainees from different backgrounds who attend programs at central training institutes. The reason for the difficulty could be attributed to an inconsistency between the environment and resource endowment of the workplace and the context of their learning. Training institutes may have to organize specially commissioned programs for particular departments. Trainers from the central training institute can visit groups of potential trainees for a better understanding of the process needed for effective learning transfer. Subsequent visits can follow up on the progress of the transfer and also evaluate the effectiveness of the programs. However, this is possible only in the case of specific and long-term programs.

The results of evaluation, as seen in the publications of the central training institutes in India and Hong Kong, indicate that there is a high level of satisfaction in relation to the relevance of training. But personal interviews revealed common complaints based on a lack of practical and suitable content in courses, a need for support in implementing learning in the workplace, and the limited impact of training, as officials are unable to apply new knowledge and skills at their workplace.

For all training, especially for management and project planning (consultancy) training, there is some scope for trainers to facilitate the process of learning transfer. Trainers can employ different techniques for this, including participation, role plays, case studies, simulations and action plans; some programs can also include post-training projects assigned to the trainees to be completed in their workplaces. The actual workplace plays a decisive role in either making or breaking the objectives of training programs (Baldwin, 1988, p. 38). Transfer of learning is not an automatic process, but an issue to be addressed at the design stage of training programs.

Matching Needs and Training Packages

The effectiveness of training depends on the relevance of the training package to the trainees' needs. If training addresses needs, the trainee attains a high level of satisfaction and describes the training as effective. However, another person, attending the same package, but gaining no benefit, due to a wrong choice of package, might consider it irrelevant and ineffective. Sometimes, government departments commit resources (time and money) without determining if training is an appropriate solution to a perceived problem. The cause of poor performance could be a lack of skills or knowledge, and training can help in such cases. But the problem could be related to other factors, in which case training will be counterproductive.

LBSNAA largely contributes to training for probationers in the public service through an extensive training package. Many of the areas included in the training package are not directly related to the tasks officials have to perform in their workplace. The trainees claimed that they had learned a lot from training and were certain that the new knowledge could be applied. Many officials anticipated difficulties in applying training to their jobs, as the context of their agencies and operations were quite different. Probationers have practically no idea of the skills required to perform their jobs, and are not in a position to evaluate the outcome of the training. The Academy continues to deliver the same pattern of training to all of the trainees without evaluating its practical utility. The present cohort of trainers, who have been deputed from civil service departments, agree that the training is irrelevant, but are not able redress the issue. The relevance of training can best be assessed with reference to job requirements, but LBSNAA makes no attempt to that end.

At CSTDI, public officials attend training programs according to their availability in order to get away from workplace. Public officials from different departments apply to join training programs through their supervisors, who play a major in nominating trainees. Supervisors are sometimes unwilling to release an employee if he is required to be at his job, even if the program may be very useful to them. For their part, trainees treat training courses as opportunities to take a break from the office. Evaluation by such disinterested trainees can be potentially misleading.

Coordination between trainers and trainees is one of the most important factors in effective training. Even if the course is well-designed and relevant to the needs of the trainees, it may fail to meet the clients' expectations unless it is delivered in an efficient and effective manner. Training the trainers can help to overcome such shortcomings. Both LBSNAA and CSTDI use the services of many invited and deputed trainers. These people are experts in their respective areas, but not in delivering training. The deputed trainers bring with them some real life and field experiences, but they are sometimes unable to train public officials effectively. Thus, even well-designed courses may not be effectively delivered and may receive negative evaluation.

Post-Training Performance

Trainees and their departments are interested in the impact of training programs on performance. Currently, evaluation is a only useful as a tool for measuring the effectiveness of the training agency. LBSNAA has yet to take evaluations seriously, while CSTDI has begun to do so. There is a need to find out if the performance of trainees improves after training. Conducting a pre-entry test for all the attendees in order to compare their pre- and post-training standards is a good method by which to evaluate the effectiveness of training. The third level of evaluation allows for the monitoring of change in the performance of trainees. LBSNAA should introduce different levels of evaluation, because it is necessary to measure the change in performance or the benefits training has on the trainees. CSTDI is selective in choosing the packages for which this level of evaluation is performed. Most of the courses offered by the Institute are extremely short in duration, and not much change can be expected in employees' performance based on these courses.

The capability of the training providers to identify the needs of the clients is crucial. When identifying training needs, the objective is to bridge the divergence between the existing capacity of an employee for a particular job and the required level for the proper discharge of functions. The stages of career progression for a trainee and the levels of responsibility he is required to have at the different stages of his career must be assessed while identifying and addressing his needs.

Trainees at LBSNAA come from different states and various government departments, which each have diverse needs and requirements. It is incredibly difficult, if not impossible, to address all of these needs in a single training package. The common areas are included in the training packages, but these are not specific to the needs of clients. These kinds of training courses are obviously not effective, even if the evaluation is positive.

The purpose and motive behind attending training also affects their effectiveness. Attending training programs in order to acquire new knowledge has a positive influence on the trainees' motivation, their reaction to the programs, and the transfer of learning. However, attending training as an obligation or an excuse to take time off from the office was found to influence these measures in a negative way. The effectiveness of training suffers if the trainees are compelled to join. The trainees appear to come with predetermined views on the training given, and thus fail to make an appropriate assessment.

Central training institutes need to increase the extent of their consultation with public officials. They must fully understand and recognize the needs of clients and then develop the objectives of training accordingly. They need to develop performance measures to assess the level to which those needs are satisfied. So, it is fair to comment that LBSNAA and CSTDI perform well in providing service-related courses in general, but do not meet the expectations of individual employees.

Trainers have been evaluating their programs for several years. But, until recently, there has been no effort made to use valid and reliable methods to conduct such evaluations. Furthermore, some trainers collect data for evaluation, but do not analyse these data in order to identify trends or improve existing training programs. Such omissions can be damaging, especially in light of the huge amounts of resources that are spent annually on training efforts as a result of demographic, economic, and technological changes.

In order to ensure that better services are provided to trainees, it is necessary to attach importance to the results of evaluation, assess the consequences of training and make further modifications to the training package. If an evaluation shows that a training program has fallen short of achieving its intended objectives, some modification in the program contents and/or methods are usually recommended in order to make the training more effective. It was observed that both LBSNAA and CSTDI are keen on the evaluation procedure, but their publications do not contain any information on changes introduced on the basis of those recommendations. The data collected from India and Hong Kong shows mixed views from the trainees on whether training is modified based on the results of evaluation. Many trainees believed that evaluation results led to changes in training programs, and doubted that evaluation results were considered unimportant. In contrast, the publications indicated that trainees had evaluated most of the training programs as adequate and relevant, and they received extremely positive evaluations. Since the programs are always so positively assessed, the reliability of feedback is often in doubt.

Future Directions of Public Service Training

The public service has changed considerably in recent years. In the past, human resource departments would instruct public officials on their duties, but now individuals manage their own careers. This includes the task of selecting training programs they think can help with their respective jobs. New training strategies have been developed to help trainees learn faster, with a greater degree of retention and with greater ease. Computers and interactive technologies in the classroom are now used to help accelerate learning, and training courses encourage meaningful participation by the trainees.

LBSNAA is presently more responsive to the needs of trainees, as compared to the past.[21] Though the publications of the institute indicate the continued use of traditional training methods, LBSNAA has been upgrading its programs and there is an evident shift from mere theoretical input to more practical aspects.[22] Trainers from the public civil service help introduce practical experience in the programs. CSTDI is a relatively new agency and is still in a developmental stage. In recent years, Hong Kong has gone through a number of significant changes with a change of sovereignty, the introduction of a voluntary retirement scheme and administrative reform, and the CSTDI had to develop and alter training packages to prepare the public officials for these changed circumstances.[23] The Institute has not been entirely successful in coping with the demands of the new circumstances due to its limited experience and heavy workload.[24]

The role of training institutes has greatly risen in importance and relevance in recent years, largely in response to globalization and the increasing complexity and challenges of development. Owing to the rapidly changing scenario and governments' increasing involvement in international affairs, there are continuous efforts to promote every nation's interests. Governments are keen to respond to the challenge presented by globalization and organize proper training for public officials, in order to give them the new job-skills and knowledge required of them. Life-long or continuous learning has become essential for all. Furthermore, with the transformation that has been revolutionizing the role of the state in most countries, it has become increasingly important to reform the training institutes that train future public officials.

The notion of future-oriented training analysis involves an examination of an organization's corporate objectives and strategies. According to Hall, 'Thinking through the link between the organization's basic objectives and need for future top executive skills is the core of strategic succession planning and must be the basis for identifying the future training and development needs of these individuals' (Hall, 1986, pp. 235-65). Progress in technology, competitiveness, economic imperatives, the international environment and other related factors have caused a knowledge explosion. As a result, new types of training and management development have emerged.

India and Hong Kong need to think ahead in order to be better prepared for these changes, instead of reacting to events as they unfold. Investing in officials through training and development is fundamental for the success of public organizations. Updated knowledge and skills can make public officials confident to take on new challenges. Future needs can be described as those required by changes in the work prerequisites of specific departments in order to meet the challenge of constant changes. Interestingly, both LBSNAA and CSTDI seem to consider future-oriented training as synonymous with enhancing the capability of public officials in information technology.

Central training institutes must have foresight. Constant changes in government and administrative environments require alteration and revision of the training packages they offer. These transformations have forced training institutes to anticipate and prepare for changes in order to provide public officials with the skills necessary to master and understand the political, economic and technological progress of a rapidly changing society.

Figure 6.5 shows a logical sequence of the implementation of future oriented training packages. The central training institutes in India and Hong Kong are recognizing the need to face demand in order to develop further and progress. They are well aware of the need to develop forward-looking training packages, as they are service-providing agencies.[25]

LBSNAA has a team of experts, as well as trainers deputed from the public services, who meet frequently to modify and update the training packages based on the needs they anticipate. The Academy identified a greater input on technology related training and training in support of administrative, civil service and economic reforms as the future needs of the public service in India. Nevertheless, 38.2 per cent of the trainers disagreed and only 2.9 per cent agreed that LBSNAA is proficient in identifying future training needs.

Thirty per cent of the trainers strongly agreed and 43.3 per cent agreed that the CSTDI identifies future training needs. The Institute keeps close contact with its customers, and makes an attempt to cater to their demands by offering tailor-made courses that address the needs of the clients. However, it has to conduct ad hoc courses to address the immediate demands of the customers. The main areas identified by the CSTDI as future needs were: the need for a greater influx of technology related training, promotion of continuous learning culture, training in support of the voluntary retirement scheme and training in relation to the public service reform initiatives.

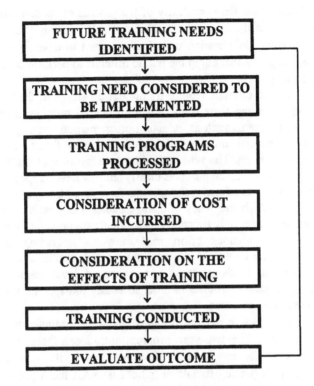

Figure 6.5 Anticipation and Response to Future Training Needs

The training institutes in both India and Hong Kong claim that they are forward-looking and respond to new initiatives by helping the public services manage changes. However, from the discussion above it is clear both that neither of the institutes fully realizes these objectives and that the objectives of civil service training are unlikely to change in the near future. Improving the skills, knowledge, ability and attitudes of the employees in order to achieve the targets of government departments will continue to be the main objectives of LBSNAA and CSTDI.

A Model Training Structure

Central institutes are the main training providers in a country, and public sector organizations depend upon them to deliver relevant programs for upgrading the quality of public services. The principal objective of the central training institute is to enhance the level of efficiency and prepare public officials for good performance. Their other aims include raising the awareness of public officials about critical issues in relation to the economy and administration of the country.

Globalization and the complexity of the process of modernization have made the achievement of these objectives more difficult in recent years. The developments accompanying globalization underline the need to develop a wide range of new training programs that equip the public officials to perform both at the national and international levels.

Public officials require training at all stages of their careers and need to continue upgrading their skills. An ideal central training institute will arrange a variety of programs such as induction or orientation training, job-based in-service training, enhanced training, unconventional and future oriented training and continuing training. The schematic diagram (Figure 6.6) describes each stage and level of training. The emphasis is clearly shifting beyond specific programs such as induction and job related training, and there is a strong emphasis on continuous learning. The high frequency of change makes it impossible for public officials to keep up with them only by attending training programs through nomination. There must be a continuous effort made towards upgrading skills and updating knowledge. In a competitive work environment, public officials have to perform many different kinds of tasks. An enhanced level training can increase the capability of public officials in order to satisfy job-specific needs and allow them to venture into new areas.

LBSNAA provides extensive induction training to all recruits to the public service. The two-year program introduces them to the structures and operations of the government. However, this is the only mandatory training received by all public officials in India. LBSNAA has a provision for specialized job-based in-service training, but it is not popular. Every state (the provinces are called states in India) and each department in the public sector has a training department and there are several agencies that cater to the specific needs of the public and private sector in India. But there are still many cases in which there is a mismatch between the increasing skill and knowledge requirements for new jobs and the skill levels of available workers. In a huge country like India, a single central training institute may not be able to deliver programs commensurate to the needs of public sector employees, at either an individual or community level, unless it is consciously linked to the specific tasks and needs of the agencies in the public sector. Sometimes, public officials in India do not receive training for several years, although training facilities are available. Therefore, it may be useful to make it mandatory for public officials to receive a specified number of training hours. LBSNAA does not offer enhanced level training and neglects future-oriented training, although there are plans being made to provide continuous training. LBSNAA has the resources and is in a position to develop the different levels of training that would enhance the quality of public officials at all levels. Thus, there is a need to include the other levels of training in their repertoire, along with the induction programs. The training process in India could be made effective if planned and implemented in coordination with the training departments at the state and central levels.

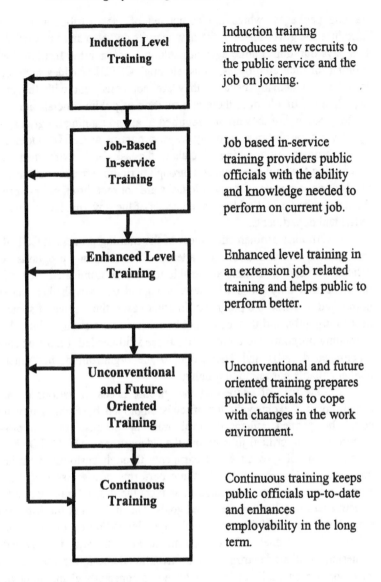

Figure 6.6 Five Point Training Structure

Note: Public officials must be given a minimum number of training hours per year, and should choose from the first four options. However, the last option should be available to everyone all at all times.

According to documents published by CSTDI, public service trainees in Hong Kong receive all the levels of training discussed above. However, in practice, the bulk of their programs concentrate on job-based, in-service training. Moreover, the distinction between the levels of training is not clear. CSTDI offers induction-training packages, which are comprised of the distribution of documents that introduce the government to the new recruits and also arrange workshops of one to two days duration. Public agencies seldom approach the Institute for this level of training for their employees. Thus, although CSTDI provides such programs, there is not much demand because they are not consistent with the needs of client departments. In addition, there is a rotation of public officials across departments in Hong Kong, but they are not required to attend training programs prior to taking up new responsibilities. In many ways, programs at CSTDI address the needs of the government by orienting officials to the tasks and environment of government on entering the public service and through periodic refresher courses. However, the needs of departments with specific tasks are not met through these programs. Thus, the training at CSTDI addresses the needs of the government as a whole but not of individual departments.

Another problematic aspect of the training process at CSTDI is related to the system of nomination for attendance in training programs. Often public officials in need of training are unable to become nominated. Several respondents informed that only those who were ion good terms with their supervisors were nominated to attend the programs. In other cases, the service of some officials was needed urgently, and they could not be released for training. Thus, the participants at training programs were not always those who needed it most or could take back much-needed skills and knowledge to the organization, but others who were neither suitable nor required training.

One way of addressing the specific needs of various departments is to design courses exclusively for officials employed by them. Tailor-made courses could be termed enhanced level training because they improve trainees' performance on critical jobs within their department. The CSTDI responds to the special needs of government departments through customized, in-house training programs. Upon request, the Institute performs needs assessments, recommends plans, designs customized courses, conducts the desired training, and evaluates its effectiveness in achieving the stated goals. The duration of this kind of training can range between a half-day or several days, depending on the level of the groups' needs and the request of the department. Such training is provided only when requested by client departments. Unconventional and future-oriented training is the most popular, as public officials operate in a constantly changing environment, but these courses are seldom available, mainly because training institutes prefer to design programs that can be offered to larger groups of participants.

The Cyber Learning Centre (CLC) was officially launched by CSTDI in March 2000 and provides a wide variety of self-learning resources through the Internet (http://clccontent.cstdi.gov.hk/default.asp). There is a proposal to use it to organize experience-sharing sessions hosted by fellow civil servants or celebrities on cases of successful learning.

CSTDI is an interesting case study because it does not appear to be nearly as successful as claimed in its publications. The Institute has received good support from the government in terms of resources and the number of public service employees in Hong Kong is not high. But it seems that the Institute is unable to cope with the demands for its services. CSTDI tries to cater to all the needs of the government, but it must undertake a rational assessment of its capacity and concentrate on areas where its strengths lie. Further, Hong Kong does not have a policy of mandatory training for public officials. Thus many officials avoid attending training programs for years, while those who are interested may not get an opportunity to receive training.

A SWOT Analysis: LBSNAA

The existing training process at LBSNAA appears to be inefficient. The Academy's efforts to prepare public officials for rapid changes are slow and cumbersome. Some of our interviews also pointed to a lack of transparency in the process. There is particular concern related to the evaluation of programs and the identification of future training needs. However, other interviewees described this as a 'flexible process', and considered it a major strength of the current system. On the basis of our observations, an examination of documents, and the responses to questionnaires and interviews, the following is an attempt to identify the strengths, weaknesses, opportunities and threats in the current state of training at LBSNAA.

Strengths

LBSNAA has a large campus and the facilities are impressive. The location and environment are conducive to learning. The trainees from various departments and states assemble and train together for specific periods of time. This helps with co-ordination and allows for interaction between the trainees and trainers. There are opportunities for informal chats and a free exchange of views. Constant interaction among public officials from diverse work and personal backgrounds strengthens the bond and widens outlook of public officials in India.

LBSNAA receives adequate financial support from the central government. The Director expressed satisfaction with the availability of funds and the trainers supported this view. Obtaining sufficient funds for effective operation is a great advantage for the Academy.

Traditional values continue to dominate most of the programs at LBSNAA. However, new ideas and orthodoxies are gradually taking hold in the public sector as the country embraces specific aspects of new public management, particularly market principles, a customer-oriented approach and performance measurement. These new norms have their advantages, but they too are limited and may have more adverse impact on public services than is apparent. Therefore, one of the strengths of LBSNAA is a continuing emphasis on traditional values, which remain relevant to the effective operation of public sector management.

Most of the trainers at LBSNAA are deputed from the public service. The trainees are exposed to the theoretical elements of public administration, which are then tested and reinforced through exposure to the practical aspect, related by public service officials from their hands-on experience. Thus, the enrichment of the training process by interaction with practitioners adds considerable strength to the programs of LBSNAA.

District experience presentation sessions at LBSNAA are useful. The trainees are provided with knowledge about the workplace and guidance. They can, therefore, deal more effectively with similar problems at their respective workplaces. Participants in the programs can contribute to the training process through constructive thinking and by being involved in case studies.

The Academy has a research unit. A research base is essential for providing information about training and education activities and it also allows for the compilation of contemporary and leading-edge ideas. If a training agency does not indulge in rigorous thinking, conceptualisation and analysis, its teaching and learning cannot reach a high standard.

LBSNAA strives to fill the skill gap of the trainers by sending them for training both within and outside the country. Overseas training allows trainers to compare their skills and achievements with international standards and identify areas for improvement.

Weaknesses

The process of documentation deserves attention at LBSNAA. Proper documentation and a suitable mechanism need to be instituted for disseminating, updating, storing and retrieving information regularly. The Academy would benefit from a resource and documentation centre to serve as a repository for modules, case studies and relevant information on training.

LBSNAA is unable to respond quickly to changes and the needs of clients. The trainers at the Academy display rigidity in their thinking and cannot adapt to new challenges. Both the trainers and trainees are more comfortable in confronting the problems they area familiar with, and hesitate to venture into new and unknown areas.

The approach at LBSNAA is academic rather than professional in nature, with relatively less emphasis on the practical aspects of work. Recruits to the public service receive theoretical input[26] in pre-entry education, but need to be informed about the application of these theories in the real world. The curriculum for management education and training and development needs to be made consistent with the actual job requirements. Training curricula driven by customer demands can be more effective than provider-driven efforts.

Although LBSNAA receives adequate financial allocation, these funds are under-utilized and the surplus is returned to the government every year. This reflects a lack of ability to take advantage of available funds.

Additionally, the location of the Academy is one of its major drawbacks. It is located on a beautiful campus in the resort town of Mussorie, far away from any of the major cities. Travelling to LBSNAA is arduous, and it discourages trainees who may not wish to remain in such a place for a long period of time. It is difficult to persuade guest speakers to visit, and this deprives the trainees from getting the benefit of listening to experts.

LBSNAA has a regular inflow of trainers from all parts of India, but they come only for a short period of time. The maximum period of their stay is three years, thus they are able to complete only one full training session for the new recruits. By the time they familiarize themselves with the training culture at LBSNAA, it is time for them to leave the Academy and a new set of trainers are deputed. They are able to identify problems and areas for improvement during their stay at the Academy, but they do not stay long enough to resolve and implement them.

LBSNAA is weak in standardizing procedures and programs, as a result the training programs are extremely flexible and there is no pressure to follow clear plans. It is necessary to strike a balance between rigidity and flexibility, and establishing clear standards would help. This also relates to the issue of the relevance of training material. The duration of the courses at LBSNAA is exceedingly long. In some courses, irrelevant input results in wastage of resources, and the lack of a clear focus affects the level of interest among trainees and trainers.

The process of evaluation has been pointed out as a weak point for LBSNAA. Training is not an end in itself and can be considered successful or useful only if it leads to better performance. Although great importance is accorded to training by the government, there is an increasing demand for proof that investment in training leads to improvements in the trainee as well as the output of the organization. Trainers and training institutes judge training with reference to the success of the process and the achievement of the learning objectives. The supervisors of trainees are obviously interested in the improvement of performance on the workforce, while the government is keen to ensure worthwhile investment in training. Many of these objectives are intimately related to the proper evaluation of training.

Opportunities

Public service training may require specially structured programs at a reasonable cost. Public organizations in need of such services should be able to request LBSNAA to prepare customized courses in specific areas.

Another strategy to motivate public officials to become more interested and involved could be to initiate a system of conferring diplomas or certificates on trainees after the completion of the courses. Consideration of performance on training courses for personnel decisions could be beneficial.

As public organizations have to respond to changes on a regular basis, strategic, cohesive and comprehensive human-resource policies and programs can enable them to anticipate and deal with these changes in a systematic and integrated way. Training is an appropriate tool for this purpose. Training programs may fail to achieve the desired ends for various reasons. Central training institutes should identify the problems and develop new training programs to resolve them. Experts can be appointed to audit training activities and make recommendations to guide the training institutes.

LBSNAA could play a vital role in the development of a national resource centre for public officials serving in the regions and out in the fields. Distance learning packages or resource support would help make learning an ongoing activity. Sharing of success stories, analysis of failures, video and slide documentation of social development programs, and case studies are tested methods for such purposes. The Academy can fill this vacuum by providing resource support to field officials who are keen to obtain new information and knowledge after they are posted to the remote areas of India.

Threats

Policy appears to be a neglected aspect of management at LBSNAA.[27] Faults in developing, formulating and analysing policies can render a sound system of public management ineffective. It is essential to strike the correct balance between the degree of emphasis on both management and policy.

The rigid mindsets of the Indian bureaucrats do not accept change easily and willingly. Even after being equipped with information and skills obtained from training about modern systems and processes, public officials are unwilling to accept changes in their styles and methods of work. They have pre-determined views about training and its providers, which affect their evaluation of the training program. Rigid mindsets and perceptions have an impact on the culture of the public service and are obvious threats to the successful operation of LBSNAA.

Some of the training programs at LBSNAA are termed irrelevant, but they still account for items of expenditure in the Academy's budget. This irrelevance is also a threat to the reputation of the LBSNAA. Most of the in-service officers who were interviewed at their respective work sites did not express any desire to be trained at the LBSNAA because they had no interest in the outdated, useless and traditional programs offered. Thus, the Academy is facing the threat of limited expansion, and may have to restrict itself to acting merely as the agency for training new recruits in the government.

The in-service training programs at LBSNAA may not be effective because most senior public officials are not interested in them. The rate of attendance and participation in these courses is poor, mainly because the officials do not expect to receive any benefit from this kind of training. Several steps can be recommended to deal with this problem, including the improvement of the content and design of training programs, as well as efforts to ensure attendance and quality participation. Incorporating performance evaluation in the assessment reports of public officials may help in this task.

A SWOT Analysis: CSTDI

Many interviewees and questionnaire respondents believed that the current process of training at CSTDI is far from perfect. There are problems at all stages of training and the Institute's attempts to modify and upgrade programs are not always successful. At the same time, CSTDI is strong in a number of areas and has the potential to strengthen its position. In the following pages, an attempt is made to recognize the strengths, weaknesses, opportunities and threats noticed at the CSTDI.

Strengths

CSTDI offers custom-made courses to departments with specific needs. This arrangement helps bridge competency gaps and encourages public officials to enhance their knowledge in order to adapt to changing environments and face new challenges. The result is improved individual and organizational performance and enhanced competence on-the-job. The programs at CSTDI cover a wide range of topics, including national affairs, leadership, public policies, management, language, information technology, professional training and work skills. CSTDI invites officials from the public service to deliver courses on management. Training delivered by a mixture of professional educators and practitioners provides a better perspective. Some of the programs aim to help public officials cope with the recent initiatives for reforming the civil service in Hong Kong, and input from incumbent senior officials is very effective, in this regard.

Interaction among officials from different departments and exchange of experience by officials while attending training programs is very useful. Of late, CSTDI has opened up its training programs to personnel from the private sector as well. Sharing of experience between officials in the public and private sectors adds a valuable dimension to understanding and operating for public officials.

CSTDI receives generous financial allocation from the government. In addition, the Institute raises substantial revenue by charging government departments for training. Besides, specialists with a wide range of experience are invited to the Institute, and this ensures a good blend of trainers with practical and theoretical knowledge. A mix of professional educators and practitioners is of great value.

The Civil Service Bureau (CSB) supervises the operation and management of the CSTDI. This arrangement, which includes accountability to a higher authority, is useful. Through this partnership, the CSB is also responsible for providing the Institute with direction and guidance.

Another area of strength in CSTDI is the diversity of training programs. Research carried out at the Institute adds to a database on training and education activities. This base of information helps in the process of planning training programs.

Weaknesses

Although, CSTDI organizes training programs on its campus, there is no facility to allow trainees to live there. A likely reason is the short duration of the programs, which do not require overnight stays. Therefore, the trainees do not have an opportunity to immerse themselves in a training environment. During the course of the training program, they remain pre-occupied with their work, since they have to return to the office after only a short period at the Institute. This factor also reduces the possibility for sharing experience among the trainees, who cannot take advantage of the lessons learned on the job by other members of the public service. There is little scope for informal chats and freely expressed views. Interaction among the trainees over a certain length of time could help achieve a better understanding of the operation of the public service and establish useful networks. The short duration of the courses is also an impediment to the better acquaintance between trainers and trainees. In addition, half-day courses do not meet most of the objectives of public service training.

Generally, a trainee at CSTDI is required to fill in a form, obtain approval from the head of his unit, and submit the form directly for enrolment. Sometimes, a supervisor does not approve an application due to personal considerations and the applicant cannot attend the training program. A frustrated trainee complained about the process: 'The supervisor tends to send his favourite subordinates for the courses instead of nominating the most suitable employee. Sometimes the supervisors do not nominate any personnel to attend the courses because the department cannot spare their services in view of heavy workload' (Interview, 12th September 2000). Allowing public service employees to apply directly to the CSTDI, which would select the most suitable candidates, could simplify the process.

Training is not an end in itself and can be evaluated as successful or useful only if it equips the officials to perform better on the job. Departments spend substantial funds on training of personnel and are keen to see results in the form of increased productivity and improved behaviour. Several programs at CSTDI are short in duration, ranging from a half to a full day. It is impractical to conduct the three levels of training evaluation on courses of such short duration, and the evaluation based on immediate reaction can be misleading. Therefore, CSTDI does not always receive feedback that would enable it to improve its training courses in order to be more effective. Much of the advantage of the allocation of adequate resources and service from a group of qualifies trainers is lost due to the problems of evaluation and feedback.

Opportunities

The opening up of training facilities to the private sector is a positive development for CSTDI. The horizons of civil servants should be widened not only through the exchange of inter-departmental experiences, but also through an interface with private sectors and other administrators. The traditional concept of career civil service in Hong Kong is undergoing a transformation, and public officials no longer expect to adhere to the same sector until retirement. This opens up the possible necessity for introducing new ideas into public service, and thus cross-fertilization between the public and private sector is desirable. It might be a good idea to expose the trainers at CSTDI to the assumptions and practices current in the private sector.

Training is a continuous process, and distant learning packages and resource support provided by CSTDI have helped make learning an ongoing activity in the Hong Kong public service. The delivery of training services can be improved through wider use of tailor-made courses at departmental and individual levels. In this regard, departments should be encouraged to identify their needs and adopt a more proactive approach towards training and development.

Threats

The most noticeable threat to CSTDI is the inconsistency between the input received by trainees during training and its application in the field. In most cases, trainees approach programs with a number of solutions to their specific problems in mind, and expect to achieve them immediately. This expectation is unrealistic, as training packages are not designed to meet with the needs of specific individuals or departments.

There is some concern over the tendency of CSTDI to advertise unrealistic objectives in order to sell their programs. A trainer defended this position: 'We have a supportive role and have a penetrating objective based on the needs of the departments. We support the needs of the departments and if we do not, they will reject us. The course will not get any response. They will go to outside consultant departments for help, which is not good for us' (Interview, 23rd October 2000). The statement reflects the tension and insecurity felt by the trainers at CSTDI. In spite of the claim that the departments would choose alternative sources for delivery training, the fact remains that the Institute has an assured market and that could be the reason for less enthusiastic efforts to respond to the suggestions from the trainees. Lack of competition has affected the improvement and development of both CSTDI and LBSNAA.

CSTDI is unable to cope with the task and responsibility of training the entire public service. The trainees found it difficult to get nominated for training, as the numbers of places are limited. Officials who are in need of training are unable to attend courses due to over subscription. Hence, the demand-supply equilibrium of training at the Institute is not balanced.

Training programs are attended on a voluntary basis at CSTDI. There are no compulsory courses that all public service officials are required to attend at some stage of their career. This makes CSTDI appear more like a commercial organization, which serves its clients and in turn charges them for services rendered, than a service provider for public sector employees and an organ of the government. The institute has a provision offering induction training to new recruits, but is seldom approached by client departments demanding this level of training. The departments prefer to provide their own induction training to new employees. The CSTDI, if approached, provides only documentary assistance by supplying notes introducing the government.

The problem of securing the release of staff from their departments is the biggest threat faced by the institute. In most departments, the volume of work has greatly increased, owing to the reduction in the number of employees and the government's new initiatives and developments, which have added considerably to the workload. This makes it very difficult to release employees to attend training programs. But, departments still want to participate in training programs, and at times, send employees who are not the most suitable. The supervisors either choose people with lower workload or those they like.

The Common Problems of Public Service Training

In considering the structures, functions, organization and operations, a number of observations can be made on public service training in India and Hong Kong. First, the process of needs assessment is unsatisfactory, which leads to a number of problems, such as inappropriate content, irrelevance and failure to achieve the expected outcome from training programs. Apathy, resistance, confusion over training and an inadequate supply of training packages further affect the outcome of training as trainees are unable to appreciate the problems on the ground and resolve them.

Second, in spite of the expansion and development of the training institutes and their programs, the choice among training programs offered is extremely limited. There is an inadequate supply of the training necessary to meet the needs of the clients, and often the programs are adjusted according to the availability of resources. Thus, officials attend training programs because they are available and not because they are needed.

Third, training is not treated with seriousness by the client departments. Only employees with lighter workload and/or personal relationships with their supervisors are selected for training, and these are only released at the convenience of the department. In other words, training is not systematically organized and officials fail to understand the importance and impact of training.

Fourth, both CSTDI and LBSNAA are well endowed with financial resources, but are inadequate in the areas of human and material resources. They have difficultly hiring good instructors, especially in India, owing to the location of the training institute. Although substantial funds are available, they are not properly and fully utilized.

Fifth, the monopolization of training institutes by the government is a serious problem, especially in India, where the central government is protective of the training institute and does not encourage links with private training organizations. In Hong Kong, the system is more relaxed and the training institute co-operates with other training institutes and universities for the development of training programs.

Notes

[1] Information based on the interview with Patricia Tam, Senior Training Officer, CSTDI on 15th November 2000.

[2] Trainers at both institutes claimed that they were future oriented as they delivered technology related inputs and used modern training techniques.

[3] Based on the interview with Subrahmanyam, Deputy Director, LBSNAA, 21st June 2000.

[4] Based on the interviews with all the trainers who claimed that the institute was given adequate funds. The trainers interviewed were very satisfied with the amount sanctioned and commented that there was never a shortage of funds faced. The institute also gathers sufficient funds by means of course fees from different departments.

[5] The Director, during the interview indicated that the institute is developing web-based learning and also distance learning as it has been realized that training and learning is a continuos process.

[6] Informed during interviews with Manisha at LBSNAA and a training officer, CSTDI, who requested not to disclose her identify.

[7] The statements given by trainees during interviews and unofficial meetings can justify this statement. Trainees both in India and Hong Kong voiced their views that the training requirements do not match with the training provided by the training institute. Moreover, the trainees also added that the departments let the institutes know about their requirements but by the time the training is organized, new needs are developed and old ones outdated.

[8] As informed during interviews, most senior officials at CSTDI attended only half the sessions and in India, the senior officials were reluctant to accept the training inputs and often condemned the training contents.

[9] The government employees informed that it was extremely difficult to get a chance to receive training at the institute. The trainers admitted that the demand was higher than the supply of training.

[10] An officer at the Ministry of Personnel, India, admitted this as a major drawback in the working of the institute.

[11] An officer at the Ministry of Personnel, India, admitted this as a major drawback in the working of the institute.

[12] Based on the interviews with the trainers of CSTDI.

[13] A government official indicated that the only time he and his colleagues visited the institute was when they underwent the induction training. He indicated that most of the officials prefer to go to other institutes for training.

[14] As observed during the training sessions at LBSNAA. The trainers as well as the trainees at CSTDI indicated that they were contended while delivering and receiving training through new and modern techniques.

[15] The analysis is done on the basis of the interviews with the government employees. The trainees felt that they should directly apply to the institute and the institute should finally choose the appropriate trainees.

[16] Singapore civil service is the first in Asia to introduce compulsory training hours each year for its civil servants. Hong Kong and India should consider adopting the Singapore model.

[17] Based on the interview with Subrahmanyam, Deputy Director, LBSNAA, 21st June 2000.

[18] The trainees, during interviews, termed training at the CSTDI and LBSNAA as general and not job specific. The trainers explained that the courses are to cater the employees of the civil service at large and unless the training is developed on request (tailor made courses in the case of Hong Kong), it is unable to meet with the requirements of the attendees.

[19] The trainers at LBSNAA informed that each state has its own training institute and moreover, India has many training institutes, which provide training on more specific areas. All government officials are given the right to apply to such institutes for training. The trainers at CSTDI expressed that most of the departments have their own training units that provide more job specific training. The senior government official are entitled to occasional overseas training as well. Furthermore the institute provides customised training upon requests from client departments. The departments can also request to get a trainer from the institute deputed to assist in the departmental training.

[20] Based on interviews with trainers. However, the trainees informed that they rarely experience the second and third levels of evaluation.

[21] The trainers deputed from the civil service indicated that the institute is more responsive to needs as compared to the time when they themselves received training.

[22] As observed, during the training session apart from the lectures, there are role-plays, case-studies, and real life experiences, which indicate a more participative approach towards training.

[23] Patricia Tam, Senior Training Officer, CSTDI, indicated the changes faced by the institute since its short existence.

[24] A common concern from the trainers and the trainees during interviews was the increasing demands for training and the ability of the institute to cope with such demands.

[25] Based on interviews with trainers at CSTDI and LBSNAA.

[26] The entrance exam for the IAS exams requires the candidate to possess adequate theoretical knowledge of many areas.

[27] The training at the institutes focuses its training on management and neglects issues related to policy.

Chapter 7

Conclusions

Globalization has ushered in unprecedented changes in every area of activity undertaken by modern governments. A rethinking and reformulation of the basic premises and practices of public administration have compelled governments to reconsider their priorities, goals and practices. In light of the issues shifts occurring under globalization, the significance of training has increased considerably as the demands and pressure exerted by the forces of globalization must be balanced with the indigenous need to enhance the efficiency of public services. It is possible to identify problem areas and concerns in the central training institutes and present recommendations for dealing with them.

We have examined the organization, operation and role of central training institutes in dissimilar territories, with the LBSNAA in India and CSTDI in Hong Kong as case studies. The task was accomplished through an evaluation of the trends, techniques and the capability of central institutes to anticipate future training needs, as well as the level of effectiveness and the process for determining priorities in planning, designing and delivering training programs. The concepts and prescriptive models presented in this study can be applied generally, although some modifications may be required to suit the specific circumstances existing in different countries. While the findings of this study are context specific, they can be applied to similar cases under similar circumstances. For instance, some elements of the study such as the information sources for needs assessment, the factors influencing the effectiveness of training, the identification of training priorities and the logical structure of training institutes can be applied broadly, while others are more context specific.

A Review of Findings

Centralized training institutes are autonomous bodies responsible for training across all government departments and training has been regarded as an important element of the public service in both India and Hong Kong. In India, public service entrants are initially recruited on probation, and later are appointed as full-time officials in a branch of service. Over the span of their careers, public officials in India attend programs at different institutes for job-related training. The ministries and departments to which they belong are responsible for providing them with specialized and skill related training.

In Hong Kong, basic training programs are not mandatory for all public service entrants, except for those entering the disciplined services. The police, customs and immigration services have arrangements by which to provide training to their new recruits through their own departmental resources. Subsequently, public officials are subjected to training from time to time to upgrade and update their skills. The main objective of training as stated by the Civil Service Bureau is to enable public servants in Hong Kong to acquire the necessary knowledge, skills and attitudes to meet operational requirements and changing circumstances, and to assist grade/departmental managers in realizing career development plans for individual officers and succession plans of grades/departments (CSB, 1999). Under the current scenario of major administrative, financial, and civil service reforms, there is an increasing demand for frequent and effective training for the public service.

Both India and Hong Kong have separate central and departmental training agencies. They have different levels and types of jurisdictions, but they need to work with common objectives in mind because their combined efforts are crucial for good performance of the government. However, in spite of the identification and adoption of measures to address specific needs, training remains an inconsistent tool in the pursuit of effective performance. The lack of consistency results from poor coordination between departments and the central training institutes. Thus, one of the essential elements for successful and effective training is competent coordination between training institutes and the government departments.

Training at LBSNAA is not structured in a way that caters to the explicit requirements of all the trainees. There is no structure in place by which the departments can negotiate with the central training institute on the basis of their specific requirements. Although CSTDI maintains close contact with its clients, the task-specific requirements of the government departments are not adequately met, as these cannot be addressed by the generalized training offered at the central institute. While, CSTDI addresses this problem by offering customized training packages, LBSNAA does not yet have such a system in place. There is a need for closer interaction and co-ordination among the different agencies of the government and the central training institutes.

Needs assessment is considered important because it not only reflects an organization's requirements, but also the ability of the training provider to correctly diagnose deficiencies that require attention. From the perspective of efficiency, effective needs assessment leads to an identification of legitimate goals and strategies, which, in turn, lead to relevant training. However, in spite of the importance of the process, the absence of a systematic and logical model hinders the identification of needs in both LBSNAA and CSTDI. These needs may vary in size, in relation to the capacity of their administrative system, and in relation to other factors specific to their situations. The size of a need refers to its scope; for instance, whether needs are assessed for one organization, a group of organizations or the government as a whole. It should also be borne in mind that public officials work in a variety of organizations and are required to perform diverse tasks. Thus, identifying training needs for government officials is a complex task because they have to discharge multifarious duties and perform different roles.

Public service training at both CSTDI and LBSNAA is mainly driven by supply and not by demand. The customers have to choose between available packages and are not in a position to make demands according to their needs. In Hong Kong, tailor-made courses are demand driven, to a certain extent, allowing the customers to have training to address their needs directly.

In terms of future training needs, both LBSNAA and CSTDI concentrate primarily on the use of modern learning techniques and training related to information technology. They seem to disregard the fact that activities that help public officials respond to the needs of the country and prepare them to deal with the changing environment should also be within the scope of future training needs. Attention to customer satisfaction and efficient service delivery with the aid of technology are examples of activities that could serve both purposes.

As central training institutes, both LBSNAA and CSTDI principally address general needs relevant to the maximum number of employees in the public services. Thus, the training curricula at both the institutes are basically similar. The latter emphasizes practical issues, while training at LBSNAA includes a blend of theory and practice. The main areas of training are management, language, and information technology at both institutes, but the duration of training programs differs. The maximum period of most of the training programs at CSTDI is approximately three weeks (except for the 3-year 'Training and Development Program' launched in 2001/02). However, even the shortest programs at LBSNAA extend over a much longer period.

The lack of an appropriate and logical training structure is a problem for both institutes. A central training institute must be able to provide a variety of training at all levels of a public official's career. Changes within and outside the government require regular upgrading of the skills of public officials. Training institutes, therefore, must offer the entire range of services including induction or orientation training, job-based in-service training, enhanced training, unconventional and future oriented training and continuing training.

The evaluation of training is a major area of concern at LBSNAA and CSTDI. In most cases, LBSNAA undertakes the first stage of evaluation in the form of documenting reactions at the end of each session. Most of the questions in the evaluation ask for the ideas and comments of participants on the actual training, and do not consider the practical implications of training. As the dominant service provider, LBSNAA has no competition and therefore does not make an effort to elicit information on post-training performance from its client organizations. On paper, CSTDI claims to undertake three levels of evaluation, but these are not applied to all training programs. In most cases, programs are subjected to only the first level of evaluation, while a few go on to the second and third levels. Neither institute makes the evaluation results public. A continuous and rigorous, rather than casual, training impact evaluation is essential for effective performance.

Both LBSNAA and CSTDI invite experts from the private sector to attend as well as deliver training. This practice is conducive to the interaction and exchange of ideas between personnel from the public and private sectors. Besides, the personal experiences of the faculty and guest speakers allow the trainees to appreciate different points of view. Also useful in this regard are the research activities and case-studies that are prepared at the institutes, as they often highlight the successful initiatives of public officials.

There have been changes in the nature, approach and content of training programs at LBSNAA and CSTDI. Initially both the institutes focused only on general programs that could be attended by officials from a variety of backgrounds. Later, CSTDI introduced tailored courses, which are directly relevant to the requirements of the client departments. A general trend is a shift in focus from input of a theoretical nature to more practical knowledge and from the lecture mode to a more participative mode.

The Two Cases

Lack of proper documentation and standardization of training packages is noticeable in both CSTDI and LBSNAA. The syllabi at LBSNAA are reviewed and updated every ten years, and thus fail to keep up with the rapid pace of change. However, trainers have the autonomy to adjust training objectives according to the requirements of the trainees, whenever appropriate. It is not possible to gather an accurate picture from the publications of the institute, which include information and claims that could not be substantiated by evidence. The training programs at LBSNAA are too flexible and easily changeable, which hinders the strategic planning process. The problem becomes more complex because both transparency and productivity are difficult to monitor as well as measure.

A sound monitoring process is critical for the effective performance of central training institutes, and a specific body or agency must be entrusted with the authority to perform that task. The Ministry of Personnel of the Government of India is authorized to supervise the operation of LBSNAA. However, it is hard to find any evidence of the Ministry's active involvement in this respect. The Director of the Academy exercises a wide range of power and generally does not seem to be answerable to any agency or committee. An annual report on the operation of LBSNAA is submitted to the supervisory authority, the Ministry of Personnel. The report is accepted without question: there is no effort made to suggest improvements or demand explanations for any aspect of its function.[1] Such lenience and the absence of a system of responsibility to the higher authority hinder the proper functioning and regular development of LBSNAA.

CSTDI identifies service-wide training needs and the departments communicate their specific requirements to the Institute. The trainers consult public sector agencies and government departments and agencies to facilitate the process of needs assessment.

CSTDI is under tremendous pressure from the ever-increasing demands of public officials for training. As a result, the Institute has had to contract out some of its work to private training providers. The trainees do not have much confidence in the outsourced programs because the backgrounds of such service providers are unknown to the recipients. Moreover, government departments can garner the services of contractors to fulfill their needs on their own, instead of going through the central agency.

A major problem in the training structure at CSTDI is securing the release of officials from the departments in which they are employed. Recent cutbacks in budgets and personnel in the public service of Hong Kong have resulted in a high workload for public officials. Consequently, officials are often selected for training on the basis of their availability rather than their needs.

A number of observations can be made on the operation and performance of LBSNAA. The Academy is unable to provide resource support to field officers, who, as a result, do not have access to new information and knowledge when they serve in remote districts. There is a tendency to sometimes overlook the human resource development aspect of training programs, and the focus is seldom on problem solving and the development of appropriate public management skills that could improve delivery systems in government. The trainees view training as a tool for improving their capacity for career advancement, whereas the trainers consider it a means for improving the skills of the trainees so they will perform better on their jobs. Lack of regular contact between the various departments of the government and LBSNAA is another problem.

LBSNAA and CSTDI have different ways of assessing training needs. LBSNAA considers job specifications in order to identify the abilities and skills required to perform effectively. Data is collected by trainers through questionnaires sent to a sample of employees and their managers in order to learn about the actual tasks they perform and to see whether these tasks vary or are similar to those identified by the Academy. LBSNAA has to take a variety of sources—notes of discussion meetings, interviews, feedback and performance appraisal data—into consideration, as it is impossible for them to solicit information from every government department to assess their needs, owing to the huge size and diversity of the population and regions of the country.

In addition, the programs at LBSNAA are more general in nature, reflecting an attempt to cover areas of common concern. The trainers have autonomy to identify needs based on the information obtained from different sources, such as job analysis, discussion meetings, and interviews with employees, supervisors and work experts, information from departmental training divisions, feedback from evaluations, questionnaires and reviews of performance appraisal data. The forecasts and predictions of trainers, international trends, conferences, demographic changes in the workforce, and anticipated changes in government and society also impact the process of needs assessment.

CSTDI undertakes an annual customer survey to help assess training needs. It also solicits suggestions from the departments on methods by which to improve performance. Regular meetings with public organizations yield information on the kind of training needed in the public service. CSTDI is guided in the process of needs assessment by instructions from the Civil Service Bureau (CSB), the assessment of trainers, and input from government departments.

The Challenges of Training for Public Service

It is extremely difficult to measure the effectiveness of training but, at the same time, it is essential to do so in order to ensure the performance of public services. LBSNAA and CSTDI consider evaluation techniques as important means by which to measure the effectiveness of the training they deliver. In addition, other factors, such as the transfer of learning, the ability of trainers to deliver and trainees to absorb, the capacity of training agencies to recognize and address needs, and matching training packages to the requirements of trainees also influence effective training. An efficient process of needs assessment helps in making decisions related to the continuation and improvement of training programs and the allocation of resources for training.

Elements of both centralized and decentralized approaches to training were noticed in India and Hong Kong, but the demarcation and division of responsibility between these two areas were not clearly outlined. There is no indication as to which areas and types of training would be allocated to either the central or regional jurisdiction. For instance, CSTDI offers induction training for new recruits, but most of the government departments in Hong Kong prefer to arrange induction training on their own. As a result, there is mot much demand for the induction training arranged by the Institute. The specification of jurisdiction and a clear division of work in this area could be more productive.

Both central training institutes make a number of claims in their prospectus and annual reports. LBSNAA concentrates on three new knowledge areas, i.e. negotiation and coordination, scientific management and personal productivity—and strives to develop them. There is also an attempt to inculcate conceptual skills as well as knowledge on policy related issues, which have largely been ignored in the past. CSTDI has a somewhat different emphasis, and seeks to design new programs to fulfill training needs, expand the mode of delivery beyond classroom training, and facilitate the development of a learning culture (CSTDI, 2000, p. 6). However, the interviewees in both India and Hong Kong found training objectives misleading and were unwilling to accept the claims regarding the performance and success made by LBSNAA and CSTDI.

In the past, the training institutes addressed only issues of a general nature, but the changed circumstances have compelled them to consider the diverse needs of public organizations. There are conscious attempts to bridge competency gaps and encourages public officials to acquire new knowledge in order to adapt to changing environments and deal with new challenges. However, the limited choice of training programs was found to be an obstacle in this process. In addition, the irrational practice of selecting trainees on the basis of availability of public officials, rather than the needs of the organization and state, results in poor returns from investments in training.

Similar problems prevail in the development of techniques for the identification of future training needs. This process involves a fair amount of forecasting and anticipation of the problems that are likely to emerge in the future and the skills required to deal with them. It is difficult to make accurate forecasts because public organizations operate in a political environment and the influence of strong national and international forces contribute to rapid shifts in direction.

Recommendations

An ideal central training institute should be able to provide training for public service officials at all levels of their career. As such, jurisdictions must be clearly demarcated and responsibilities must be allocated in order to streamline the operation of central training institutes. The targeted clientele and area to be covered by the training course must be clearly stated. Regional or specialized branches may be created to deal with specific demands and resolve problems as they arise.

The problems around the leadership of central institutes merit more attention. This is too large and complex a responsibility to be entrusted to the office of a single senior public servant.[2] Specialized sub-institutes, responsible for different levels of training should be placed under the leadership of other experienced trainers. These sub-institutes may be located within or outside the central training institute, and their leaders must be held accountable to the head of the central institutes. They would be responsible for organizing training in designated areas.

Figure 7.1 suggests a structure for central training institutes with reference to their duties and responsibilities. Increased autonomy and responsibility will enable the leaders of sub-institutes to operate in an efficient and effective manner. The customers, too, will be able to indicate their preferences and choose training packages that are most relevant to their organization, leading to greater satisfaction, efficiency and effectiveness. The sub-institutes will be allotted adequate resources and will be made aware of their objectives and responsibilities. It will be possible to detect weaknesses and failures quickly and accurately, and effective steps can be taken to deal with them. These changes would require a considerable reorganization and restructuring of the training institutes.

Information gathered from different sources for the purpose of assessing needs must be carefully reviewed. Training works best when the trainee is motivated to ascertain the knowledge and skills required of him and works toward achieving them. The identified training needs must be refined and categorized into areas such as technical, technological, language and management. Technical and technological skills are basic requirements and deserve attention first, because the officials will be unable to function without these skills. At the same time, management and language skills should not be ignored. These are essential for improving morale, facilitating teamwork, and developing employees as they look for and face new challenges.

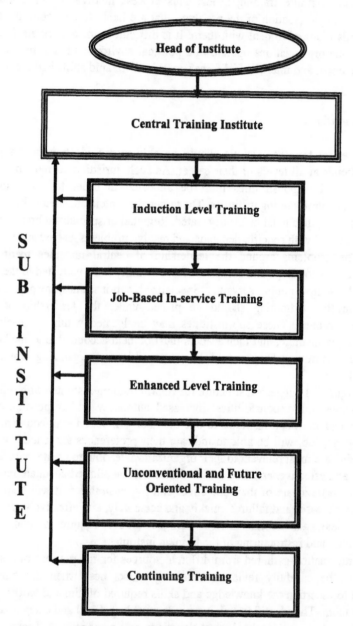

Figure 7.1 Proposed Duties and Responsibilities

Training must enhance the competence of public officials in performing the tasks of government, which are increasingly becoming more complex. The trained personnel must be able to shoulder higher responsibility and further improve their decision making ability. The stages of career progression and their corresponding levels of responsibility are two other areas of importance in public service training, and should be taken into account when identifying training needs. Needs will differ for officials at the junior, middle and senior levels. Induction training, besides providing a strong foundation that allows officials to settle into their new environment and perform the tasks at the junior level, also inculcates values, skills and perspectives that are useful throughout their career. Over the course of service, public officials should attend various types of in-service training that are designed to provide them with the necessary skills and expertise required to handle jobs at the middle and senior levels.

The information obtained from the evaluation of training packages is ambiguous and incomplete because it draws upon subjective observation of the trainees. Follow-up interviews with the participants or their supervisors, after the completion of training, could yield valuable information on the impact and sustainability of training. This may involve higher costs, but it would be worthwhile in that it would ensure the achievement of training objectives. On a smaller scale, the central training institutes could select samples from participants and their supervisors at random and interview them extensively. In the case of India, the casual approach used to measure the effectiveness of training must be replaced with a more serious one and a standardized process for evaluation must be initiated. This will entail implementing three levels of evaluation, instead of the current practice which predominantly uses just one level.

LBSNAA devotes maximum attention and effort to its induction training programs. When public officials are sent to districts to acquire practical knowledge at the field level, it would be useful to provide an opportunity for the trainers to observe their performance. That would allow trainers to obtain information on the application of skills in the field. Feedback could then be obtained from the officials who supervise training at the field level. The trainers could select a number of states[3] and departments, and visit them without prior notice to assess the real impact of training.

Central training institutes should devote more time, resources and effort to ensuring the quality and credibility of their output. This may entail streamlining the quality and quantity of training packages, with a strong emphasis on their relevance to public service. The duration of training packages requires adjustment. For example, the length of training programs at LBSNAA could be reduced, as the trainees find it extremely difficult and disorienting to be away from their workplace for such a long period of time. This lengthy duration also affects the degree of their concentration and ability to absorb new information and acquire skills. On the other hand, the duration of training programs at CSTDI may be adjusted in the opposite direction, as they are generally too short.

There is a need to improve the system of record-keeping with regard to public service training. A detailed report, to be retained in official records, should be prepared at the end of a training program and could include the nature of the course, its content, relevance to work, and an account of the performance of the trainees. This kind of documentation could help officials to assess the requirements of their assignments and could also serve as a data bank for the government to draw upon when needed. It is necessary to develop methods for proper utilisation of the manpower available to the government, in view of the substantial investments made to develop human resources for a nation.

There should be an appropriate balance between centralized and decentralized approaches to training in the public service. Both arrangements have their merits, but a clear division of responsibilities between the two is critical. Training agencies at the departmental levels must be able to organize training programs directly relevant to the tasks performed in their units. It is, therefore, recommended that institutes adopt a decentralized approach for training in specific areas, but maintain centralized training for strategic or cross-sector activities.

As states around the globe introduce public sector reforms and undergo changes, central training institutes have a major role to play. These changes require the active involvement of central training institutes in the planning as well implementation of reforms. After taking stock of the state of the manpower available to face new challenges, central training institutes can assist governments in setting targets and developing policies and programs to achieve them. Close cooperation between the government agencies managing human resources (the Ministry of Personnel in India and the Civil Service Bureau in Hong Kong) and the central training institutes is essential in this respect, as public sector reforms have extensive and long-term consequences.

Finally, globalization has thrown up new challenges for governments and their training institutes. The free movement of capital, goods, commodities and ideas across borders have had a significant impact on the thinking patterns and behaviour of states and bureaucracies. There is strong pressure for convergence and conformity with the standards set by the dominant powers in the international arena. As a result, reform agendas and the directions of change are strongly influenced by external forces, which very few countries can avoid. This makes it critical for the central training institutes to monitor changes and strategies, and ensure that the country has an adequate supply of trained manpower that can operate effective public organizations.

Globalization and Public Service Training

The task of providing public training has become increasingly challenging in view of the new circumstances, expectations, tasks and implications of public administration. The cases of India and Hong Kong highlight the need for a serious reassessment of the existing state of affairs and an effort to embark on a path that will make the quality and content of training consistent with the needs of the time.

One of the most noticeable impacts of globalization is the drive for uniformity and a standardization of practices and procedures in several areas, including public services. Consequently, public service training programs are becoming more standardized in approach, content and methods. As new and more interactive methods of delivery become commonplace, central training institutes are eager to adopt them. However, not all are adequately equipped and prepared to do so. Besides, the rigid and hierarchical structure of the bureaucracy of training institutes is not conducive to the free exchange of ideas and the use of interactive methods that could have a positive impact on training practices.

Another noticeable trend stemming from globalization is the emphasis on computer skills and information technology. These areas are perceived to reflect modernization and progress, and there is considerable interest among trainees to acquire skills that can be used to quickly obtain information and respond to inquiries and requests from the public. Developments in IT also make the process of public service delivery more flexible as citizens can access information around the clock through the internet. However, many training institutes in developing countries devote time to imparting basic knowledge to trainees on the use of computers. The real benefit comes from an established system of electronic service delivery. It is not helpful to invest in training programs on information technology if the infrastructure for electronic service delivery is inadequate.

Globalization has resulted in increased international exposure and states are compelled to interact with partners outside their borders. The emergence of powerful international bodies such as the United Nations, World Bank and International Monetary Fund has initiated a process of change, which has been accentuated by the forces of globalization. World bodies play an influential role in setting the agenda for reforms, and have various means and methods by which to enforce this agenda. The circumstances in the public sector have become more complicated with the parallel growth of transnational corporations, which have become major players in countries benefiting from these sources of revenue. These developments have implications for public service training, as training programs need to inform trainees about these new demands and realities and help them acquire skills to cope with them. The tendency to concentrate on changes in the international arena can have adverse consequences for the country, as local issues tend to be ignored. While the trainees learn about the rules and strategies for dealing with international issues, the task of preparing them to deal with more pressing local concerns may be remain unfulfilled. Globalization has shifted attention away from the local and towards the international scenario.

On reflection, the role of central training institutes in India and Hong Kong has evolved to reach the current stage, in which most of the programs have been consolidated, and it is likely that a similar process will continue for years to come. The general framework of training is similar in terms of program design, evaluation, and adjustments to adapt to the changing circumstances. The strategies and procedures for identifying training needs and conducting programs are not that different, with more or less similar techniques and mechanisms to ensure a competent public service. New challenges have often pushed institutes to consider and develop additional programs, but their main emphasis remained unchanged. The additional initiatives have been introduced on a piecemeal basis, and cannot be completely effective because they are not properly integrated with the plan for training public service officials in India and Hong Kong. One of the principal forces behind the development of training programs has been government objectives and priorities, and the perceptions about the future direction of public service training in India and Hong Kong are also compatible.

A way forward can be ensured by attending to the problems identified in this study. A rational structure followed by central training institutes will help reduce, if not completely eliminate, many of these problems. This should be supplemented by a competent system of collecting and analysing information. The process of evaluation must be made objective in order for the quality of the training programs to be ensured. Accurate records must be maintained and the data used to assist with the deployment of officials to the appropriate positions. The benefits of both centralised and decentralised approaches to training must be appreciated, and central training institutes should take a proactive role in facilitating the process of administrative reform through its activities. As globalization continues to usher in change, all public institutions will need to keep up in order to provide quality, efficient and responsive public services to citizens.

Notes

[1] This was revealed by one of the officials of the Ministry of Personnel, India, at an interview conducted in July 2000.
[2] In both India and Hong Kong, central training institutes are headed by Directors who are senior members of the public service.
[3] The 'states' in India refers to provinces and are governed by provincial governments, and include a figurehead Governor, who is appointed by the central government.

Appendix A: List of Selected Officials Interviewed in India

1. Mr. Ajit Jogi — Chief Minister, Chattisgarh.
2. Mr. A.K. Arora — Joint Secretary, Department of Personnel and Training, Government of India
3. Dr. V.K. Agnihotri — Additional Secretary, Department of Administrative Reforms and Public Grievances, Government of India
4. Mr. Vijay Singh — Principle Home Secretary, Government of India
5. Mr. B.S. Baswan — Director, LBSNAA
6. Mr. Binod Kumar — Joint Director, LBSNAA
7. Mr. Tarun Shridhar — Deputy Director (Sr.), LBSNAA
8. Mrs. Manisha Shridhar — Deputy Director (Sr.), LBSNAA
9. Ms. Geeta Mishra — Deputy Director (Sr.), LBSNAA
10. Mr. A. Santosh Mathew — Professor, LBSNAA
11. Mr. Yaduvendra Mathur — Deputy Director, LBSNAA
12. Mrs. B. V. Umadevi — Deputy Director, LBSNAA
13. Mr. K. N. Kumar — Deputy Director, LBSNAA
14. Mr. T.V.S.N. Prasad — Deputy Director, LBSNAA
15. Mr. M. H. Khan — Deputy Director, LBSNAA
12. Mr. Chandan Sinha — Deputy Director, LBSNAA
16. Mr. B.V.R. Subrahmanyam — Deputy Director (Management), LBSNAA
17. Mr. D. Banerjee — Professor & Cord. (Law), LBSNAA
18. Mr. L. C. Singhi — Professor (Law), LBSNAA
19. Dr. A. Subrahmanyam — Reader (Law) LBSNAA
20. Dr. M.M. Mishra — Professor (Language) LBSNAA
21. Dr. Unnithan — Assistant Lecturer (Language) LBSNAA
22. A Nallasamy — Assistant Lecturer (Language) LBSNAA
23. T.V.S.N. Prasad — Coordinator & Vice Chairman of Centre for Rural Studies, LBSNAA
24. P.R. Hari Krishnan — Sr. Programmer Computer Centre

25. Anjali Chauhan	LBSNAA Research Associate Gender Studies
26. Mr. D.S. Mathur	LBSNAA Principle Secretary, Government Administrative Department, Government of Madhya Pradesh
27. Mr. M.M. Upadhaya	Commissioner, Jabalpur, Madhya Pradesh
28. Mr. Surrender Nath	Labour Commissioner, Government of India (Rtd.)
29. Mr. Sanjay Bandopadhaya	Collector, Government of Madhya Pradesh, Jabalpur
30. Mr. Padamvir Singh	Ex-Deputy Director, LBSNAA
31. Mr. C. P. G. Unni	Inspector General of Police, Government of Madhya Pradesh, Jabalpur

Appendix B: List of Selected Officials Interviewed in Hong Kong

1. Ms. Patricia Tam — Senior Training Officer CSTDI
2. Dr. Joshua Mok — Associate Professor, City University of Hong Kong and Invited Trainer CSTDI
3. Dr. Brian Brewer — Associate Professor, City University of Hong Kong and Invited Trainer CSTDI
4. Dr. Hon Chan — Associate Professor, City University of Hong Kong and Invited Trainer CSTDI

Note: A comprehensive list of interviewees of Hong Kong is not presented due to the request of confidentiality of identity.

Bibliography

Alam Manzoor M. (1990), *Civil Service Training and Development: Assessing the Role and Significance of Higher Civil Service Training in Less Developed Countries,* Administrative Development Agency, Helsinki.

Analoui, F. (1996), 'A Socio-Technical Framework for Effective Transfer of Training', *New Series Discussion Papers No. 70,* Development and Project Planning Centre, University of Bradford.

Austin, M., Brannon, D. and Pecora, P. (1984), *Managing Staff Development Programs in Human Service Agencies,* Nelson-Hall Publishers, Chicago, IL.

Avasthi and Maheshwari (1996), *Public Administration,* Lakshmi Narain Agarwal Press, Agra.

Babbie, E. (1995), *The Practice of Social Research,* Wadsworth Publishing Company, Belmont.

Babbie, E. (1998), *The Practice of Social Research,* Wadsworth Publishing Company, Belmont.

Baron B. (1981), *Systematic Training in Managing Human Resources,* Edward Arnold, London.

Berg Bruce L. (1998), *Qualitative Research Methods for Social Sciences,* Allyn and Bacon, Boston.

Boston J. (1996), *Public Management: The New Zealand Model,* Oxford University Press, Auckland; New York.

Buckley, R. and Caple, J. (2000), *The Theory and Practice of Training.* Kogan Page, London.

Caldwell, Lynton K. (1962), *Improving the Public Service Through Training,* Agency for International Development, Washington, D.C.

Camp, R., Blanchard, P. and Huszczo, G. (1986), *Toward a More Organizationally Effective Training Strategy and Practice,* Prentice – Hall, Englewood, New Jersey.

Civil Service Bureau, June (1998), *Civil Service Newsletter,* Issue No.3. Government Printer, Hong Kong.

Civil Service Bureau Feb. (1999), *Civil Service Newsletter,* Issue No.1, Government Printer, Hong Kong.

Commonwealth Secretariat (1979), *National Policies and Programs for Public Enterprises Management Training,* Report of a Meeting of Senior Officials, 5-7 November, Author, London.

Cowling, A. and James, P. (1994), *The Essence of Personnel Management and Industrial Relations,* Prentice Hall, New York.

CSTDI (1996), *Civil Service Training and Development Institute Prospectus,* Government Printer, Hong Kong.

CSTDI (1998), *Civil Service Training and Development Institute Prospectus*, Government Printer, Hong Kong.

CSTDI (1999), *Civil Service Training and Development Institute Prospectus*, Government Printer, Hong Kong.

CSTDI (2000), *Civil Service Training and Development Institute Prospectus*, Government Printer, Hong Kong.

CSTDI (2001), *Civil Service Training and Development Institute Prospectus*, Government Printer, Hong Kong.

Denscombe, M. (1998), *The Good Research Guide of Small–Scale Social Research Projects*, Open University Press, Buckingham.

Dror, Y. (1986), *Policy Making Under Adversity*, Transaction Books, New Brunswick.

Foley, B.J. (1985), 'Designing Training Systems' in William Tracey, (ed.), *Human Resources Management and Development Handbook*, Amacom, New York.

Goldstien, I.L. (1986), *Training: Program Development and Evaluation*, Brooks/Cole Publishing Company, Monterey, California.

Hall, D.T. (1986), Dilemmas in Linking Succession Planning to Individual Executive Learning, *Human Resource Management*, **25** (2), 235-65.

Hall, D. and Goodale, J. (1986), *Human Resource Management: Strategy, Design, and Implementation*, Scott, Foresman Company, Glenview, IL.

Haralambos M. and Holbom (2000), *Sociology: Themes and Perspectives*, HarperCollins, London.

Heady, F. (1991), *Public Administration: A Comparative Perspective*, M. Dekker, New York.

Heneman, H.G. and Schwab, D.P. (1986), *Perspectives on Personnel/Human Resources Management*, R. D. Irwin, Homewood, Ill.

Hong Kong Government (1978) *Annual Report*, Government Printer, Hong Kong.

Huque, A.S., Lee G.O.M. and Cheung A.B.L. (1998), *The Civil Services in Hong Kong: Continuity and Change*, Hong Kong University Press, Hong Kong.

Jahns, I. (1981), 'Training in Organizations,' in Stanley Grabowski (eds.), *Preparing Educators of Adults*, Jossey-Bass, San Fransisco.

Jain R.B. (2001a), *Public Administration in India: 21ˢᵗ Century Challenges for Good Governance*, Deep and Deep Publications, New Delhi.

Jain R.B. (2001b), 'Towards Good Governance: A Half Century of India's Administrative Development', *International Journal of Public Administration*, **24** (12), p. 1299.

Kaufman, R. and English, F. (1979), *Needs Assessment: Concept and Application*, Educational Technology, Englewood Cliffs, NJ.

Kerrigan, J.E. and Luke, J.S. (1985, June), *Management Training Strategies for Developing Countries*, USAID.

Kirk, J. and Miller, M. L. (1986), *Reliability and Validity in Qualitative Research*, Sage Publication, California.

Kirkpatrick, Donald L. (1967), 'Evaluation of Training' in Craig, Robert L. and Bittel, Lester R. (eds), *Training and Development Handbook*, McGraw-Hill, New York.

Knowles, M. (1984), 'Adult Learning: Theory and Practice' in Leonard, (ed.), *The Handbook of Human Resource Development*, Wiley-Intersience Publication, New York.

LBSNAA (1996), *Annual Report*, National Academy of Administration, Mussoorie.

LBSNAA (1997), *Annual Report*, National Academy of Administration, Mussoorie.

LBSNAA (1999), *Annual Report*, National Academy of Administration, Mussoorie.

Maheshwari, S.R. (1993), *Administrative Reform in India*, Jawahar Publishers, New Delhi.

Mandell, Milton M. (1959), 'Personnel Standards' in Marx (ed.), *Elements of Public Administration*, Prentice Hall, New York.

Marx, Fritz Morstein, (1954), *The Administrative State: An Introduction to Bureaucracy*, Chicago, University of Chicago Press.

McCalman J. and Paton R.A. (1992), *Change Management: A Guide to Effective Implementation*, P. Chapman, London.

McGehee, W. and Thayer, P. (1961), *Training in Business and Industry*, John Wiley, New York.

McIntosh, N. and Daniel, W.W. (1972), *The Right to Manage: A Study of Leadership and Reform in Employee Relations*, Macdonald, London.

Miller, V. (1987), 'The History of Training,' in Robert L. Craig (ed.), *Training and Development Handbook: A Guide to Human Resource Development*, McGraw-Hill Book Company, New York.

Miners, N. (1995), *The Government and Politics of Hong Kong*, Oxford University Press, Hong Kong.

Moore, M., and Dutton, P. (1978), *Training Needs Analysis: Review and Critique*, Academy of Management Review.

Moris, J. (1977), 'The Transferability of Wester Management Concepts and Programs: An East African Perspective' in Stifel's *Education and Training for Public Sector Management in Developing Countries*, The Rockefeller Foundation, New York.

Nadler, L. (1984), 'Human Resource Development' in Leonard Nadler (ed.), *The Handbook of Human Resource Development*, John Wiley and Sons, New York.

Paul, S. (1983), *Training for Public Administration and Management in Developing Countries: A Review*, World Bank, Washington, DC.

Paul S. (1985), *Training for Public Administration and Management in Developing Countries: A Review*, World Bank Staff Working Paper-584, Washington D.C.

Qureshi, A. (1967), *California State Training Division: A Study in Institution Building*, (Doctoral dissertation), University of Southern California.

Reilly, Wyn. (1979), *Training Administrators for Development*, Heinemann, London.

Revans, R.W. (1982), *The Origins and Growth of Action Learning*, Chartwell Bratt Ltd, Bromley, UK.

Robinson, Mary E. (1961), *Education for Social Change: Establishing Institutes of Public and Business Administration Abroad*, Brookings Institution, Washington, D.C.

Rubin, H.J. and Rubin, I.S. (1995), *Qualitative Interviewing: The Art of Hearing Data*, Sage Publication, Thousand Oaks.

Sachdeva, K.L., and Gupta, J. (1990), *A Simple Study of Public Administration*, Ajanta Prakashan, New Delhi.

Sarantakos, S. (1993), *Social Research*, Macmillan Education Australia, South Melbourne.

Scott, I. and Burns J.P. (1984), *The Hong Kong Civil Service, Personnel Policies and Practices*, Oxford University Press, Hong Kong.

Shafritz, J.M. (2001), *Personnel Management in Government, Politics and Process*, Marcel Dekker, New York.

Sherwood, F., and Fisher, F. (1984), 'Institutional Self-assessment and Planning: Report of an Experience in Kenya.' Paper presented at the 1984 Annual Conference of the International Association of Schools and Institutes of Administration (IASIA), Bloomington, Indiana.

Smith, N. (1974), 'Employee Development Methods' in Kenneth Byers (ed.), *Employee Training and Development in the Public Sector*, International Personnel Management Association, Chicago, IL.

Steadham, S., and Clay, M. (1985), 'Needs Assessment' in William Tracy, (ed.), *Human Resources Management and Development Handbook*, Amacom, New York (pp.1338-52).

Strauss, Anselm L. (1987), *Qualitative Analysis for Social Scientists*, Cambridge University Press, Cambridge.

Subramaniam V. (1990), *Public Administration in the Third World: An International Handbook*, Greenwood Press, New York.

Taylor, F. (1911), *The Principle of Scientific Management*, Harper and Bros., New York.

Tompkins J. (1995), *Human Resource Management in Government: Hitting the Ground Running*, HarperCollins College Publishers, New York.

Torrington, D. and Chapman, J. (1983), *Personnel Management*, Prentice-Hall, Englewood Cliffs, New Jersey.

Treffman, S. (March, 1978), 'The Development of Training in Organizations.' Paper presented at the National Workshop on Extension Staff Development, New Orleans, Louisiana.

Tummala, K. K. (1996), *Public Administration in India*, Times Academic Press, Singapore.

United Kingdom (1944), *Report of the Committee on the Training of Civil Servants*, HMSO, London.

United Nations (1966), *Handbook of Training in Public Service*, United Nations Publications, New York, U.S.A.

United Nations (1978), *A Manual and Resource Book for Popular Participation Training*, Vol. I, United Nations Publications, New York.

Vadhanasindhu Chindalak (1994), *The Thai National Civil Service Training Center*, UMI, Ann Arbor, Mich.

Subject Index

76-77, 80-81, 83, 90, 93, 96, 117,
122-123, 130, 137, 142, 144-153,
155, 157-158, 160-164, 166, 169-
170, 174-175, 177-179, 182-183,
185-188
job-related, 51, 164, 178
methods, 1-3, 7, 9, 12, 14, 16, 19, 23,
25-26, 28, 32, 39, 42, 46, 55-56,
64-65, 69, 71-73, 86, 93-95, 101-
104, 108, 127-128, 134-135, 147,
152, 155, 160-161, 182, 186-187
phases, 26, 30, 47
pitfalls, 42
priority, 2-3, 6, 10, 14, 16, 79-80, 97,
99, 104-105, 126, 130, 134, 136,
138, 141, 150-151, 177, 188
scope, 1, 15, 54, 85, 108, 134, 145,
158, 172, 179
specialized, 1, 8, 16, 37, 39, 44-45,
59-61, 83, 115, 152, 164, 177-178,
183
standardization, 1, 145, 180, 187
standardized, 1, 85, 178, 183
strategies, 3, 14, 16, 31, 39, 46, 56,
65, 71, 90, 96, 98, 148, 157, 161,
179, 186-188
structure, 2, 8, 11, 15, 35, 47, 49, 62,
67, 71, 84, 88, 94, 98, 103, 147,
152, 165, 177-179, 181, 183, 187-
188
techniques and mechanisms, 10, 14,
16, 93, 125, 152, 188
trends, 3-4, 6, 10, 13-16, 77, 100,
102-104, 108, 128-135, 141, 148,
150, 160, 177, 181-182

types, 2, 15, 28, 32, 42, 45, 47, 52, 91,
94, 108, 150, 156, 162, 108, 178,
182, 185
Training Models
collaborative, 35
continuing education, 35
diagnostic , 34
induction-training, 35
in-service training, 35
menu, 34
organizational learning, 35
orientation-training, 35
pre-entry education, 35
prescriptive, 141, 177
special order, 34
Training needs, 3, 10-16, 22, 26, 28-29,
31, 34, 42, 46, 53, 64, 68-69, 72-74,
81, 83, 89-93, 95, 98-99, 105, 121-
126, 129, 131-132, 136, 141, 146-151,
153, 160, 179-183, 185, 188
Training, types
continuing, 164, 179
in-service, 3, 32, 35, 37-38, 43-46,
59-61, 68, 71, 81-82, 91, 99, 145,
164-165, 170, 179, 185
orientation, 3, 32, 35, 38, 44, 46, 61,
80, 132, 134, 164, 179
post-entry, 3-4, 32, 38, 110-111
pre-entry, 3, 37, 43-45, 51, 81, 110
project related, 37, 39, 43
self development, 21, 39
Transfer of learning, 86, 157, 160, 182